D1624999

*THE RELIGIOUS CARE
OF THE
PSYCHIATRIC PATIENT*

THE RELIGIOUS CARE
OF THE
PSYCHIATRIC PATIENT

by
Wayne E. Oates

THE WESTMINSTER PRESS
Philadelphia

Scripture quotations from the Revised Standard Version
of the Bible are copyrighted 1946, 1952, © 1971, 1973
by the Division of Christian Education of the National
Council of the Churches of Christ in the U.S.A., and are
used by permission.

BOOK DESIGN BY DOROTHY ALDEN SMITH

First edition

Published by The Westminster Press ®
Philadelphia, Pennsylvania

PRINTED IN THE UNITED STATES OF AMERICA

9 8 7 6 5 4 3 2 1

Library of Congress Cataloging in Publication Data

Oates, Wayne Edward, 1917–
    The religious care of the psychiatric patient.

    1. Church work with the mentally ill.   2. Pastoral
theology.   3. Pastoral psychology.   4. Mentally ill—
Care and treatment.   I. Title.
BV4461.O18 1978   259   78–18454
ISBN 0–664–21365–0

To
John Schwab, M.D.

CONTENTS

ACKNOWLEDGMENTS

For their specific contributions to this book, I am deeply indebted to my colleagues who have joined minds and pens with mine in the chapters that follow. I gratefully express my appreciation to Paul Schmidt, Ph.D., a clinical psychologist in the city of Louisville and a member of the Staff of the Children's Treatment Unit at Central State Hospital, for his specific interpretations of the Backus Sin Test material in the chapter on the religious care of the schizophrenic patient. In the same chapter, I am indebted to four theological student colleagues at the Louisville General Hospital Psychiatry In-patient Unit. They worked one whole semester in a case conference with Dr. Schmidt and myself as we explored the nature and theological significance of the experience of the schizophrenic patient. They are Steve Perkins, who prepared the case history at the conclusion of the chapter, and Jackie Ammerman, Ed Gouedy, and Sister Rita Ann Wade.

Further, David McNeely, M.D., Medical Director of the Norton Psychiatric Clinic and Associate Professor of Psychiatry and Behavioral Sciences in the School of Medicine of the University of Louisville, has been my leader and friend as we developed together the chapter on religious symptom pictures of psychiatric patients. Curtis Barrett, Ph.D., Director of Adult Psychological Services and Associate Professor of Psychiatry and Behavioral Sciences in the University of

Louisville School of Medicine, has collaborated in writing the chapter on psychotherapy and pastoral counseling. To both these colleagues I am deeply indebted.

John Schwab, M.D., professor and chairman of the Department of Psychiatry and Behavioral Sciences, has led our colleagues and me in patiently building a unique program of care for mental patients of all stations of life. He has made a microcosm of the larger community of the multiple specialists in our department. He has been my senior officer, my teacher, my friend, and, at times needed, my physician. I express gratitude to him and all my colleagues in the department for the dialogues out of which this book has grown.

Mrs. Bonnie Lakes has done the final draft of this book, and her competence and dedication show through the manuscript from page to page. I give thanks to her and her family for her services.

The patients, from whom I have learned on their pilgrimage from disorder to order, confusion to clarity, and despair to hope, are due my deepest gratitude for their trust, friendship, instruction, and companionship.

WAYNE E. OATES

Louisville, Kentucky

PROLOGUE

The common ground, the mutual concern, of the clergy and the physician is the human body itself. The physician is dedicated to the scientific exploration of the structures, functions, and balance of the human body. The clergy are concerned with the human body as the chosen instrument of the revelation of God to humanity. The proclamation of the good news of God is through persons. Both clergy and physician are confronted in daily practice with the impacts that the events of life have on the health and welfare of the human body in relationship to itself and to other human beings. Both clergy and physician are faced daily with human suffering. The ways in which human beings can devastate and exploit the bodies of other human beings are the stuff of their work. Both clergy and physician share a common commitment to the care and restoration of the human being to its originally intended existence in the intention of God, the Creator.

Such a commitment commonly shared by both the clergy and the physician is often realized by one or both of them. The very living, moving, and breathing organism of the human body focuses both the physician's scientific scrutiny and the clergyperson's basis of appeal to those to whom he or she is sent to communicate God's love.

The meeting ground of the human body itself is painfully real to the physician upon encountering a cadaver as one of

1

the first assignments in anatomy class. Yet, as medical education progresses through the preclinical years (before patients are assigned to the medical student), the mountainous quantity of detail about microbiology, microphysiology, biochemistry, etc., which the student has to memorize crowds out the vivid awareness of the wholeness of the human body as it is when alive. Even the physician in the making begins to lose clear focus of the totality of the living organism of the human body. The process of learning all this *about* the human being obscures and depersonalizes the body considerably. The medical student may feel depersonalized along with it. Yet, as the doctor-patient relationship is activated, the medical student comes alive to the matters of birth, life, and death that are represented in the growth, development, aging, deterioration, and death of the human person.

The human body is the critical issue in the education of a clergyperson, although in a much more subtle way. The apostle Paul said that we have the treasure of ministry in earthen vessels. The body is the temple of the Holy Spirit. We consecrate our bodies as living sacrifices to God. The needs of the body for food and marital love are the pattern of creation. The sources of the satisfaction of these needs are good when received with thanksgiving and prayer. None of this hits the emerging minister until he or she realizes the meaning of the way God reveals himself to humanity. The process of learning Greek, Hebrew, textual content and criticism of the Scriptures can depersonalize the theological student. The purpose of ministry does not become personal until the student is confronted by the prophets of the Old Testament and Jesus and the apostles in the New Testament. The brunt of the Judeo-Christian understanding of God is that God speaks through human persons, human bodies. In the Christian gospel, the real stumbling block even to many professed Christians is that God in Christ was incarnated in the flesh, the human body. Jesus was more distinctly human than most of us have the courage to be. The persistent heresy throughout history is the Gnostic heresy. Gnosticism denies the reality, the sanctity, and the importance of the human body. Yet the good news is that God chose to reveal himself fully in the human body of Jesus. The medium of the human body became the message itself. The Word was made flesh and dwelt among us, full of grace and truth. Therefore, the minister of that Word cannot make an artificial distinction between the spiritual and the bodily conditions of the creation in the human body. God does not defy the creation in his revelation to humanity; God uses the creation itself in the redemption of humanity. The aim of the revelation of God is the restoration of humanity to its original specifications in creation.

The minister who takes the intentions of God seriously cannot skirt, ignore, or consider out of his or her realm of interest all known means of understanding the human person in sickness and in health. The more seriously he or she takes the human person in sickness and in health, the more common ground there is for the medical doctor and the minister to meet in dialogue. The ideal way of learning for both is in conjoint education in the same clinics, hospitals, prisons, etc. Then artificial distinctions of separate territories, roles, and power bases dissolve in the sweaty struggle in behalf of the best interests of the patient. The substantive data of each other's disciplines represent different angles of vision for perceiving the care and cure of persons as human bodies. Human suffering's demands overflow the banks of neatly separated roles.

Consequently, the common commitment to sharing these perspectives enables the doctor and the minister to rise above pedestrian roles and achieve larger perspectives through demonstrated competence in each other's disciplines. The point of view expressed in the following pages of this book will therefore be somewhat jarring to persons educated in the 1940's, 1950's, and early 1960's. Little is made of professional rivalries, tension, and role competition. Much is made of the unpretentious exchange of technical data, interpretations, and perspectives back and forth between ministers and physicians on the common ground of the care of psychiatric patients. The reader who expects neat packagings of the separate professions into compartments of ministry and medicine will be disappointed. The point of view here seeks to rise above that. I have the audacity to suggest that detailed technical knowledge of the religious culture of the patient and the religious concerns of the patient can go a long way toward a more effective diagnosis and treatment being rendered by the physician. I will get the most resistance, I suspect, from the minister who protests that the "average minister" cannot be expected to know anything about the human body, its disorders, its chemicals, and its visceral demand for community with people who love that person. Yet, with equal audacity I insist that such knowledge explicates the meaning of grace.

The "body" is a term often used to refer not only to the individual person but also to the corporate community. The ecology of human health and illness in community cannot be separated from the processes of treatment. The quality of the community cannot be separated from the redemption of the individual. The psychiatric patient can be hospitalized. This creates a specialized kind of community for a limited span of time for the intensive treatment of the person. Upon discharge, however, countless patients have no place to be, to exist, to call their own. They have no community of persons who understand and support them through the dark days of convalescence when, their confidence in themselves having been severely shaken, they begin to try to find housing, a job, self-sufficiency in a competitive society. The critical meeting ground of physician and clergyperson, therefore, is in the liaison between their chosen territories—the hospital and the church and synagogue. In years past, we have somewhat esoterically discussed the interaction of the minister and the physician. Only recently have we begun to raise the issues of the interaction of the hospital with the congregations as corporate communities within the larger society.

A person who works most of the time with psychiatric patients in a community is acutely aware of the atmosphere

of silence that surrounds community concern about the illnesses of psychiatric patients. These persons are not mentioned routinely along with those who have physical illnesses,
in requests for prayer in public meetings of churches. Psychiatric patients are not besieged with well-wishing visitors.
They do not get cards, letters, flowers, and choice morsels of
food as do patients with more "socially acceptable" diseases.
I am not suggesting at this time that the patients' privacy be
invaded or the "cover" of their illness be "blown." They
themselves more often than not prefer anonymity in their
illness. Yet I cannot help sensing the most recurrent characteristic of these patients, regardless of diagnosis: isolation and
loneliness. I ponder how it could happen, for churches and
synagogues could share some of their overabundance of respectability with these patients.

Therefore, in the pages that follow you will sense my own
preoccupation with the character and construction of the
healing community that is neither hospital, home, nor school.
Here the deepest wounds of people, wounds that draw no
blood, may be shared in a life support system of acceptance,
grace, and restoration. The Old Testament refers to the congregation as the "people of God." The New Testament rarely
if ever refers to the church as a building, as a system of voters
who decide who is in and who is out. To the contrary, it more
often refers to the church as the body of Christ. The body of
Christ is the church that *happens* in the most unexpected
and unlikely places. These events are the tissue of humanity
meeting humanity in openness of both bondage and deliverance, suffering and healing, despair and hope. I have experienced these happenings in the settings in which I work
in hospitals and teaching clinics. I have recorded disciplined
observations which I hope will be the seedbox for many
highly specific and carefully designed researches for both
ministers and physicians in the years to come. However, if
either the minister or the physician is willing to settle for
being "average," he or she should lay this book down now
and lean back on averageness, on the least common denomi-

nator of pastors and physicians. But how far can averageness go without being mediocrity?

Education has a very real way of beginning its most exciting phase when a person with an inquiring mind finishes formal schooling. The above-average clergyperson and physician is one who captures the freedom from depending upon professors and learns from direct experience. I hope that the following data bases will be a handbook for the comparison of my direct observations with yours.

The reader will immediately see that the primary purpose of this book is not to provide techniques of pastoral counseling. Pastoral procedures are made evident, but that is not my primary purpose. The objective is to develop background understanding and wisdom which the reader will infuse into techniques that are natural to his or her concern for the best interests of the suffering person. Techniques follow the shape of the person who is using them. The main rationale of the book is: (1) to inform and acquaint the whole psychiatric team concerning the religious care of the psychiatric patient; (2) to provide a data base that is unique to the religious care at the same time that the technical data of the psychiatric understanding of schizophrenia and depression in the context of religious history are carefully noted; and (3) to provide effective models of how informed ministers, informed psychiatrists, informed psychologists, and informed nurses and social workers do in fact work together in creative learning concerning the deepest yearnings for the healthy religious life of psychiatric patients.

It may be asked why I have chosen to give separate treatment to depression and schizophrenia and not to other psychiatric disorders. These two disorders comprise the majority of the patients under care at any given time. Persons are more likely to be totally disabled by these disorders than by any others, except for organic brain syndromes such as toxic conditions, seizure conditions, delirium conditions, and cardiovascular disorders. I perceive these latter to be in need of separate treatment because of the "behavioral neurology" that is required for their understanding. Also, I have not considered here the neuroses or the character disorders, because I consider these to be more nearly disorders of learning than are depression and schizophrenia. I have dealt with depression and schizophrenia, also, because they call for specific medical modalities of treatment by a psychiatrist, whereas many persons suffering from neuroses and character disorders may or may not be urgently in need of a psychiatrist. Furthermore, the neurotic person and the antisocial person are more likely to "use" psychiatry as an occasion to justify personal irresponsibility than are depressed and schizophrenic patients. Rational measures are more likely to be effective with the former than the latter.

Of course, candor requires that I say also that the length of the book would be prohibitive if I sought to be thorough in the treatment of all the disorders listed in the fifteen hundred pages of the *Comprehensive Textbook of Psychiatry—II*. The neuroses and the character disorders deserve separate treatment in other volumes. I have not dealt with them for these reasons. However, the reader who concentrates with me on depression and schizophrenia will find that more profound approaches to the positive mental health of the other disorders will surface in the process.

1

THE CLINICAL APPROACH
TO THE RELIGIOUS CARE
OF PSYCHIATRIC PATIENTS

In nontechnological communities both in the past and in the present the treatment of emotionally disturbed persons was and is dealt with by appointed persons who are seen both as healers and as priests. In highly complex technocracies such as our own, the religious care of the psychiatric patient tends to go in one or more of the following directions:

1. A religious cult promises that through faith healing, group solidarity, and forced indoctrination the person can be healed without outside help.

2. The particular psychiatric hospital or comprehensive mental health center attempts to heal the emotionally disturbed person by medical and psychological means, with no reference to the person's religious beliefs, practices, or affiliations.

3. The psychiatric treatment of a patient involves the mainline church life of the patient in relation to the parish clergyperson or the synagogue rabbi if the psychiatrists and social workers think these persons can contribute to the positive recovery of the patient. They tend to avoid the religious situation if they think the clergyperson would be of no use or would work against the recovery of the patient. The general parish or synagogue clergy participate when they are found to be credibly helpful to psychiatric patients. Therefore, a person of the clergy does not have to be a "specialist"

in psychiatry to have a place in the religious care of psychiatric patients.

4. The psychiatric hospital has on its staff, a fully participating chaplain as a theological specialist in the care of psychiatric patients. Religious assessments are considered along with other assessments by psychologists, social workers, etc. Such a "specialist" approach is not at all unusual in the psychiatric communities today. Collaboration with the parish clergypersons is a strong commitment of most specialized pastoral counselors.

This book is written to a wide audience by reason of the four different approaches I have identified above. Therefore the content will pose difficulties for the reader. I am writing to the parish or synagogue clergyperson who is not a "specialist" in this field. The psychiatric concepts and terms used will be strange. A medical or psychiatric dictionary will be useful. Most of the terms are either defined in the text or are available in an unabridged dictionary. Too many of these terms are loosely used in the daily newspapers for a clergyperson to avoid the discipline of learning their technical meanings.

I am writing to medical students, psychiatric residents, and psychiatrists. These persons will have some trouble understanding specialized religious language. Yet this is the language used by the patient. Some of it may be the ordinary, everyday speech of thousands of persons in the community. These words also appear in an unabridged dictionary. In this text I have sought to define them. Any well-educated minister can explain their meanings. In any event, the medical student, the psychiatric resident, and the psychiatrist will understand the patient better if he or she goes to the trouble of learning this nomenclature.

Consequently, I readily recognize that speaking to such widely specialized groups of readers is to invite you to a struggle—a struggle to understand other worlds of communication than your own. The struggle has a reward. You will move out of your own "conceptual ghetto" and discover continents of fellowships with others of which you were unaware. If you will struggle with my writing, I will struggle with your need for me to be as clear as possible.

Psychiatry and religion have in common the fine art of broad generalization. These pages will be bespeckled with broad generalizations as a result. "Paddling up the stream" of global statements is a clinician's job. Consequently, writing a book on the religious care of the psychiatric patient requires a commitment on the part of the author: that is, inasmuch as possible, the clinical approach to the patient's religion will prevail over broad generalizations, global statements, and appearances of infallibility. Or the contrary, in the spirit of prophetic religion, the sense of knowing in part and prophesying in part is the essence of both effective psychiatry and creative religion. My commitment, therefore, is made at the outset: that the religious care of the patient will be approached from a clinical understanding of the day-to-day care of the patient as we professionals find him or her.

WHAT IS THE CLINICAL APPROACH?

The clinical approach to the patient's religion has several characteristics.

First, the clinical approach to the patient's religion evaluates the patient's symptoms in terms of (a) what they mean to the patient, (b) what they mean in the light of the long history of the patient, (c) what they mean in the light of the immediate stresses the patient is under, and (d) what they mean in terms of the possible future hopes and ongoing spiritual integrity of the patient as a person. The patient's symptoms, particularly the patient's expressions of religious concern, are not evaluated in terms of the particular prejudices of the minister, the psychiatrist, the social worker, the psychologist, and the nurse on the therapeutic team. These religious prejudices must be confronted frankly and honestly. They cannot be the basis of the evaluation of the patient. Rather, they can be the basis of the self-evaluation of the person who holds the bias. It is best that everyone take a close look at one's biases or prejudices about religion. For example, some religionists and physicians who are not psychiatrists will feel that the whole profession of psychiatry itself is a mistake. They feel that if a person would simply use "willpower" or faith in God, the apparent psychiatric condition would "go away." With a shrug, they will say, "a little common sense is what is needed". Another example is the psychiatrist, social worker, or nurse who sees *all* religious conversation of the patient as evidence that the person is mentally ill. The sources of these defensive kinds of prejudgment in the life of the persons who hold them *can* be a source of self-knowledge that will strengthen the therapeutic ability of any helper of persons.

Second, the clinical approach to the patient's religion assumes that the patient is idiosyncratic, but not exclusively so. The religion of the patient also says much about the culture and the subcultures from which he or she comes. It is an index to the kind of community milieu from which the patient comes and to a knowledge of how to enhance the process of reentry into that community. Therefore, the subcultural symbols used in the religious thinking of patients quite often confuse the mental health professional who does not understand them to such an extent that a wrong diagnosis could occur. For example, a black man was interpreted by the admitting resident as being delusional. The patient had said his name was Elijah. Upon closer questioning by the therapeutic team in staff, the patient gave his name as Elijah, and said further that his "slave name" was Leroy Jones. Closer questioning revealed that he was involved in the Black Muslim movement. The diagnosis was finally that he was depressed but not delusional. Superficial disregard for his religious subculture could have led to the wrong medication for this patient.

Third, the clinical approach to the religious life of the patient focuses on a careful recording of religious data. More precise instruments for the assessment of the religious life of patients are being devised. Examples of instruments are the

Draper Religious Ideation Questionnaire and the Backus Sin Test as well as the Allport-Vernon Religious Attitudes Inventory. The minister on the therapeutic team will often gather data that may not be accessible to other members of the team. These data can be recorded and/or communicated verbally to the appropriate team member with proper regard for the patient's sense of privacy. In a teaching hospital the exchange of needed data about a patient is a part of the patient's chart record. Only what is needed is recorded for the best interests of the patient. The clinical approach to the patient's religion is characterized, therefore, by its data orientation. Conclusions about the patient's religious life must be based on accurate data from the patient or from the patient's family, or from both.

Fourth, the clinical approach to the patient's religion is characterized by a nonpropagandistic appreciation of the patient's dilemma as a sick person. Heavy demands for decisions about the patient's religious connections with various churches or the patient's ascribing to the particular set of dogmas represented by a religious group are not laid upon the patient. The emphasis is upon the patient's personal grasp of the forgiveness and friendliness of God, the reality of hope even in the face of disappointment, and the importance of personal faith as a source of courage rather than verbal assent to doctrinal statements. One of the threats that hangs over the psychiatric team when religion is mentioned is that the team and the patient will be submitted to some kind of forced indoctrination about a particular religion. To the contrary, the clinical approach is concerned with finding the basic cross-cultural constants, such as personal hope, interpersonal effectiveness, and social concern, that all living religions worth the name create in the life of a person. In turn, these are bases for the religious care of the patient.

Finally, the clinical approach to the religion of the patient is an educational one. The best care of patients is often done by students. Yet these students of the ministry cannot go unsupervised. The patient's religion is appreciated in the context of a fellowship of learning from the patient, from a clinically educated supervisor, and from the other members of the therapeutic team. Learning takes place best when medical students, theological students, social work students, and psychology students are taught alongside one another in the care of patients. Learning happens best when the teaching staff of a unit are in dialogue with one another across disciplinary lines. Education need not be as confusing as at first it may sound if the teaching staff genuinely related at a functional level with patient care as the center of teaching. The staff rise above the special pleading of each profession most often when the early recovery and lasting usefulness of the patient to himself or herself and to others is the primary commitment. I have chosen to call this a "transdisciplinary" approach.

RELIGIOUS CARE OF THE PATIENT
IN A TRANSDISCIPLINARY SETTING

A psychiatric team is composed—optimally—of the psychiatrist, the nurse, the social worker, the psychologist, and the minister. The minister who does this work well has submitted to intensive clinical pastoral education under supervision. The supervisor who does this supervision is educated in the supervisor process and certified nationally by the Association for Clinical Pastoral Education. Ordinarily, the clinically educated minister has had supervised clinical education in a hospital, in specialized study and casework with a variety of persons in distress. This is in addition to part of the minister's basic theological education of three years. Many pastors have a doctor's degree involving research, residency education, and personal psychotherapeutic exploration and are specialists in chaplaincy, pastoral counseling, and teaching in hospital settings.

Such education equips the minister to assume a full share of the responsibility on a transdisciplinary professional team for the religious care of the psychiatric patient. By "transdisciplinary" I mean that each member of the psychiatric team has a secure identity in having become competent in a specific base of data. Each is well enough educated in the data of the other members of the team that he or she can function in a smooth relationship with other professionals. Furthermore, "transdisciplinary" implies that the different team members have "risen above" the territorial imperatives of professional roles. Territorial defensiveness insulates and stresses many treatment teams with competition and status hassles. The concern here is primarily for the most complete understanding of and care for the patient as a total person and not as "booty" for warring factions of professional competition. Such transdisciplinary function is most possible when the team members are competent in their own field, secure in their own identity, and intellectually concerned to understand one another's particular skills and insights.

The focus, therefore, of this book is not on the "domains" or "sanctuaries" of different professions. The focus is upon functional competence of the professions related to one another in the total care of the patient. I assume that the religious life and needs of the patient are clinical realities that deserve conjoint diagnostic and therapeutic attention along with the medical, psychological, sociological, and nursing needs of the patient. All these needs are interfused in one patient. Adequate diagnostic care and therapeutic care interfuse at a transdisciplinary level to meet these needs.

A TECHNICAL VS. A POPULAR APPROACH TO RELIGION

When the professional person today confronts the possibility of the religious needs of his or her patients being a valuable part of the diagnostics and treatment of those patients, confusion can be the result. What do I mean by "the religious needs of the patient"?

To clarify this confusion, one must identify its sources. The professional person may think that I mean the popular religion that he or she "graduated" from when no longer required to go to Sunday school and church. The professional may think I mean the kind of religion that is promoted and propagandized through such television shows as those of Bob Schuler, Billy Graham, Oral Roberts, and others. Or the professional may think I mean the particular institutions of religion, such as the patient's affiliation with a Catholic or a Protestant church or a Jewish synagogue.

Essentially, I mean these things only when they affect the health and welfare of a given patient. The social reality of the psychiatric side effects of popular religion is clinically significant.

More specifically, by "religion" I mean the patient's need for freedom from bondage to fear, hate, and despair. The patient's need for love, forgiveness, and hope is a cross-cultural religious constant. The patient needs companionship in the face of loneliness, responsibility in the face of the denial of any part of that patient's own ill-fortune, and a life support system when discharged from the support of the treatment. These become "religious" when they are related to the patient's feelings toward God and the people of God. By "religion" I mean the patient's need for a sense of serenity in the face of change and the process of aging. I mean the patient's need for God as functioning adults need God, as opposed to their need for magic, as a little child would view God. By "religion" I mean the patient's need for conviction of personal responsibility for his or her own deeds as well as an assurance of the forgiveness of God for real or perceived wrongdoing. Finally, by "religion" I mean the patient's need for a personally chosen set of ethical standards. Personally chosen ethical standards grow out of a person's own experiences of hurt and damage in the past rather than the relatively petty moral codes that are wholesaled by both secular and sacred moralists of the past and the present.

Contrasting a popular approach to religion with a more technical approach is like contrasting folk medicine and patent "over the counter" medicines with prescription treatment resulting from medical diagnosis. The technical approach to religion involves basic technical knowledge of the history, linguistics, and subcultural forms of religious groupings. Technical knowledge of the Bible and church living are the "anatomy" and "biochemistry" of the education of the disciplined pastoral clinician. Systematic knowledge of various beliefs or theological systems as well as their corresponding ethical teachings becomes something of the "pharmacology" of the technical preparation of a pastoral clinician. Some of these beliefs and ethical teachings are more potentially "toxic" than others. All of them have their toxic level which must be assessed and regulated. The technical approach to the religion of psychiatric patients involves a comparative study of religion and involves an awareness of the "cross-reactions" of one set of beliefs on each other in the decision-making process. Pastoral care, like medical care, is a "contact" profession. Pastoral care has its skilled intervention procedures and its more supportive rehabilitation and restoration procedures. The basic sciences of linguistic and exegetical Biblical studies, church history, theology, and ethics are not easily applied in the classroom. Theology and ethics become applied learning in the clinics under careful supervision.

LEVELS OF RELIGIOUS CONCERN
IN PSYCHIATRIC PATIENTS

Religious concern varies in depth and seriousness among the mentally ill in similar, if not the same, ways as it does in the general population. In two studies I have made, one including 73 patients and the other 52 patients, only about 52 percent of the patients showed much if any religious concern at all. (Wayne E. Oates, *Religious Factors in Mental Illness,* Association Press, 1955; and Wayne E. Oates, *When Religion Gets Sick,* The Westminster Press, 1970.)

Among those patients who do express religious concern, the depth and seriousness of their concern may be classified in five groups: superficial concern, conventional concern, compulsive concern, character disordered religious concern, and authentic concern. Each of these deserves separate discussion.

Superficial Religious Concern

The religious concern of some patients may well be more apparent than real. In some instances, religion is a sort of "plank" that a patient grabs as he or she is decompensating into a psychotic episode. This "plank-grabbing" syndrome is exemplified in the patient whose previous history shows little or no concern about his or her relationship to God. Yet at the onset of a severe psychotic episode, such a patient may go to a religious meeting with her boyfriend and shortly afterward be admitted to a hospital ward with hallucinations about Jesus "cutting open her heart." When the psychotic episode is in remission, she may have little or no interest in finding out more about Jesus of Nazareth or pursuing the religious concerns evident in her psychotic state.

Superficial religious concern may appear as a convenience for the manipulative patient. A patient who is in the hospital as an alternative to legal prosecution for sexually molesting small children may suddenly develop a religious interest if he thinks the chaplain may be influential in shortening his stay in the hospital. When he discovers that this is not true, his religious concern vanishes. Another example is the female patient who wants to debate finely trivial theological points as a means of diverting attention from her plans for an extramarital affair with a recently discharged male patient. Such religious concern can be confronted for what it is—a game. More often than not, the religious concern simply evaporates when the issues are clarified. The patient would rather have done with a staff member's company than to change his or her ways.

Conventional Religious Concern

Faithful church members become mentally ill, and as one patient put it, "our religion suffers along with the rest of our lives." Their relationship to their church may be primarily a social contract and only conventionally a religious one. This may be either a positive or a negative force in the treatment process. If the patient's family minister knows the patient and the family, he or she can visit the patient during hospitalization and be a vital support when the person reenters the community. "Reentry" is a major problem in the convalescent patient's life. The members of the parish can enable and facilitate the care of the patient by sending cards, letters, and small gifts such as food and flowers. In short, they can reduce the ostracism and stigma which the patient receives and feels by looking upon the patient's illness as they would surgical interventions. Thus conventional religion can positively "lend" some of its respectability to mental disorders.

On the negative side, as will be seen in later chapters, conventional religious groups are often the last to know— if they ever do know—about the mental illness of their people. These are stigmatized sufferings that are borne by many outside the camp of religious rectitude. The isolation of the illness itself may be negatively reinforced by the conventional religious group. In the process of diagnosis and treatment, conventionally religious mental patients often discover some of the deeper personal significance of beliefs to which they have hitherto given only lip service. For example, the feeling of being "in grace" or being accepted, though unacceptable to oneself, is a discovery often described vividly by mental patients. Also, the discovery of the strange sense of gratitude for the modern chemical treatment of emotional disorders. Lithium is one of these medications. For example, a patient writes:

WAITING FOR LITHIUM

What nightmares they endured
I can but guess,
What scourge of hopelessness
Besieged each breast.

And how they say I spent
Those deadened days
Seems no more me
Than actresses in plays,

Though certain horrors I
Remember well
Enough to comprehend
Their anxious hell.

Persistently they waited
Till the end
And planted roses just
For me to tend.

(Janet B. Erwin, *Surviving Hopeful,* p. 35. Privately published. Copyrighted by the author, 1974. Poems used by permission of the author.)

Furthermore, the conventionally religious patient is often a crowd-oriented, gregarious person. In a mental illness the person may discover what the value of privacy and solitude is. As the same poet wrote:

A PLEA FOR PRIVACY

With all the talk
Of brotherhood
("Community," I think they say—
A laudable idea, indeed)
I shrink away—

Away to a spot
Where nature reigns,
With no one there but me;

Away to a room
I call my own
That locks with a key;

Away to gather courage,
To listen to my heart
Beat its peculiar rhythms
When apart—

Apart from all the people,
Even those I love the best
To sort through my collection—
Confessed and unconfessed—

Of hurts that, hidden, fester,
Of joys I scarce believe,
Of thoughts in brain cell prisons
Awaiting their reprieve.

Grant me this reassessment—
Not even forty days,
Just minutes in a closet
While life prays.

        Janet B. Erwin, from
        Surviving Hopeful (p. 56)

Compulsive Religious Concern

A third quality or level of religious concern is the much-written-about compulsive obsessional kind of religious concern. Freud universalized this kind of religious ideation and behavior when he said that "one might describe neurosis as individual religiosity and religion as a universal obsessional neurosis." (Sigmund Freud, "Obsessive Acts and Religious Practices," 1907, *The Standard Edition of the Complete Psychological Works of Sigmund Freud,* Vol. IX, pp. 126–127; London: Hogarth Press, 1959.) At the same, he spoke more clinically and more accurately when he likened the compulsive act as a private ceremonial act whereas religious ritual is a communal, public ceremonial act. "While the minutiae of religious ceremonials are full of significance and have symbolic meaning, those of neurotics seem foolish and senseless." (*Ibid.*, p. 119.) The accuracy of Freud's comments about compulsive religion is reasserted again and again in the clinical care of patients. However, Volney Patrick Gay does a linguistic analysis of Freud's German and says that "Freud describes the anti-instinctual mechanism typical of *Verdrängung* (repression) and that which is typical of religious acts as *Unterdrückung* (suppression) or *Verzicht* (renunciation)." (Volney Patrick Gay, "Psychopathology and Ritual," *Psychoanalytic Review,* Fall 1975, p. 499.) This would suggest that compulsive religiosity is a function of the superego, whereas more healthy religion is the function of the ego—an important distinction made by Zilboorg. From my point of view, Freud's concept is not broad enough to encompass the whole of pathological manifestations of religious concern, not to mention the expressions of healthy religion. For example, the schizophrenic and depressive patients present two additional aspects of the pathology of religion. The sociopathic or character-disordered person presents even a third aspect on the spectrum.

The compulsively religious person is usually someone with a long history of disturbed religious thinking along with a long history of defective religious training and emotional deprivation. This group of patients comprise about fifteen percent of groups of patients studied. They present stubborn symptoms that defy psychiatric treatment more successfully than many other disorders. The compulsive religious concern is "dyed in the wool" and "woven into the cloth" of the personality of the patient.

Quite often, a patient with a compulsive obsessional kind of religious concern enters a hospital suffering from a superimposed depression. Chronic thought patterns of self-negation become acute in a state of depression. Through the use of present medicines these patients are brought through the depression. The obsessional thinking in the religious sphere of their lives continues.

In religious literature, this level of concern has been described. The apostle Paul called this kind of religiosity "bondage to the law," by which he meant the ceremonialism of his ancestral religion. He felt that "all who rely on works of the law are under a curse" (Gal. 3:10). To the contrary, he felt that "he who through faith is righteous shall live." Paul rejected "religion" and affirmed a life of faith, hope, and love. The Catholic Church identifies compulsive religion as scrupulosity, with which Martin Luther was afflicted. The churches of the Great Awakening in America lay much emphasis upon the religious "revival." A revival is a series of religious meetings led by an evangelist preacher who calls upon the "unsaved" to repent, walk down the church aisle during the "invitation," while salvation hymns are being played, and confess faith in Jesus Christ. They are then "born again" into a new life in Christ. The assumption is that this "new birth" wipes out past sins and starts a "new life in Christ." Compulsive religiosity appears too among revivalist church members in their preoccupation with whether they are "saved" or not. These persons often make repeated professions of faith in revival meetings. Sooner or later even members of these religious groups begin to identify this as a "sickness."

Enough has been said here to identify compulsive levels of religious concern. More will be said later.

Religious Concern in Character Disorders

An even more difficult level of religious concern among psychiatric patients is with sociopathic uses and misuses of religious concern. This may be called the "Elmer Gantry" syndrome, after the character in Sinclair Lewis' novel *Elmer Gantry*. These persons use religion as a platform for their exhibitionism, as a medium for the seduction of the opposite sex, and as a means of "ripping off" their followers for money and power. Such persons do not often appear in psychiatric treatment. Occasionally when they have just been caught or are about to be caught in deviant behaviors, they will run for cover in psychiatric treatment. For example, a religious leader may be caught by members of the church in the aberrant sexual exploitation of other persons. Or, another person is on the verge of being exposed for the misappropriation of funds collected by the congregation.

In a sense, admission to a psychiatric hospital is almost or actually a manipulation of the "health delivery systems." It may be just a more respectable form of self-imposed imprisonment for wrongdoing. Pleading insanity may be a way of appealing to the sentiments and sympathies of those who would otherwise hold the person legally and morally responsible for obvious and gross wrongdoing.

The separation of the sociopathic qualities of religious motivation from the "acting out" behavior of a genuinely depressed person is a matter of differential diagnosis for later discussion. In Biblical terms, such diagnosis is "testing the spirit." In I John 4:1 the admonition is given: "Beloved, do not believe every spirit, but test the spirits to see whether they are of God; for many false prophets have gone out into the world." The false prophet is one who is "depraved in mind and bereft of the truth, imagining that godliness is a means of gain" (I Tim. 6:5).

Authentic Religious Concern

A considerable number of psychiatric patients are authentically concerned religiously. The ego functions are at work in the fray of the psychiatric illness. The patients are seeking for a genuinely meaningful interpretation of the chaos that has come upon their lives. These patients are usually acutely ill. The degree of their desperation is high. Furthermore, they tend to work at trying to solve the greatest problems of life: e.g., the problem of deliverance from old patterns of life and discovery of new patterns for existence; the problem of a durable meaning to life in spite of tragedy; the problem of integrity before God in a world that places more value upon appearance than upon reality; the problem of forgiveness for failure and recovery from the shame of never being able to achieve a much-cherished goal in life. These are existential problems that call for developing one's own interpretation of life to be large enough to encompass if not to explain the problems. The struggle of being becomes one of a "joined battle" between the forces of redemption and the forces of destruction.

For example, Anton Boisen, a devout Congregational minister, had three schizophrenic psychotic breakdowns in the course of his life. He recovered each time to make an extensive scholarly contribution to the understanding of the religious aspects of mental illness and to the instruction of other ministers in the understanding and care of the mentally ill. He published a research study of 173 cases of severely psychotic patients. In eight of the cases he found that "most striking is the tendency of the panic reaction to produce change either for the better or for the worse. Not only do we find the largest proportion of social recoveries and of improvements in the panic group, but we also observe that when panic occurs in the warped personality it may serve to break up the shell of delusional misinterpretation and set the victim free." (Anton T. Boisen, *The Exploration of the Inner World: A Study of Mental Disorder and Religious Experience*, p. 43; University of Pennsylvania Paperback, 1971.) Boisen says further that these eruptive types of experience may be growth producing, a chaotic sort of personal development. "Such disturbances often serve as a sort of judgment day, the patient blurting out what before . . . he would not have dared to say. Just as inflammation in the physical organism is an attempt at repair or elimination, so the emotional disturbance serves to purge out accumulated poisons and break up malignant concealment devices which have been blocking development." (*Ibid.*, pp. 158–159.)

Yet this kind of interpretation assumes a considerable amount of effective and creative religious experience and education as a background, a strong religious life support system as a fellowship, and a remarkable amount of human strength on the part of the patient. We do see these factors in wholesome confluence in psychiatric settings where the staff are religiously aware enough to make careful clinical assessment and use of them. Authentic religious experience among mental patients, as among the prison population, in fact does happen. Boisen's case is only one among many on record.

The above classification of levels or qualities of religious concern has been developed over a period of years of listening intently to what psychiatric patients have to say. General though it is, specific cases of illustration have been used to lower the fog index. If this classification is kept in mind, the more specific case presentations in the later chapters will make the classification clearer. Also, the terms "superficial religious concern," "conventional religious concern," "compulsive religious concern," "religious concern in character disorders," and "authentic religious concern" provide a convenient shorthand for evaluating the role of religion in the life of a psychiatric patient.

Assessment is a task of clinical judgment. Religious assessment can be done technically and clinically. Adequate assessment is the basis for the religious care of the patient.

2

RECURRENT RELIGIOUS TEACHINGS
AND
THEIR PSYCHIATRIC IMPLICATIONS

The American psychiatric team face a bewildering collage of different religious groups as they seek to take seriously the religious care of the psychiatric patient. There are approximately three hundred separate religious groups in America. How can one bring some sort of continuity and order out of these many subgroups? Many problems emerge as one tries to do this. First, one is prompted, by the sheer numbers of patients, to associate mental illness with the particular religious group that is most numerous in the area. For example, in Jackson, Mississippi, one would quickly associate pathology with Southern Baptists. In Idaho or in Utah one would tend to associate psychiatric difficulties with the Mormons. In Boston, one might associate mental illness with Catholicism. This does not necessarily follow upon closer scrutiny on a nation-wide basis.

Second, one is likely to make a global statement about all religious groups and use a "lumping procedure," i.e., all religious interest or concern is either *ipso facto* "therapeutic" or malignant in its effect upon the psychic health of persons. In doing so, one makes a philosophical judgment rather than a clinical assessment.

Third, one is likely to attempt a classification of different religious groups on the basis of their organizational presence in the American scene. This is the most often attempted effort to bring order out of chaos. However, the cultural impact of religious ingroups on each other makes this approach both confusing and unreliable.

Rev. J. E. Runions, M.D., a Canadian psychiatrist and minister who is an associate professor in the Department of Psychiatry at the University of Alberta in Edmonton, Alberta, sought to classify different religious faiths according to their organizational or denominational structures. He has a fourfold classification: Baptistic Denominations, Holiness Denominations, Ethnic Denominations, Major Denominations (United Church of Canada, The Anglican Church of Canada, and the Roman Catholic Church). (Rev. J. E. Runions, M.D., "Religion and Psychiatric Practice," *Canadian Psychiatric Journal*, Vol. 19, 1974, pp. 79–85.) The sociological and political context of Canada provides more usefulness for Canadians for this classification than does the context of persons in the United States. The history of a state-supported church is more recent and vivid in Canada. The extensive union of different denominations is more effective in Canada than in the United States. However, the classification of the religion of psychiatric patients used by Runions is at best problematic because of the way in which denominational structures represent political and power considerations which are usually irrelevant to the psychiatric conditions of patients. For example, Runions is a Baptist minister himself. Twenty-six out of seventy, or 37 percent of his sample of psychiatric patients, came out of the Baptist population. Do Baptists represent that percent of the population in Canada? One could also ask: Are Baptists overrepresented in the sample because of an unusual degree of mental illness among Baptists? One does not know this. Are they overrepresented because the psychiatrist himself is a Baptist and has a level of acceptance and acquaintance among Baptists that he does not have among other faith groups? Maybe this is true; one does not know. Runions points out that half of the patients were referred by religiously committed physicians. A religious "ingrouping" may be surmised, but not with certainty.

The *degree* of religious commitment or devoutness is more important as a variable than is denominational affiliation. This conclusion has been supported by studies of large samplings of persons such as the Kinsey studies of human sexuality. Kinsey made the distinction among religious subjects along devoutness lines rather than ecclesiastical connections: (1) Devout, (2) Moderately Religious, and (3) Religiously Inactive. (Alfred C. Kinsey *et al., Sexual Behavior in the Human Male,* pp. 55–56; W. B. Saunders Company, 1948.) Lenski affirms the importance of what he calls devotionalism, another word for degree of devoutness, in his choice of devoutness as a basis of the evaluation of the religious factor in human experience. He says that the religious factor can be defined in terms of devotionalism, i.e., the practice of prayer, the study of sacred Scriptures, the adherence to the religious rules of discipline of one's faith group, and active affiliation with its community of persons. (Gerhard Lenski, *The Religious Factor;* Doubleday & Company, Inc., 1961.) In another study, James E. Enstrom makes practice of the religious faith a criterion for evaluating the strength of the religious factor, even though he chooses one faith group, the Mormons, in his study of cancer mortality among members of the Church of Jesus Christ of Latter-day Saints in Utah and California.

I affirm the importance of devoutness and practice as criteria rather than denominational affiliation. I add to them the nature of the religious teaching and practice as a basis of the classification of religious subgroups. These teachings tend to pervade a variety of different denominational connections. They are themes running throughout many rather than just one religious denomination. The different textures of belief and practice are the bases of classification I would suggest for bringing some sort of order out of the confusing pantheon of religious belief and practice among Americans, and especially among psychiatric patients. When we do this, different patterns of religious belief and practice tend to be present in greater or lesser intensity in a variety of different power structures of religious denominations:

1. Advent or "end of the world" teachings and practices
2. Sacramental-liturgical teachings and practices
3. Deliverance and ethnic teachings and practices
4. Communal and theocratic teachings and practices
5. Spiritual gifts and Spirit possession teachings and practices
6. Mystical teachings and practices
7. "Escape from freedom" teachings and practices
8. Positive thinking and health teachings and practices

A given denomination will espouse beliefs and practices that would represent it in several of these groupings. If one is eager to see where one's own denomination is to be classified, one would find the set of teachings and practices that is most representative of one's group. From the point of view of the religious care of the psychiatric patients, the position taken here is that the degree of devoutness in holding to a particular religious attitude and practicing a particular kind of behavior provides the most reliable basis for appreciating the relevance of the religion of the patient to the patient's psychic health or illness. As was indicated in the previous chapter, religious concern in the psychiatric patient is significant in the diagnosis, treatment, prognosis, recovery, and prevention of recidivism in terms of the superficiality, the conventionality, the compulsiveness, the sociopathy, and/or the authenticity of the patient's religious belief and practice.

Each of the eight groups of teachings and practices needs description, illustration, and referencing for further study. This chapter is, therefore, a discussion of each of the eight groups. The concern is with religious belief as behavior as it is defined by the specific group to which a patient belongs. This is where the rubber of life hits the concrete of reality and makes a difference in lives in progress. The purpose of this chapter is (1) to see American religious groups in terms of larger themes of belief, teaching, and practice, (2) to use illustrative religious groups as case examples while listing other similar groups alongside the illustrative groups, and (3) to identify some psychiatric side effects commonly seen in adherents to these particular groups.

ADVENT OR "END OF THE WORLD"
TEACHINGS AND PRACTICES

"Advent" has a double meaning in Christian teaching. It refers to the Advent season, when most Christians celebrate the coming or the birth of Jesus of Nazareth. Adventism refers to the teaching that the Kingdom of God is expected to come on earth immediately. A person expresses a distinct and urgent concern for Christ's Second Coming to set up an earthly kingdom in which believers in Christ will become a part of the ruling power of the earth. Then the person's position in the world is suddenly shifted from persecution, obscurity, and powerlessness on the earth to national and international prominence, acceptance, and political strength.

This belief has a long history. Jesus' own disciples expected him to set up this kind of world order in his time. Some evidence suggests that for a time Jesus himself held this hope. He said, "Truly, I say to you, there are some standing here who will not taste death before they see that the kingdom of God has come with power" (Mark 9:1). Later, he also said: "But of that day or that hour, no one knows, not even the angels in heaven, nor the Son, but only the Father. Take heed, watch" (Mark 13:32–33). Yet this hope was transformed in his life to the realization of the inevitability of his own death on the cross. He promised to send the Holy Spirit as a continuing counselor and guide to his followers (John, ch. 14). Along with this promise was the commitment to return in the same way in which he left at the time of his ascension into the heavens (Acts 1:6–11). Some Christians have interpreted this "return" as the gift of the Holy Spirit. Some have insisted on the hope that not only would they receive the Holy Spirit but they would also live to see the visible takeover by the returning Christ to rule the earthly kingdom. The precise setting of times, the precise manner of the ruling power, and the specific choice of the believer and rejection of the nonbeliever have been predicted.

From the beginning of Christian history, several profound emotional and sociological side effects have accrued to the belief in the early second coming of the Messiah. They can be listed here:

1. There is a shift of values about sex and marriage. If one *really* believes that the end of the age is at hand and that, as Jesus said," they neither marry nor are given in marriage, but are like angels in heaven" (Matt. 22:30), then several types of behavior might result. For example, those persons would not marry, not because they considered sex as evil, necessarily, but because of the extreme brevity of time remaining. Hence, celibacy could emerge. Or, again, if those persons did marry, they might not consider it wise or necessary to have children. The Shakers of the middle of the eighteenth century rejected both marriage and procreation. They devoted themselves to the care of orphans in the post-Civil War period in Kentucky and other parts of the country. They held so devotedly to this belief that they contributed to the end of their own sect by not reproducing their own kind. Thus, many initial Christian teachings about sex are not based upon Greek ideas about the evil of the flesh; they are outgrowths of the trivial nature of sex in the light of larger and more pressing possibilities of the end of the age. Or, again, the attitudes of the believer might affect his or her devotion to work. In Thessalonica, because of belief in Christ's imminent return the temptation to idleness, being a busybody, and doing no work was tending to become widespread. Therefore, the apostle Paul said: "If any one will not work, let him not eat" (II Thess. 3:10).

2. There is an unusual shift in the attitude toward death. When a person believes that he or she will live *as is* until the end of the age, then the fear of death becomes neutralized. Decisions about medical care, insurance, and the prolongation of life become contradictions of the belief in the imminent coming of the Kingdom of God. Participating in war becomes anathema. The thing to do is to let the children of darkness fight it out in some kind of Armageddon. (Armaged-

don is the name of a place mentioned in Revelation 16:16 where the forces of evil and the kings, rulers, and authorities of the world will assemble for battle on "the great day of God the Almighty." Adventists, especially millennialists—those who believe that Christ will rule for a thousand years prior to the final resurrection—believe that this battle will be a historical fact.)

3. There is a particular shift in attitude toward earthly authorities, persecution, and pain. Persons who genuinely believe in the imminent return of the Lord Jesus Christ are likely to develop a group relationship in which all members are considered ministers. They reject the idea of a priesthood. They will resist encroachment by governmental authorities on their lives in such things as the education of their children, the treatment of their sick, the paying of taxes and responding to military service drafts, etc. In turn, they are likely to be willing to go to prison, take verbal abuse, or even be put to death rather than renounce their faith. These attitudes are particularly relevant to the work of the psychiatric team with patients who embrace and act upon these beliefs. They are reluctant to accept the authority of *either* the doctor *or* the minister; legal measures used in committing patients for psychiatric care are challenged on religious grounds. Latent or manifest paranoid constructions put these patients in the position to attack the establishment rather than to defend their own position.

Two groups of religious devotees are most illustrative of these attitudes which I have described. One of these, the Jehovah's Witnesses, is a newer group than the other, i.e., the Seventh-day Adventists. The Jehovah's Witnesses were founded by Charles Taze Russell soon after 1870. He taught that the end of all things was slated for 1914. The early Jehovah's Witnesses were called "Russellites," and later were believers in Rutherfordism, after the name of Russell's successor, Joseph F. Rutherford. They believe that "millions now living will never die," although the first setting of the date of the end of all things did not happen.

In their earlier history, the Jehovah's Witnesses refused to own real estate. They rented instead of buying real estate. Though they still believe that "millions now living will never die," that they will see the final end of Satan's rule in God's war of Armageddon, they have begun to buy real estate.

Another belief that is most often met by physicians and chaplains is the Jehovah's Witness belief that blood transfusions are forbidden by Scripture. They base this on such passages as Lev. 17:13–14, Deut. 12:16, and Lev. 17:10. These passages refer specifically to the eating of animals' blood. The same prohibitions are made in Acts 15:28–29. They have been so persistent in this that physicians have taken it as a challenge in at least one instance. A group of surgeons treated forty-six Jehovah's Witness patients who underwent aortocoronary bypass surgery. Only two of these patients died, a mortality rate of 4.3 percent. Neither death was related to the lack of blood transfusions. Their results caused them to conclude that their policy would be to avoid blood transfusions whenever possible in all operations. (F. M. Sandiford, "Aortocoronary Bypass in Jehovah's Witnesses: Review of 46 Patients," *American Surgery*, Vol. 42, No. 1, Jan., 1976, pp. 17–22.)

The psychiatric team have a different set of problems with which to deal in the care of the Jehovah's Witness patients. As has been indicated, the belief system and practices of the Jehovah's Witnesses encourage them to invite persecution and prompt them to take a grandiose position in relation to the beliefs of anyone else. A study was made in Australia of fifty Jehovah's Witnesses admitted to the Mental Health Service of Western Australia. Followers of the sect, according to this study, are three times more likely to be diagnosed as suffering from schizophrenia and nearly four times more likely to be suffering from paranoid schizophrenia than the rest of the population at risk. The question is raised by the study as to whether or not pre-psychotic persons are more likely to join the sect than normal persons and what part (if any) membership in the sect has in bringing about such a breakdown. (J. Spencer, "The Mental Health of Jehovah's Witnesses," *British Journal of Psychiatry,* Vol. 126, June 1975, pp. 556–559.) An additional question needs attention: To what extent does joining the sect socialize a psychotic episode and prevent the person from becoming a patient in a hospital? The Australian study raises the similar question: Is the opiate of the religious belief such as to make the use of psychotropic drugs either unnecessary or undesirable, or both?

The Jehovah's Witnesses are a relatively new and radical example of the belief in the return of the Lord as a ruler of the political order of things on earth. One can see that resistance to medical care is at base a way of expressing the belief that death will not reach them, but only the Satan bound. A less radical and more creative example of this same belief and its appropriation in life is the Seventh-day Adventists.

The Seventh-day Adventists are an older group of believers in the immediate return of the Lord. William Miller (1782–1849), a Baptist minister, studied Archbishop Ussher's chronology published in the margins of editions of the King James Version of the Bible beginning in 1701, which began by stating that the earth was created in 4004 B.C. Miller calculated, along with the help of his promoter and publicist, Joshua V. Himes (1805–1895), that the date of the coming of the Lord would be finally October 22, 1844. Thousands of people began preparing for this date, the last definite date to be set by the movement's leadership. Yet a hard core of believers survived what they later came to call "The Great Disappointment." A third powerful leader arose in the person of Ellen G. Harmon (later Ellen G. White), who poured out a new version of Adventism which held the Ten Commandments to be the tested and true expression of the character of God. They emphasized therefore worship on Saturday, instead of on Sunday, the first day of the week. They emphasized heavily the giving of a tenth, or a tithe, of their income and offering much more than this. Their per capita giving is about $500 a year from their membership of

2,145,061 in 16,726 churches.

From the point of view of the physician and the other members of the psychiatric team, the most significant teachings of the Seventh-day Adventists are those which concern diet, health, and medical care. They are vegetarians. They have developed food stores that present foods prepared as meat substitutes. They abstain from anything with caffeine in it—coffee, tea, cola drinks, etc. Alcohol is forbidden. Obesity is frowned upon. Outstanding among their hospitals and clinics established in the latter part of the nineteenth and the earlier part of the twentieth century has been the Battle Creek Sanitarium, founded by their vegetarian protégés the Kelloggs, who were outstanding physicians. They experimented with foods and invented and developed the breakfast cereals that bear the Kellogg name today. A very modern medical center is operated by the Adventists in Glendale, California. This medical center concentrates on both treatment and prevention. It has an alcoholic rehabilitation program, a program aimed at dealing with obesity, a pulmonary clinic that combines treatment of upper respiratory disorders with the treatment of addiction to tobacco and the abuse of other smoking substances such as marijuana. The cancer mortality rate over the period from 1958 to 1965 of persons of the Adventist faith who were over thirty-five years of age was about 60 percent less than that of the California population as a whole. (James E. Enstrom, "Cancer Mortality Among Mormons," *Cancer*, Vol. 36, No. 3, Sept. 1975, p. 825.)

When one compares and contrasts the Jehovah's Witnesses and the Adventists, from a psychiatric point of view and a general medical point of view as well, one sees that their belief in the coming of the Lord prompts them to handle seriously the reality of impending death. The Jehovah's Witnesses use the belief to deny that the "elect" will die: "Millions now living will never die." This belief was also present in the earlier and older expressions of Adventist life. As the Adventists endured "The Great Disappointment" of October 22, 1844, however, they stepped back. They reassessed their practice of their faith. They began to affirm the reality of death and to seek the secrets of longevity. They found this in the health emphases of their rigid dietary practices, the austerity of their use of money, and the subtle labor significance of their worshiping on Saturday. In contemporary American society, to worship on Saturday almost assures that there will be *two* days and not one day of rest, and thus they challenge the addiction to work. Furthermore, the psychiatric significance of the belief in the *end* of time is demonstrated as being an impetus toward the conservation and care of life instead of martyrdom. In the next chapter, when we discuss the common religious symptom pictures of the psychiatric patients, the relevance of the "end of the world" belief for the suicidal lethality of a patient's thinking will be assessed.

Sacramental-Liturgical Teachings and Practices

The hope of the end of the age gradually faded in the life of the early Christian church of the first century. Even within the Biblical story of the New Testament, the hope of an immediate second coming was pushed into the background by the hope that the church itself would *be* the earthly embodiment of the City of God. As churches developed, they gradually became interested in the care and nurture of children. They renewed interest in marriage between men and women as like unto the relationship of Christ to the church. They developed ways of sorting out the difference between true and false prophets and of settling differences between contending Christians. Examples of this can be found in Ephesians, chs. 5 and 6, Matthew, ch. 18, and the whole book of James. Widows were appointed and given a widow's supplement of money to be comforters of other widows. Deacons were appointed because Greek widows were uncared for and the administration of food to the needy was detracting from the apostolic task of preaching and teaching. A priesthood was beginning to develop.

In the early days of the Christians of Rome, they were set over against the Roman state and were put to death as enemies of the Caesars. Then came the recognition of the church by the state under the leadership of Emperor Constantine in A.D. 313 in the Edict of Milan, which proclaimed "Christianity on a full legal equality with any religion of the Roman world, and ordered the restoration of all church property confiscated in the recent persecution." (Williston Walker, *A History of the Christian Church*, rev. ed., pp. 101–102; Charles Scribner's Sons, 1970.) Whereas Constantine did not establish an imperial state church, his conversion and the establishment of the bishop of Constantinople began the struggle of the papacy to become the Imperial State Church. Finally, after the Council of Nicea established the Nicene Creed, Rome did become the sacred city of the papacy. The church became a focus of both political and ecclesiastical power. The pope and the priesthood under him became the custodian of the "keys of the kingdom of God." Salvation meant being a part of the Roman Catholic Church, the dispenser of forgiveness and hope. The hope of the immediate return of the Lord to rule was now a realized hope in that the church itself *was* the earthly counterpart of the heavenly rule of God. To be in the church meant to be safe from eternal punishment in hell and to be assured of eternal happiness in heaven. Elaborate explanations of the afterlife were developed, even including the idea of purgation after death to make one completely safe in heaven.

The Roman Catholic Church, as well as other groups such as the Greek Orthodox Church, the Russian Orthodox Church, and the Anglican Church, developed systems of discipline that take into account the common crises of the human life cycle. This system is called the sacramental system. The Seven Sacraments parallel in an unusually similar way the stages in the development of a person from birth to death. The church is involved in priestly ways at the times of the medical care of the patient in the premarital examination; the obstetrical and gynecological care of women; the pediatric care of newborn infants; the threat of an impending divorce; the possibility of remarriage after a divorce; guilt over a past divorce, which is so often involved in psychiatric treatment of patients; in the events of bereavement; and in the encounter with death. These Seven Sacraments are as follows:

1. Baptism: Takes place at birth
2. Confirmation: Takes place at or about puberty
3. Eucharist, or the Mass: A sharing in the communal by participation in the mysterious Meal of the Body and Blood of Christ. Takes place weekly and on high holy days and is shared by all who have been confirmed.
4. Penance: The confession of sins to a priest acting as confessor, for absolution by that priest. Takes place at least once a year and is expected on an as-needed basis.
5. Orders: The sacrament of initiation into the priesthood, into an order of sisters, etc.
6. Marriage: Marriage itself is a sacrament and no marriage is to be "outside" the church. If persons are married under conditions "otherwise than as God's Word doth allow, their marriage is not lawful." A member of the church who is divorced and wishes to marry again must be able to demonstrate that the marriage was not an authentic marriage from the outset. It is to be annulled before remarriage can take place. Divorce is not recognized, but annulment through ecclesiastical courts is recognized.
7. Extreme Unction: The Last Rites, to be administered when death threatens or is imminent.

When one places these rites on a spectrum with the developmental eras of human life and compares them with the responsibilities of the medical team in the care of patients, it can be seen that they coincide with each other in time and circumstance. Critical issues of medical judgment are placed vis-à-vis the teachings and practices of the sacramental-liturgical churches. Some of these issues are listed below.

1. The problems of medical intervention in attempts to control the birth process through artificial means of contraception. Only the rhythm method of birth control is approved by the Roman Catholic Church. Recent surveys indicate that 80 percent of Catholics practice artificial contraception in spite of these teachings. However, the degree of ambivalence, guilt, and inadvertency that the teachings themselves introduce into the thinking and behavior of persons who have been reared as Catholics is periodically psychiatrically significant in cases of depression. One does not have to be a Catholic to be affected by these teachings. The teachings pervade the beliefs of many Protestants.

2. The problems of medical intervention in impending childbirths to produce a medically induced miscarriage. Some Catholic patients ask whether it would be murder if, let us say, a child that will predictably be a mongoloid or Down's syndrome child is thus aborted. Quite apart from the case of medical intervention in extreme situations, the problem of legalized abortion puts the physician and the rest of the therapeutic team in conflict with the teachings and practices of the church. Furthermore, persons who have had an abortion may present guilt over the abortion months or even many years later in psychiatric syndromes encountered in the religious care of the psychiatric patient. This, however, is not by any means always true.

3. Patients who have been divorced, and especially those who are remarried, will present long-standing ruminations about the sinfulness of their behavior and their remorse over their excommunication from the life of the church.

It is easy for a Protestant to take all these issues and begin special pleading for Protestantism, and especially for his or her own particular brand of Protestantism. However, clinical casework in the care of the psychiatric patient will repeatedly affirm that the teachings and practices of the sacramental-liturgical churches have become the moving assumptions of a broad spectrum of Protestant groups at the point of attitudes that determine behavior. A Wesleyan Methodist may present "unamended" Catholic concepts of marriage, divorce, childbirth, child rearing, etc. Similarly, a Baptist may have interpretations of marriage and divorce that are indistinguishable from the Catholic teachings.

The Catholic, Anglo-Catholic, and other liturgical communions were primarily challenged by Protestants on their concepts of personal freedom and the power of the papacy. These were basically political issues. The popular expressions of a wide range of Protestant groups suggest that they have —quite without protest—accepted and espoused teachings concerning marriage, sexuality, divorce, and child rearing that recapitulate the teachings of Catholicism. They have done this without developing a system of enforcement and instruction such as the Catholic Church has. Therefore, the individual is bound with the heavy burden of certainty that one's place in heaven or hell is assured by the way one behaves in these matters. In short, many Protestants are bound and laden with these demands and guilts. They are given none of the political, social, institutional, and liturgical support that the Catholic Church provides for its faithful adherents.

Therefore, an unexpected thing has occurred in the development of a sacramental attitude and practice among some churches that have had the most vociferous objection to Catholicism. These churches are usually in *the tradition of the religious revival meeting.* They have built elaborate denominational structures on the following assumptions:

1. They assume that salvation comes through conversion from sin to a profession of faith in Jesus Christ, who saves them one by one *when* they confess their faith in Jesus Christ and make a public announcement of this during a religious service, either at a revival meeting or at a regular Sunday meeting of the church.

2. They assume that the urging and encouraging of people to make such "decisions for Christ" in order to be "saved" is best done in a communitywide revival meeting such as is exemplified in the Billy Graham and Oral Roberts revival

meetings *or* in a revival meeting conducted by a local church, usually with a "visiting evangelist," i.e., a guest speaker. Sometimes the pastor of a church will conduct these special revival services. In some churches, the assumption is that these revivals will be conducted every weekend and the main task of a Christian is to "win souls to Christ," i.e., to persuade other persons not affiliated with the church to join upon a profession of faith. Extensive programs for training persons to be "soul winners" are conducted. Highly specific formulae are devised whereby a person is affirmed by the minister and the congregation as having been "saved," or "born again."

3. They assume that this act—a profession of faith—is sufficient for dealing with one's emotional problems, for producing happiness, and for securing one's right of entry into heaven. The failure to make such a profession explains why a person is depressed, unhappy, and in danger of going to hell. If the person would have the experience of "getting right with God," then he or she would not have all these problems. This experience of "getting right with God" is often called "being born again" after the passage in John, ch. 3, where Nicodemus is told by Jesus that he must be born again in order to enter eternal life. This experience may be a traumatic, life-shaking encounter such as the apostle Paul had on the road to Damascus; it may be the dramatic turn-around of a person such as Charles Colson, who, after the Watergate scandal, was converted, though already a nominal church member, and writes of it in his book, *Born Again;* or it may be the relatively routine experience of children, youth, and adults who are essentially simply "joining the church" without such upheavals of the inner life.

The revival tradition cuts across denominational lines almost indiscriminately. It is very evident among Southern Baptists, Wesleyan Methodists, Cumberland Presbyterians, the Church of Christ, the Church of God, Charismatic churches, Pentecostal churches, and a large number of Independent Baptist churches.

From a psychiatric point of view, all the data that have been set forth here are simply a prelude to an observation that compulsive obsessional rumination and depressive self-rejection collect around the symptoms of which we have been speaking. In the content of the thought of psychiatric patients, recurrent themes of the fear of being excommunicated from the Mass and the fear of not being "saved" though one repeatedly has been to revivals occur. The purpose of going into this much detail is to give the members of the psychiatric treatment team the cultural subgroup language and some of the behavioral patterns with which to assess the thinking of the patient. More specific symptom pictures will be discussed in the next chapter.

Yet the obverse of the threat of condemnation is true also. The presence of an understanding priest or pastor whose attitude of care countermands the self-condemnation clutching a patient "can be a source of immeasurable encouragement for patients. They [the presence of the priest and the sacraments] become concrete and almost tangible evidence of God's love and concern during a time of fear and anxiety." (Cornelius J. Van Der Poll, C.S.S., "Pastoral Care. Presence: Sacraments, Ethics, and Community," *Hospital Progress,* Vol. 56, No. 5, May 1975, p. 81.) The need for "tangible evidence" is greater, it seems, in psychiatric patients, in line with the concreteness of their thinking.

DELIVERANCE AND ETHNIC TEACHINGS AND PRACTICES

The appearing of the Lord and the kind of salvation that brings redemption from bondage takes on a whole new context in the lives of people who are in slavery as oppressed minority groups. Inevitably, yearning for deliverance from slavery and oppression finds a profound religious expression among them. Religious language and ethnic language are closely tied together. The music of oppressed people charges words with emotion. Political and religious changes have been brought about throughout history by the identification of religion with a homeland, a nationality, a language group, or a race. Power bound up in the development of religious subcultures still has heavy political influence. In turn, the subcultures have their own relevance to the issues of illness and health, to the care of the psychiatric patient.

One of the oldest and most powerful ethnic groups are the Jews. Their profound religious pilgrimage is almost a working model for the appreciation of the need for deliverance and the need to belong to a unique people. Several historical events in the life of the Jews have successively reinforced their sense of need for deliverance. Religion is born in situations in which someone is in bondage. The Jews have felt this need for deliverance in situations when their relationships both to God and to each other as a people have been intensified to a maximum. The bondage in Egypt, the Babylonian captivity, and the holocaust under Hitler were situations of this kind.

1. The call of Abraham, ancestor of the people of Israel, to leave Haran, his ancestral home in northern Mesopotamia. Abraham is chosen to play a decisive role in God's historical purpose for Israel. That purpose was to "become a great nation," to receive a land of their own, and to mediate light and blessing to other peoples. Israel had God's blessing and was to curse nations that cursed them. (Gen. 12:1–8.)

2. The deliverance of the Israelites from slavery in Egypt through the leadership of Moses and the establishment of the Jews in an elaborate system of religious laws and rituals and in a new land in Palestine.

3. The return of the Jews from the Babylonian captivity to their native Palestine and Jerusalem.

4. The battle of the Maccabeans against the Hellenization of the Seleucid king, Antiochus Epiphanes.

5. The centuries of landlessness and wandering, culminating in the holocaust under Hitler which sought to stamp them from the face of the earth, killing six million of them.

6. The return to Palestine and the formation of the State of Israel.

One factor common to all these events is the Jews' faith that the future existence of the Jewish nation is dependent upon its return to the historical homeland. Another factor common to these events is the binding power of the Jewish Torah, or holy law. The family life of Jews coheres around the practice of celebrations and confessions in the context of the Jewish history and the Torah. The structure of the Jewish family, with its value upon the leadership of a wise father, held them together as individuals, families, and as a nation. Their focal rituals involve the family. As in the case of ceremonial circumcision and the Bar Mitzvah, these rituals serve as completions of the stages of maturity with their separation from mother, from childhood, etc. It could well be that the activation of psychotic potential seems to be less both in number and intensity in Jews because of *(a)* their sense of corporate destiny and *(b)* the cohesive power of their rituals in offsetting stress of separation, transition, and uncooperation. (George Pollock, "Jewish Circumcision: A Birth and Initiation Rite of Passage," *The Israel Annals of Psychiatry and Related Disciplines,* Vol. 2, No. 4, Dec. 1973, pp. 297–300.)

The present stress within the Jewish race rests upon the politicization and secularization of the children of parents in the World War II era. In a discussion of psychiatric treatment, however, Weintraub and Aronson suggest that, in the sample of the patients they studied, "the great majority of Jewish patients in our group were described by their analysis as participating minimally or not at all in the practice of their religion." Yet, they observe, the influence of religious teaching continues in the absence of formal participation in religious practices. (Walter Weintraub, M.D., and H. Aronson, "Patients in Psychoanalysis: Some Findings Related to Sex and Religion," *American Journal of Orthopsychiatry,* Vol. 44, No. 1, Jan. 1974, pp. 102–108.)

A second group illustrates the deliverance theme in an ethnic setting. This group is the American Black Muslims. They are newer to the scene of the battle for deliverance, but their life represents more acutely the relationship of religion and deliverance from oppression, poverty, disease, and family disruption. The Black Muslims have antecedents in American history for the elision of their cry for deliverance with a messianic religious fervor.

Nat Turner was a slave in southeastern Virginia in 1831. He learned to read and became a house servant for his master. Very early he became aware that he was a slave and that reading was a way to freedom. He early felt that God had called him to preach. He received increasing resistance from his owners. In a massive psychotic break, he organized a sustained revolt of slaves who went on a killing rampage against whites. The important factor from our point of view is that Nat Turner did this and died by hanging as a response to what he perceived to be a direct command from God. He felt it was his divine mission to kill all the white people in Southampton County, Virginia. That spirit of violence has been partly religiously driven periodically until its most recent outbursts in Watts, Newark, Detroit, and many other cities in the 1960's. The important reality to note is the religious fervor for deliverance.

Malcolm X was the most gifted representative of today's Black Muslims. He grew up as the son of a Baptist preacher. His father was gunned down in the streets of a Michigan town for his efforts in behalf of his black race. Malcolm X's mother struggled with poverty until she collapsed in a psychotic state and was placed in a state hospital. He himself became a street child, a drug pusher, and a pimp. He was arrested and imprisoned. In prison he joined the Black Muslims, became an avid reader, broke the habits of smoking, eating pork, using drugs, and uttering profanities. He was released and became an effective preacher and organizer of the fast-growing Black Muslims. He insisted that "not ideologies, but race, a color is what binds human beings. . . . The collective white man's history has left the non-white peoples no alternative, either, but to draw closer to each other." (*The Autobiography of Malcolm X*, p. 285; Grove Press, Inc., 1966.)

Yet a sense of doom and death lingered over Malcolm, and he was martyred in 1965. He was a fervent believer in Allah, holding to the intention of exposing "any meaningful truth that will destroy the racist cancer that is malignant in the body of America" (*ibid.*, p. 382). Although Elijah Muhammad, who died in 1975, was the titular political head of the Black Muslims, Malcolm X was its flaming oracle.

Both Malcolm X and Nat Turner demonstrate the social and family pathology that tends to germinate the religious messianism of a religion of deliverance and ethnic identity. Patients in a psychiatric hospital from the black community will display in their content of thought the claims of being a second Elijah or a second Malcolm and of refusing to be called by their "slave names." Although not all black patients react this way, especially older ones, those who do, cannot be said to be suffering from a one-factor, one-cause illness. They are ill because of any variable by which one chooses to measure them: biochemistry, poverty, crowded housing, shattered families, ethnic pressures, religious fervor, etc.

The Black Muslims attack these problems head on with their religion of a black identity. Such a religion of deliverance from being "a no-people" to being "a people" with a sense of integrity points to the kind of community therapy found in the Native American Church among the Indians of Oklahoma. Would it not be realistic to include the religious cohesiveness of these groups in therapy plans? Programs of treatment for alcoholic Indians involve the use of the resources of the church and rely on the empathy and group support "for ego-strengthening directions." (Bernard S. Albaugh, M.S.W., and Philip O. Anderson, Pharm. D., "Peyote in the Treatment of American Indians," *American Journal of Psychiatry*, Vol. 131, No. 11, Nov. 1974, pp. 1247–1250.) The long history of the use of peyote among members of the Native American Church provides peyote with a context of spiritual meaning that is absent in communities that organize *de novo* around the use of drugs as a means in themselves.

COMMUNAL AND THEOCRATIC TEACHINGS
AND PRACTICES

The ethnic need for deliverance is submerged in many religious groups in this country whose origins were in Europe. They came to this country for many reasons: work opportunity, land, freedom from persecution, and a perpetual need for a Utopia, an Erewhon, a Walden Pond, a Shangri-La, etc. Their religion held them together in the diversity of their needs, in the homogeneity of the native language, and in their common need to survive. Their religion gave ritual, sense, and substance to their life together. Many of these groups have disbanded as their people became acculturated and absorbed in the mainstream of American life. Several such communities have survived, done well, and even prospered. The relevance of their styles of life for mental health has been studied. One in particular has been of most interest because it has remained intact as an autonomous religious community. This community is the Hutterites of South Dakota, North Dakota, Montana, Washington, Minnesota, Alberta, Manitoba, and Saskatchewan. Their number in 1974 was 21,521, situated in a total of 229 colonies of mean size of 94 persons.

The Hutterites are descendants of the Anabaptist Christians of Moravia. In 1528 they joined under the leadership of Jacob Hutter, who stood for several principles of faith and practice. First, they agreed to forgo private ownership of both personal property and real estate. Second, they became pacifists. Today they will not participate in war, either with their money or with their sons. Third, they agreed to a communal sharing of their faults, that they might help one another. Fourth, as of today they insist on their children being cared for and educated by the community as a whole, without undue dependence upon the nuclear family and with the children being permitted to go only to the eighth grade. Finally, they believe in baptizing only adults. They do not permit an adolescent to be baptized until the individual has decided to "settle down." Their convictions are that the Bible is the inspired divine word, and that submissions to God's will and to the good of one's fellow human beings are the rules of obedience.

The Hutterites came to this country between 1874 and 1877, after centuries of persecution in Europe. They brought their German language with them. Today they teach their children to speak both German and English. They believe that it is sinful to marry outside the sect. Nearly all the present members are direct descendants of the original 101 couples that came to this country.

Particularly significant is the Hutterite attitude toward adolescent deviant behavior. Adolescents are taught to select a career, to work at tasks within the community, to assume personal responsibility for their behavior, and to discipline their own impulses. They are expected to have a time of "foolishness" and to get over it before they settle down to church membership, marriage, and parenthood. As Eaton says, "The Hutterite culture softens the discontinuity between child and adult roles." (Joseph W. Eaton, Ph.D., "Adolescence in a Communal Society," *Mental Hygiene,* Vol. 48, No. 1, Jan. 1964, pp. 66–73.)

As a result of their communal patterns of work, worship, and property ownership, the Hutterites have no unemployment, do not accept governmental subsidies, have no welfare program, and have little crime beyond petty theft and other misdemeanors.

The mental health of the Hutterites is a remarkable study in the effectiveness of a solid life support system in the diagnosis, treatment, and rehabilitation of the mentally ill. All types of mental disorder occurred at a lifetime morbidity rate of 23.3 patients per 1,000. Psychoses had at some time affected 6.2 per 1,000. The lifetime morbidity rates are higher than those of the general population. Yet the symptoms of mental illness are less severe. The community attaches no stigma to the illness. A person can return to health with no penalty in work assignment. They care for their own.

The Hutterites care for their own mentally ill, although they are not averse to the care and advice of physicians. They prefer that the ill person be with people who love him or her, and that occupational therapy, physiotherapy, visiting, travel to visit old friends in other Hutterite colonies, and tolerance for duration be treatments of choice. Illness is a reality to them, but they resist institutionalization and the "warehousing" of sick persons. They permit a person to be as useful as possible as long as possible.

Prayer and confession are used for the admonition and support of a mentally ill person. Emphasis is placed upon the "forefathers" and their strengths, and the future-orientation of hope. Conscious suppression of behaviors and thoughts is encouraged. The Hutterites show minimum patience with personality disorders. They are likely to use a "straighten up and fly right" approach to such deviance. They are "reality therapists" with character disorders without knowing what "reality therapy" is, doing as the more sophisticated therapist does. (Joseph W. Eaton and Robert J. Weil, *Culture and Mental Disorders*; Free Press, 1955.)

Several conclusions can be drawn for the psychiatric treatment team as to the significance of responsible and durable communal religious living. First, mental illness is reduced to one fourth in frequency. This may be due not only to the religious values of the community but also to the rural environment. Second, the intensity of the symptoms is softened by the communal care given. Third, mental disorders, particularly psychotic episodes, nevertheless *do* occur. This gives some credence to the possibility that constitutional and biochemical factors are operative somewhat independently of sociocultural factors. The study was done before the wide use of psychotropic drugs. We have no assessment of the impact of medication on Hutterites. Fourth, the Hutterite communities have successfully resisted acculturation into the mainstream of American society. The kind of community care of the mentally ill that the Hutterites give in homes would have to be artificially contrived in an open community. What "mainstreaming" the Hutterites would do to them is a question for further research.

The variables of risk-taking, kindness, religious concern, etc., as motives for caring for the mentally ill have been studied by Edward Fisher. He discovered that attitudes of helping and social responsibility rather than beliefs about mental illness prompted people to volunteer for the care of mentally ill persons in the home and community. The skewing factor in his research is that all his subjects were in one age group, i.e., 329 new students at a community college. One asks whether a sampling of parents of sons and daughters who have all grown to maturity leaving the parents in an "empty nest" might not have revealed other motives, such as the reactivation of the parental skills. These are the people who tend to "graduate" from the church after their children are grown. Could a selected number of them be equipped to care for convalescent mental patients in a home environment? (Edward Fisher, "Who Volunteers for Companionship with Mental Patients?" *Journal of Personality*, Vol. 39, No. 4, Dec. 1971, pp. 552–563.)

SPIRITUAL GIFTS AND SPIRIT POSSESSION TEACHINGS AND PRACTICES

Another cluster of religious groups is centrally concerned with the gift and the gifts of the Holy Spirit. When I say *gift* of the Holy Spirit I refer to the story of Pentecost (five Sundays after Easter) recorded in Acts, ch. 2. Hence, many of these groups call themselves Pentecostal. When I say *gifts* of the Holy Spirit, I refer to the gift of healing power, the gift of speaking in unknown tongues (glossolalia), and the gift of power over demons. Other important gifts of teaching, administering, and pastoring are mentioned in the Bible, but not emphasized by these religious groups.

A considerable number of these groups interpret illness, especially psychotic or epileptic behavior, as possession by the devil and/or demons. They have extensive healing sessions and often seek to exorcise demons. If they are dealing with essentially hysterical conditions, they quite often have varying degrees of success in restoring the person to a state of health. If they are dealing with a schizophrenic condition in a patient, they may leave the patient in a latter state that is worse than the first. William Sargent affirms that the basic conviction of possession presents "exactly similar types of possession, producing exactly similar states of intense faith . . . being explained in very different cultures as being due to the intervention of the Holy Spirit, or perhaps Voodoo gods, or Abyssinian 'Satans,' or Sudanese 'zars' or Zambia 'pepos.'" Sargent himself almost became convinced of the validity of the faith of a group he was studying. Whereas this was a fleeting and short-lived experience, he insists that the nonwhite people in the groups he studied "seemed to have acquired a supreme dignity, poise and strength of absolute faith." (William Sargent, "The Physiology of Faith," *British Journal of Psychiatry,* Vol. 115, 1969, pp. 505–518.)

Spirit-given groups are episodically influential in their insistence upon the gift of speaking in tongues, or glossolalia. This is an unusual pattern of speech, an altered state of consciousness particularly in terms of the meaningfulness of language. The externally meaningless language may have intense internal meaning to the speaker. The speaker usually thinks of the language as having meaning to God. The most extensive psychiatric study of this phenomenon has been done by Mansell Pattison, M.D., who is educated both theologically and psychiatrically. He says that the most sophisticated studies of the phenomenon fail to support an automatic assumption that glossolalia is necessarily a psychopathology. However, these studies seem to refer to the more established forms of Pentecostalism. (Mansell Pattison, M.D., "Behavioral Science Research on the Nature of Glossolalia," *Journal of American Scientific Affiliation,* Sept. 1973, pp. 73–86.)

Paul Morentz, M.D., identified six dominant personality patterns among glossolalists: (1) hostility to authority; (2) the wish to compensate for feelings of inadequacy; (3) the wish to rationalize feelings of isolation; (4) the wish to dominate; (5) strong feelings of dependence and suggestibility, and (6) the wish for certainty. (Paul Morentz, Lecture on Glossolalia, unpublished paper, University of California at Berkeley, 1966. Quoted by Pattison.)

My own evaluation of glossolalists is that they tend to fall into one or more of four groupings.

1. The "programmed" glossolalist, who is part of a group in which glossolalia is of sufficiently long standing to be an expected and culturally shared ritual.

2. The intellectual glossolalist, who probably was reared in a conventional Protestant or Catholic parish. After long years in an arid and formal, rational and nonemotional spiritual atmosphere, he or she finally gets in touch with the unutterable depths of the nonrational religious experience.

3. The inadequate personality, on the one hand, and the power-hungry leader of a "tongues" group, on the other hand, meet each other's needs to be led and to lead.

4. The glossolalist who is indeed psychotic but the contact with a glossolalia group was a final effort to maintain the collapsing ego defenses. This is the "plank-grabbing syndrome" mentioned earlier. Glossolalia is symptomatic and only peripherally related to the patient either religiously or psychiatrically.

The Spirit-led and Spirit-given person may express a basic paranoid outlook on life with "the struggle with evil spirits" and the warring with temptation. A problem of differential diagnosis to be discussed in the next two chapters is that of assessing the degree of concreteness and literality as over against the capacity to symbolize and use these concepts analogically. The former points toward a schizophrenic process and the latter toward a subcultural format for symbolizing rather specific temptations, guilts, and shames. The longitudinal religious history is the basis of such diagnosis. Context gives meaning.

MYSTICAL TEACHINGS AND PRACTICES

A mystical experience is one that brings to the individual a sense of personal fellowship with God. The experience involves a person at the nonrational level of human experience. Augustine describes it in his *Confessions:*

> With you to guide me, I entered into the innermost part of myself, and I was able to do this because you were my helper. I entered and I saw with my soul's eye . . . an unchangeable light. . . . He who knows truth knows that light, and he who knows that light knows eternity. (Bk. VII, Ch. 10, *The Confessions of St. Augustine,* tr. by Rex Warner; The New American Library, Inc., 1963)

This is an example of classical Catholic mysticism, which is evident today in the writings of Thomas Merton. Merton shows mystical wisdom coupled with an acute sense of social concern for American social and political problems. The Protestant expression of mysticism is best exemplified in the meditative spirit of the Quakers. Usually anticlerical, anti-establishment, and antiwar, the Quakers have been pro-humanity, pro-mystical. They are concerned for the inner life, insisting that "the stamp of God's spirit must be known by inner acquaintance." This inner acquaintance is available to all persons without ceremony, ritual, or priest. In order to "test" one's revelations from God, the group of friends is the special instrument of measurement. Hence, the Quakers are constantly checking solitude and community by each other. Reality testing of individual revelation is a "built in" part of Quaker belief and practice. The group "hear" the individual "concern." They assess, add to, confront, comfort, and admonish the individual. A group "concern" either blends with the individual or all "wait before God" until such a group solidarity develops among "the Friends."

However, mysticism has appeared in a new order of things in the 1970's. Transcendental Meditation is a Far Eastern expression of mystical meditation for "discovering inner energy and overcoming stress." Maharishi Mahesh Yogi, the spiritual guru from India, leads his highly organized movement for promoting the "technique of contracting pure awareness." "Neither a religion nor a philosophy, nor a way of life, Transcendental Meditation is a natural technique for reducing stress and expanding conscious awareness." (Harold H. Bloomfield, M.D., Michael Peter Cain, and Dennis T. Jaffe, *TM*, p. 10; Delacorte Press, 1975.) Sponsors of this movement deny any religious involvement, although in both origin and methodology heavy Hindu overtones are present. Some of its rituals require a reverence for if not obeisance to the Maharishi.

Other forms of Eastern mysticism are much more candid and articulate as religious meditation. Thomas Robbins records several case histories of users of illicit drugs who founded the Meher Baba religious group in Chapel Hill, North Carolina, as an effective "halfway" house between the drug culture and reassimilation into conventional society. (Thomas Robbins, "Eastern Mysticism and the Resocialization of Drug Users," *Journal for the Scientific Study of Religion*, Vol. 8, No. 2, Fall 1969, pp. 308–317.)

The presence of mystical overidentification in the religious delusions of counterculture patients is seemingly increasing in incidence among the nineteen to twenty-six age group. In my own study of six male patients diagnosed as schizophrenic, I observed that they presented histories of having been reared in conventional denominations. At about the ages of fourteen to sixteen, they "dropped out" of church attendance. Then they became involved in drug use, grew long hair, "ripped off" their parents and others for money, refused any productive work, and adopted characteristic dress, music, and foods which have been the standard fare of the counterculture. Then they entered some form of mystical group, such as Zen Buddhism, devil worship, or Pentecostalism. They were converted and swore off drug use. They became sexually ascetic. They spent much time in meditation and/or prayer with the group. If the group stayed by them, obvious psychotic symptoms were interpreted and "handled" by the group. For example, the "All the Way House" in Louisville, Kentucky, is managed by its founder, the "Earth Mother," a middle-aged Pentecostal woman who spends her whole time caring for youth who are "coming down" off drugs. She strongly advised one twenty-year-old not to use any kind of drugs. He "played games" with the group by periodically coming to an emergency psychiatric walk-in clinic and asking for Valium. The "Earth Mother" said that he was suicidal, could not yet commit himself to Christ, and therefore needed a physician and should be in a hospital. This he did only under legal commitments.

Also, if there had been no group, no halfway house, no support community other than the parental family, these young persons would have tended to become sufficiently decompensated and bizarre at being hospitalized.

Peritz Levinson, M.D., describes similar clinical manifestations in 8 out of 85 first admissions between 1970 and 1972. They presented depression, confusion, and paranoid thinking. Each subject "was admitted to the hospital with the grandiose delusion that he was 'Christ,' the 'Son of God,' or the 'Messiah.' For example, the delusion often included the conviction that he had the power to control people's minds, to read the minds of others, or to cure illness." The messianic claim sometimes meant that he had achieved Nirvana and was able to help others to do so. (Peritz Levinson, "Religious Delusions in Counter-Culture Patients," *American Journal of Psychiatry*, Vol. 130, No. 11, Nov. 1973, pp. 1265–1269.) During the acute psychotic episodes, psychotropic drugs were the treatment of choice. A remarkable factor in the convalescence process was the way in which these patients formed relationships of trust with the personnel who had the least status in the hospital chain of command. Family members themselves were taught to be "back up" therapists. The goals of treatment were the development of a realistic and possible identity, the improvement of impulse control, emotional support, and the prevention of avoidance and withdrawal symptoms. In my own study of six patients, I observed the alienation of all six from the conventional church. In three of the six cases, the informal religious groups were very helpful during convalescence. They represented reality and provided community "over and above the line of duty." In two cases no support was available, and in one case our unit staff of chaplains provided the continuing relationship for over a year.

"Escape from Freedom" Teachings and Practices

The response to a collapse of leadership and credible authority in corporate society is often the upsurge of absolute authoritarianism. This happened with the rise of Nazism. Erich Fromm described it as the "escape from freedom." He says that Fascism, Nazism, and Stalinism have in common that they have offered the atomized individual a new refuge and security. These systems are the culmination of alienation. The individual is made to feel powerless and insignificant. He or she is taught to project all his or her powers into the figure of the leader . . . to whom he has to submit and whom he has to worship. He escapes from freedom into a new idolatry. (Erich Fromm, *The Sane Society,* p. 237; Rinehart & Company, Inc., 1955.)

An example of this "leader idolatry" in recent history is the Father Divine cult, led by a black man from Georgia who migrated to Baltimore, Brooklyn, then to Long Island, and then to Philadelphia. He was first George Baker, then Major J. Morgan Divine, and then Father Divine. In Baltimore, he met Samuel Morris, an itinerant preacher who declared that he *was* the Father Eternal (I Cor. 3:16). As Father Jehovah, Morris founded a church of his own, and then associated George Baker with him as his "Messenger," or second person. In 1908, Saint John Divine Hickerson joined them, but the trio broke up because of quarrels over their places in the Godhead. Father Divine located finally in Harlem in 1931.

During the Great Depression, he established the Peace Mission. The holy communion of homage to him was bountiful dinners served free. Both black and white people became his followers. Among city officials he was seen as a "con" man who "ripped off" some of the populace and fed others of the populace. He called his locations "heavens," and when "he died in 1965 the major heavens of his kingdom were still in New York and Philadelphia," plus farms in New York State and other areas. (Sydney E. Ahlstrom, *A Religious History of the American People*, Vol. 2, pp. 578–581; 2 vols., Doubleday & Co., Inc., Image Paperbacks, 1975.)

Father Divine was a showman of the most dramatic kind. He indoctrinated his people through a publication called *New Day*. The only formal hierarchy he had was his first wife, and then his second wife, a white woman. The second wife continued as the leader of the movement after his death. In spite of his showmanship, Father Divine tackled serious social problems in behalf of his followers. He opposed racism on the part of both blacks and whites. He dramatized poverty by "feeding his sheep." He challenged war and engaged in mayoral and presidential political contests. Yet he used the social festering points in society to foster worship of himself by his followers. He used propaganda and forced indoctrination to maintain his leadership. I have attended meetings of the Peace Mission in New York and especially the teaching sessions that follow them. If one accepts Father Divine as God, then all the other teachings fit nicely. It is the socialization of the grandiosity of the paranoid pattern of thinking. Everything is somewhat coherent if the master delusion is affirmed as true. The hungry, the poor, the racially discriminated against, those who "hate City Hall" all found a Xerox copy of identity through the person of Father Divine. At that time and place, the appeal was to all age groups, who were amply present in his crowded meetings.

A present-day example of the "escape from freedom" kind of leader idolatry is the Unification Church of Sun Myung Moon. At the outset of his campaigns, this Korean preacher and teacher used a procedure similar to that of Father Divine —feeding people a free meal. He differs, though, in that he invites the leaders of the religious, social, political, and business communities to dinner at the better hotels of the cities in which he appears. Sophisticated sales and advertising procedures are used. He does not claim to be a god, but he does claim to have final answers to the world's conflicts. He does demand absolute obedience to his way. Whereas he insists that he is calling young people away from drugs, alcohol, and sexual promiscuity, the use of his multimillion-dollar enterprise has little or no programs for the care of persons caught in these troubles. He believes that Korea is a chosen nation, that "the line-up in Panmumjon is like a line-up between the heavenly world and the satanic world. We must make a show-down in Korea." Sun Myung Moon says Korea's victory, particularly against Communism, is not Korea's alone. "I came to America to bring it back to the scene of the struggle. America has been retreating from responsibility; that has happened in Vietnam. America will decide the world's destiny." (*Newsweek*, June 14, 1976, p. 62.)

The crucial contact that pastoral counselors and psychiatrists have with followers of Sun Myung Moon is in the programming and battling for the minds of late and delayed adolescents. Moon says that these persons become "dedicated followers and members" of the Moon family. Some parents say that he has brainwashed their sons and daughters, alienating them from their parents. A group of opponents of Sun Myung Moon who call themselves "deprogrammers" has arisen. Parents of the youth are most often the ones who ask for the help of ministers and psychiatrists. The youth live in "Moonie communes" which offer them a willing refuge, take care of all their physical needs such as food, clothing, and eyeglasses, give them medical care, and supply personal items such as toothpaste. In return, they work as disciples, collecting converts and money. Berkeley Rice says that this dependency increases the "degree to which groups of smiling Moonies look as though they were cloned rather than recruited." It is a "welcome refuge to those unwilling or unable to face the daily frustrations of life on the outside: no drugs, no drinks, no sex, no money, no problems, no chances, no decisions." (*Psychology Today,* Vol. 9, No. 8, Jan. 1976, pp. 36–47.)

Escape from freedom—and responsibility—is provided by other groups. Youth flock to Hare Krishna, the Children of God, the Jesus People, Maharaj Ji's Divine Light Mission, and many others. The critical issue seems to be the need for absolute authority combined with freedom from the anxiety that responsible selfhood demands.

POSITIVE THINKING
AND HEALTH TEACHINGS AND PRACTICES

The final group of teachings that the psychiatric team must deal with in providing religious care for psychiatric patients are those exemplified in Christian Science. I identify these teachings as "positive thinking" and "health" teachings and practices. They run throughout many of the mainline denominations with the force of pietistic denial of evil, disease, and death in the world. These ideas are not solely those of Christian Science. However, the positive thinking themes are most evident in Christian Science and to a considerable extent in the preaching and teaching of Norman Vincent Peale and other "positive thinkers."

The Church of Christ, Scientist, established by Mary Baker Eddy in 1879, had at the outset a program of teaching that strongly appealed to women, an appeal that it has sustained. Both men and women were trained to be Christian Science practitioners who instruct and even "treat" people with all manner of problems in living and in health. A national network of churches and reading rooms provides places of contact for the practitioners to work. They are the real competitors for all forms of medical practice, which they consider useful only for people who are unenlightened and without faith.

The key teachings of Christian Science are the "nothing-ness of matter," the total supremacy of God, and that the only reality of sin, sickness, and death is their *seeming* reality to the mind. Drugs and other medical modalities are stupid substitutes for the Divine Mind. The proper treatment is to deny the reality of pain, sickness, death. They are deceptions reinforced by medical experts.

The group of patients to whom Christian Science appeals most from a psychiatric point of view are those suffering from stress-induced psychophysiologic disorders. These are disorders that arise out of the predominant effects of emotions on bodily changes. Quite apart from their theological apparatus of belief, the Christian Science practitioners do much for persons in helping them rearrange their priorities in everyday living. They use much time listening to and philosophizing with their communicants. They guide them into less stressful ways of living. In addition to this, they use much power of suggestion, positive reinforcement, and behavioral modification. Their denial of disease as a reality does little harm to the stress-ridden patient with psychophysiologic disorders. Their denial is no more unrealistic than that of the physician who in haste dismisses such patients saying: "There is nothing wrong with you. It is just your nerves." If that physician does not have time to inquire into the stress patterns of the patient's life, to teach the patient how to manage life to his or her own health's advantage, then the Christian Science practitioner *does* have the time!

A second group of patients to whom Christian Science appeals are the patients beyond fifty years of age, or even younger, who have chronic ailments such as arthritis or arteriosclerosis, or suffer the painful emotional results of previous surgery or psychiatric help. These patients are often brushed aside by the physician and labeled "old crocks." They are told: "This is something you are just going to have to live with." Yet no instruction is given in "learning to live" with the disability. Christian Science has a full-time practice of teaching people its particular philosophy of how to live with the results of medical treatment, the side effects of the process of aging, and the threat of death that aggravates the minds of those who are no longer enjoying the illusion of deathlessness known as youth.

The psychotic patient who befuddles and boggles the mind of the Christian Science practitioner is the same patient who is mysterious to the medical profession and to conventional religionists—the schizophrenic patient. For example, a twenty-nine-year-old Jewish woman rebelled against her parents by demitting Judaism and becoming an ardent devotee of Christian Science. She developed a very dependent relationship to her practitioner, a woman. She then became openly psychotic, with grandiose ideas of how she had the power to heal her seventy-two-year-old Jewish father of his heart disorder. She became agitated, uncontrolled, and delusional. Her parents had her committed involuntarily for psychiatric help in a private psychiatric facility. She resisted treatment and demanded instead the care of her Christian Science practitioner. She considered this to be a legal right of hers as a patient, assured by the Constitution's provision of the right of a person to practice religious faith without impediment or legal restraint. This would have been a moot question if she had been a voluntary patient. However, she was there under legal restraint. She finally went out of the hospital against medical advice, with the written consent of her parents.

When I visited the patient as a minister during her hospital stay, she used both her parental Judaism and her Christian Science to thwart any conversation about her own bizarre thoughts and behavior.

The patient who has "dropped out" of Christian Science is a third challenge to the psychiatric team. Ronald Cohen, Ph.D., and Frederich Smith, Ph.D., describe a twenty-eight-year-old mother who was obsessed with fears of various diseases, both for herself and her children. She was a Christian Scientist who over a period of ten years had had her faith in "thought cure" shaken repeatedly. She finally sought psychotherapy when she lost her job and could no longer care for her child because of her obsession with the thoughts of disease. Yet she was ambivalent about her faith in Christian Science, because it had actually helped her quit smoking and lose weight. In twenty-four sessions of psychotherapy, she recovered from her obsessive thinking. Relaxation training and thought-stopping techniques were used. (Ronald J. Cohen and Frederich J. Smith, "Socially Reinforced Obsessing: Etiology of a Disorder in a Christian Scientist," *Journal of Consulting and Clinical Psychology*, Vol. 44, No. 1, 1976, pp. 142–144.) Cohen and Smith affirm that thought concentration and behavioral modification techniques are useful. Real danger occurs when they are given divine significance and assumed to be applicable to all conditions. This I could affirm and add that an effective and healthy religious interpretation of God's power and love through a given technique is, therefore, not necessarily to be ignored or avoided, but to be used prescriptively in specific instances, but not as a magical panacea. For example, an obsession can be dealt with definitely in psychotherapy, but gallstones cannot!

It would be unfair to equate with the system of Christian Science the "positive thinking" of Norman Vincent Peale, the faith healing of many Pentecostal groups, the strong affirmations of Robert Schuller's preaching, or the easy answers to life's problems in Billy Graham's preaching. Yet one must point out that the messages of these strong personalities appeal to people upon whom the doctors and conventional pastors have given up, for whom they do not have time, and who need to be told the same thing many times. Likewise, these are persons who have not hesitated to be positive and persuasive. They use the power of one personal influence and persuasion on the behavior of great crowds of people. They use the strategies of television and other media to influence mass thinking and action.

Yet they have in common with Christian Science the overuse and panacea effect of denial. In behalf of the half-truths of optimism about life, they neglect the half-truths of pessimism. There is a better way than either—a hardheaded realism that includes the awareness of the potentials as well as the limitation of human beings, not choosing to exclude either. Accepting and affirming the uncertainties of life and death, hope and despair, pain and pleasure existing in the same time frame amounts to wisdom and compassion, not bonny optimism nor crippling pessimism.

CONCLUSION

I have briefly evaluated some psychiatric implications of eight different patterns of religious teachings and practices. Wherever possible, I have used illustrative case material and technical literature. I want to reiterate that illustrative religious groups have been cited in each of the eight sets of religious teachings and practices. Yet, such teachings can be found in varying degrees of seriousness both in mainline denominations and in the subcultures of religion. The very association of a set of religious practices with psychiatric patients may be read by an ardent exponent of that group as an assumption of "put-down" or "all-badness" on the part of the author. I disclaim that here with the quaint response: Not so. All God's children have troubles. Neither your nor my religious group is an exception. My appreciation of the psychiatric patient, by long acquaintance, may just be kinder than yours.

3

RELIGIOUS SYMPTOM PICTURES
OF PSYCHIATRIC PATIENTS

JAMES DAVID MCNEELY, M.D.,* and WAYNE E. OATES,
TH.D.

The statistical incidence of religious concern among psychiatric patients is about the same as that among the general population. The basic attitudes of the psychiatric resident, the psychiatrist, or the psychiatric nurse toward religion tend to shape their reactions to the religious ideation of the patient. Several reactions can be taken: (1) One can be selectively inattentive or ignore the religious ideation. (2) One can interpret religious ideation per se as evidence of pathology. (3) One can be caught up in the religious ideation and intellectualize along with the patient through the use of theological talk. (4) We suggest that we take the religious ideation seriously as being both diagnostically and therapeutically significant of the patient's existential struggle or the absence of struggle to live. Let us suggest, also, that we take the religious affect and ideation of the patient as substantive evidence of a relationship, or lack of it, to a life support system of significant people in a religious community.

The beginning therapist, whether a psychiatric resident or a pastoral counselor, is confronted early in the exchange with patients by religious symptomatology and resistances to ther-

*Dr. McNeely is Associate Professor of Psychiatry and Behavioral Sciences, School of Medicine, University of Louisville, and Medical Director of the Norton Psychiatric Clinic, Louisville, Kentucky.

apy. Our purpose in this chapter is to describe a group of rather typical religious symptom patterns. They tend to occur most often in our experience and relate clinically useful as well as spiritually sensitive ways of meeting the patient at his or her point of concern and facilitate the launching of an effective psychotherapeutic exchange. It is our belief, in Eriksonian fashion, that the person's religious belief system *can* be an ego-adaptive, integrating, and supportive means of realizing human potential.

One should certainly not ignore it or attempt to circumvent it in the course of therapy. Religious ideation can be a source of valuable diagnostic information and should be viewed as one aspect of mental life warranting sensitive exploration and understanding. It goes without saying that often our patients come from disrupted and essentially rejecting families. The church as a community and an extended family is often the only viable social support system available to the patient. One of us (W.E.O.) has written extensively elsewhere about the distinction between "healthy" versus "sick" religion. (Wayne Oates, *When Religion Gets Sick.*) What we propose in this chapter we feel is consonant with these previously stated views. Namely, that religion when it is healthy enhances human life and potential, is affirming of human experience, is creative, not fixed or overly legalistic or ritualistic.

The "Weak Faith" Syndrome

The first type of religious symptom pattern we would like to describe is the "weak faith" syndrome. These persons are usually from a particularly devout background and feel that to be suffering from a mental or emotional illness is testimony to their lack of faith. They fall victim to the following logical inference: If one has faith no larger than a grain of mustard seed, then one can move a mountain (Matt. 17:20). To recover from a mental illness is certainly easier to do than to move a mountain; therefore, if one cannot recover from a mental illness through faith, then one's faith is too small.

The approach to this particular resistance in therapy involves helping the patient to separate religious commitment from the particular psychopathological symptoms involved in the illness. Gently encourage the patient to take into account other etiologies of the illness rather than "a weak faith." Reassure the patient that this type of illness can strike anyone, even the most devout person.

Illustrative Case Number 1: A widowed high school teacher in her middle fifties referred herself to the Norton Psychiatric Clinic after hearing one of the authors (J.D.M.) discuss grief and mourning on a local television program. She was profoundly depressed, with a great many anxiety symptoms, e.g., persistent cough, headaches, and insomnia. She was a quite intelligent woman who related her feelings to the death of her husband four years earlier. She thought of him constantly and had shut off all social life, except with relatives, while still an active and attractive woman. She had been reared in a poor family, but cultural and educational attainments were emphasized. Her father and mother were divorced in her early adolescence. Remaining with the mother, she took the loss of her idealized father quite hard. She finally worked it through by redoubling her efforts in school because it was what "he would have wanted." A devout Methodist orientation was maintained through early life and up until the time of her husband's death. At that point she lost interest in attending church. She wondered how "a loving God" could let this happen to her. She had met her husband in college. They made an attractive, talented couple —she being a pert, attractive, talented coed, and he being a large, easygoing athletic hero. The marriage had its rough moments as both worked, but she tended to dominate her more passive husband. He in easygoing fashion had allowed the customers of his small business to accumulate debts up to $40,000. When he died, she had to file for bankruptcy because she could not satisfy her husband's creditors. At the same time, she had to sell her house, which they had built themselves. Being unable to tolerate the loss of self-esteem in their small rural community, she moved back to the city with her mother. She soon found a good teaching position but had never adequately mourned her husband.

When first seen at the clinic, she verbalized active suicidal intention and was promptly admitted. Hospitalization was a blow to her self-esteem as well as her rather shaken faith. She told her doctor how ashamed she felt for not having a stronger faith. Anger toward her husband for leaving her in such miserable circumstances was strongly repressed. Diagnostically, she was thought to be suffering from an involutional melancholia, which often has a prominent dynamic pathological mourning response.

Fortunately, the patient responded to a psychopharmacological approach that included a combination of a tricyclic antidepressant and a major phenothiazine tranquilizer. Psychotherapy was oriented first toward overcoming the initial feeling of having a weak faith and allowing her to accept the medical nature of her illness. Gradually the mourning work was reactivated. She was helped to get in touch with some of the repressed affects related to her husband's death, particularly her anger at his abandoning her at a period of emotional vulnerability as her father had done in her early adolescence. An active social and church life was eventually restored and the patient remarried two years later.

THE DEMAND FOR A CHRISTIAN DOCTOR

The second symptom pattern is the "demand for a Christian doctor" syndrome. The psychiatrist is very often greeted with the question, "Are you a Christian doctor?" The implication is that only a Christian psychiatrist could possibly understand the spiritual needs of the patient, let alone the psychological subtleties of the emotional problems. By the same token, the pastoral counselor is seen as inadequate unless of the same faith or denomination as the patient. To take this problem a step farther, as the therapy progresses to a point where an interpretation of a defensive operation becomes necessary, the patient counters with: "But, doctor, that's the way I am, that's what we Baptists believe. You promised you wouldn't say or do anything that would add to or detract from my sense of religious commitment and practice." The doctor seems trapped by his or her own ethical value of not wishing to foist his or her own value system upon the patient. We call this bind and resistance the "defensive normality" of religion. It has dynamics very reminiscent of ingroup, outgroup paranoia. At times the therapist feels compelled to back off when his or her attempt to interpret character defenses is met with this defensive operation. Indeed one is wise not to enter a debate about the veracity of the Scriptures or the particular views of a given faith or denomination. Very often the sensitive pastoral counselor can help break the impasse or introduce a shred of constructive doubt as the therapist would do in any other fixed paranoid system. Once that is accomplished, then the patient can be helped to modify his or her beliefs in a more flexible, ego-adaptive manner.

Illustrative Case Number 2: Ed was a successful corporation executive who sought help at the urging—indeed, the demand on threat of divorce—of his wife, Marsha. His initial complaints related to complaints of his wife that he was "cold, distant, and not interested in me or the children." Ed came for two sessions dutifully and then stopped. Marsha was so infuriated that she launched a vituperative attack on the person of the therapist for his incompetence. As a result, another appointment was scheduled for Ed. Marsha reluctantly agreed to see a woman social worker "for support in coping with my husband's problems."

Ed was seen as a rather passive, obsessive individual who sought relief from Marsha's hysterical tirades by overinvolving himself in his work. For the past two years it had been "necessary" for him to be away from home three to five days out of every week to supervise his regional offices. Marsha was left to cope with their three sons, two of whom were in early to middle adolescence.

Ed had been reared in a pious Lutheran Midwestern household, where his father ruled with a quiet but firm hand, being distanced from the children. His mother was a warm, giving, deeply religious self-sacrificing person. Marsha, in contrast, grew up in an Eastern home, where her mother ruled by a quick wit and dramatic demonstration. Her father was a successful officer in the armed services but usually acquiesced to the mother's demands. The family religion was Catholic and Marsha had been instructed that sex was sinful but a duty to be performed within the sacred bond of matrimony. Marsha and her mother had many conflicts during Marsha's adolescence. Ed and Marsha met while Marsha was in college. Ed was five years older, already educated and holding a good job. He made no sexual demands and after a brief courtship they were married in the Catholic church, with Ed converting. The marriage was stormy from the start but settled into an uneasy homeostasis as the children began to arrive on the scene. Three years prior to onset of therapy, Marsha became increasingly dissatisfied with her lot in life. Ed was unresponsive to her needs for self-fulfillment.

Two years prior to treatment Marsha, under the influence of two summer missionaries, dramatically converted to Mormonism. She joined her new religion with tremendous fervor. She became involved to the extent that almost every waking moment involved prayer or some church activity. Ed countered by reactivating his all but ceased interest in Catholicism. Thus began a power struggle, with the children sadly caught in the middle. Father and sons began to go on camping trips together and seemed to "gang up" on Marsha, who felt that Ed was trying to alienate the boys from her affection. The increasing marital rift propelled them both into therapy.

A marital couple therapy was embarked upon but was not effective. Marsha, while threatening divorce, at the same time had received a personal revelation from "the heavenly Father" that the marriage would be saved. Meanwhile, the therapist was seen as a personal agent of the heavenly Fa-

ther. At the same time, any attempt at interpretation of her
hysterical character defenses was seen as an attack upon her
dedication to her newfound devotion. Finally, after consultation and assistance from a pastoral counselor, a collaborative
therapeutic approach, with both Ed and Marsha being seen
individually, was embarked upon and was ultimately successful.

THE "WITCH OF ENDOR" SYNDROME

A third pattern of religious symptoms that is often seen is
what we have chosen to call the "witch of Endor" syndrome
(I Sam. 28:3–25). When King Saul was confronted with a
problem, namely, a host of hostile Philistines, he first sought
advice and solace from the Lord through dreams, the sacred
lottery, and the prophets. When help was not forthcoming,
he finally sought the help of a witch, even though he had
earlier mounted a campaign to drive such people from the
land. There is a strong Judeo-Christian bias against sorcery,
and, for some, the mental health professionals with their
magic words and secret knowledge of the mind plus their
magic potions represent an evil, antireligious influence.
Often the psychiatrist is approached only as a last resort and
his or her efforts are immediately seen as evil attempts to
undermine the person's faith.

Early in the course of therapy much effort must be directed toward assuring and reassuring the patient of the
therapist's humanness and genuine wish to help. The psychiatrist does not in fact have all the answers, secret or otherwise. Emotional illness does not mean that God has ignored
the person, nor does it disqualify one from belonging to the
human race.

Illustrative Case Number 3: A Protestant minister in his
early fifties was brought to the Norton Children's Hospital's
emergency room after having taken an overdose of Valium
in an apparent suicide attempt. With much urging on the
part of his frantic son, he was admitted to the psychiatric

ward. The following history was elicited. The patient had been gradually deteriorating over the past two years. He had not been active in the pastorate for those years. He had been living with first one relative and then another, wearing out his welcome by his insatiable demands for care and feeding. His days were spent crying in an agitated manner, alternating with prolonged morose pouts. This minister had been asked to leave his second church. The board of deacons with all due tact informed him that his extremely authoritarian mode of church administration was creating dissension within the membership, resulting in the loss of some of the more faithful members. When so informed, he immediately resigned on the spot, never to return. He passed up the usual farewell social and gift, only later to resent that he had not received them.

His father before him had been a minister of the same faith and was quite effective in his pastorates through use of a benign, authoritarian paternalistic approach. However, he maintained a sense of awe and mystery about his person extending to his own family, who referred to him as "the Reverend." The patient's mother was described as being closer to the patient, who was her youngest. She had died rather suddenly of a heart attack four years prior to the patient's admission. She had been a warm and giving person but was quite stern in her religious fervor. Reaction formation was the order of the day, and no anger was allowed expression.

The patient's depression was complicated by a rather severe case of essential hypertension. The patient's complete work-up was negative, but his pressure continued to range in the neighborhood of 180/110. A persistent tachycardia also complicated the clinical picture. The cardiovascular symptoms were not controlled by either minor or major tranquilizers. Antihypertensive agents deepened the depression to the point of active suicidal intention. A trial of tricyclic antidepressants worsened the cardiovascular symptoms. A rather prolonged course of electroconvulsive therapy was embarked upon, but the depression, basically neurotic in nature, did not lift.

An active pastoral counseling approach with an older, experienced pastor proved to be helpful. In the meantime, a biofeedback approach was begun in an attempt to modify the cardiovascular symptoms. The patient's blood pressure fell fifteen points during the first biofeedback session! This so impressed the patient that finally he became an active participant in his rehabilitation. In pastoral counseling and in psychotherapy with his psychiatrist he began to get more in tune with his own feelings, particularly anger. Anger toward God and subsequent guilt with self-castigation was a prominent dynamic. His social support system was reestablished through active social casework with his family. When he left the hospital, he seemed hopeful. He planned to find a small pastorate where he could put into practice a new style of ministry more in keeping with some of his own emotional needs.

MISTAKEN IDENTITY

The fourth set of symptoms found in the religious views of psychiatric patients is what we call the indicators of "mistaken identity." The search for identity is not a recently named struggle of the human spirit. The religious quest of persons since Moses has included the question, Who am I? under the pressure of a felt sense of calling. Mental patients are no exception. They too struggle with their sense of identity. Mental patients become confused about who they are— who they think they are and who they really are. Usually, mistaken identities appear in patients who perceive themselves to be the Christ, to be God, to be Solomon, to be the Virgin Mary or some Catholic saint in the case of Catholic patients. A cluster of case references shows various aspects of the syndrome of mistaken identity.

These persons feel that they are Christ, that the whole world has come to an end, and that after dying and being buried, they were resurrected as the Christ to rule a new age. It is always important to notice, in Christian patients who believe they are the Christ, or in Jewish patients who see themselves as the Messiah, whether the patients perceive themselves as having died. Has their world come to an end or it is yet to come to an end? In the first instance, the therapist will find the patient often to be a chronic schizophrenic person perhaps of a paranoid type. The patient feels that the whole world is persecuting him or her and that the world has already come to an end, so there is no use struggling or fighting anymore. Professor Anton Boisen *(The Exploration of the Inner World)* measured the sense of the messianic calling of people by the degree of struggle and desperation that they were experiencing. Those who believe they have already died, been buried and raised again, show little struggle and seem to be self-satisfied. There is a long-term, poor prognosis for this kind of patient.

The patients who perceive themselves as having become the Christ and as being in an intense struggle as to whether they will live or die, and are about to be crucified, would be classified differently for the simple reason that the degree of desperation is so acute. There seems to be a much better prognosis and a much better future for the anguished person than there is for the dead-and-risen, self-satisfied person in the first example. The degree of desperation is the clue.

A therapist may find that patients perceive themselves not as the Christ but as some other outstanding Biblical character. One patient, for example, saw himself as King Solomon and was extremely erotic. He perceived all women as being his gift from God. One can readily imagine that this person got into all sorts of difficulty when he was in an open community and came into contact with women. This was what got him into the hospital: to protect himself from embarrassment as well as to protect other people. The degree of desperation in this man was rather mild; he seemed to be enjoying his fantasies and was something of a simple schizophrenic person.

The newer long-term antipsychotic drugs, such as Prolixin, have been of exceptional help in restoring these more chronic patients to a more secure and appropriate way of life.

Instead of finding that a person is identified in a mistaken way with Solomon, one may find that a person is identified with a Catholic saint. One sees this occasionally in Catholic patients.

Illustrative Case Number 4: A woman was thoroughly disabled by heart trouble until she had open heart surgery at the age of fifty-two. This rather dramatic surgical intervention restored her to a normal way of life. Then she had to take up her responsibilities in relation to her husband, who, much to her chagrin, was alcoholic. The conflict between her and her husband was so intense that she went into a postsurgical psychotic episode. She told her husband that she was Saint Theresa. She said she made mistakes but was free of all sin. She was caught in the clutches of the impossibility of deciding clearly about her life situation. The psychotic episode gave an unsatisfactory resolution of some of the tension, but it led to her hospitalization as a psychiatric patient. We confronted here the desperate situation of a person who was, strangely enough, enjoying the good results of successful open heart surgery. She was having to readjust to life. She could no longer depend on the heart symptoms that had previously protected her from responsibility.

Interestingly enough, she became Saint Theresa. Studies of the original Saint Theresa reveal that a "lancer" came and touched her heart. Ever after that, she had pains in her side and times of great mental confusion in which she saw visions, etc. This particular patient also had pains in her side, just as the original Saint Theresa did. But hers was a case of mistaken identity. As long as she could sustain her ego strength by maintaining that she was Saint Theresa, she did not have to face up to the hard reality that she was a sexually active woman in her fifties. She was married to a man who was very difficult to live with and from whom she would have liked to be separated. As a deeply convicted Catholic person, divorce for her was a total taboo. For her, illness was a fitting solution to her problem. First, but unsatisfactorily, a heart disorder and now a psychotic disorder seemed to "solve" her problem. Yet both were maladaptive. The long-term prognosis of this particular patient was very poor because of the strong habit system built through the years of her dependence upon her heart symptoms. However, some of the more recent behavioral therapy techniques used with this person might resolve some of her troubles. This example of a religious symptom picture illustrates the search for identity arising in the mistaken identity of a patient being some great person.

DEMONIC POSSESSION

The fifth type of religious symptom picture of psychiatric patients concerns cases of demonic possession and diabolic possession. One has to take very great care to separate the cultural dimensions of demonic possession from any psychotic component that may be present. There are devil worship cults today. The therapist may have seen members of his or her own circle of friends or of the larger community who are under the influence of the coercive leaders of such groups. These groups "program" their members to believe in demons and to believe in devil possession. This is a culture-related phenomenon. Anxiety-ridden and pre-psychotic people do gravitate toward these groups. They gravitate on the same basis that other people gravitate toward coercive, authoritarian leaders. They gravitate on the basis of feeling greatly inadequate themselves. A "borrowed" sense of personhood comes to them when they align themselves with a strong leader who will make their decisions for them. They do not like the insecurity of being independent, accepting responsibility on their own, and thinking their own thoughts before God. They prefer the security of a hypnotic and coercive leader who will "take over" for them.

This is not the first era in our history in which these particular mass cults and groups have appeared. Demonology is a prescientific psychology in its own right and deserves to be respected as such. Definite correlations can be found between contemporary psychotherapeutic findings and prescientific expressions of demonology. We are not discounting the validity of all the prescientific psychological truths in Biblical understandings of demons. However, we do see at least two expressions of demon possession and devil possession that bespeak a derangement in psychiatric patients. When we refer to a psychiatric patient we mean someone who has lost the ability to function adequately on the job, in the family, and in interpersonal relationships with the valued surrounding community. Yet these patients have no evident physiological symptoms to explain the somewhat bizarre behavior they express.

Demon possession symptoms appear in the so-called "three faces of Eve" syndrome. A person will perceive himself or herself to be one person at one time and another person at another time. Sometimes, this neurotic dissociative reaction presents the idea that at one time the subject is a demon and at another time an angel and at another time himself or herself. This is, in psychiatric circles, thought of as the dissociated personality. The process of dissociation is a neurotic manifestation and quite often does not cause the person to be hospitalized. The person may be able to function well on a job, although suffering a great deal of confusion in the process.

The psychotic person, however, comes to the point of simply being unable to function at all. Here is the case of such a person.

Illustrative Case Number 5: A man from the skilled laboring class of people felt that he saw the devil rear up in front of him and then was overwhelmed by him. He was so terrified by what he saw that he dashed out of his bedroom, screaming and beating his head against the wall. He took an overdose of medicine. Before the medicine took effect, he headed back toward his bedroom. There he met a demon, he says, in the hallway of his home. He was so terrified by this that he hardly knew what to do. He said that he refused to run from the demon and hence was overcome by the demon.

In this particular case, when asked what the devil was, he said: "It was my evil past rising up in front of me. It was the evil part of myself." This man did not mythologize the devil into being a separately projected personality. However, when he began to think about the demon that he saw, he did haggle in his mind as to whether this demon was a personality separate from himself or whether it was only a projection of his evil self.

The important thing the therapist needs to look for here is whether the person is actually projecting the demon or the devil into a separate personality or is simply using the idea of a demon or devil to symbolize his or her own conscience factors. The person may be referring symbolically to self-condemnation because of his or her past behavior. This particular patient had a good prognosis because he did not project *all* of the evil onto the devil. He accepted responsibility for his "own evil past," as he called it. A part of his perception lies in the realm of the conflict that he was having then with his third wife. He was desperately afraid that he would lose her, as he had lost his first two by divorce. He was suffering the fear of failure again. His depression overwhelmed him. He became frightened and panicked. His fear of failure became so great that he went into a psychotic state. We received him into one of our hospitals. He responded quite well to the psychotherapeutic treatment of a psychiatric resident who chose to work conjointly with a pastoral counselor. Only a minimum of medication was needed in treating this patient. However, he did need considerable marriage and family counseling. The involvement of his wife in family therapy was instituted alongside his individual psychotherapy.

The idea of demon possession and devil possession provokes a considerable amount of interest as to the demonic possession and devil possession reported in the New Testament. In the New Testament and the Old Testament, for that matter, spirit, demon, or devil possession was always related to the idolatrous worship of that which was not God. There was a process of deception, both of self and of God, going on.

The New Testament speaks most clearly in the words of Jesus when Jesus himself identified the demonic as the father of deception or of lies. Jesus himself quite often referred to demons as spirits rather than as ectoplasmic personalities separate from a human being. In our understanding of the New Testament, the apostle Paul speaks of the spirits of bondage, the spirits of fear, the spirits of slavery. In the New Testament, Paul's clear message is in Galatians, where he said that we are not to become worshipers of the beggarly elemental spirits of the universe. Paul said that these spirits are not gods but that we are to have done with this because "for freedom Christ has set us free" (Gal. 5:1). In another part of the New Testament, the teaching asserts that God did not give us a spirit of fear but of power, and love and self-control. In even another part of the New Testament, we find the teaching that "whenever our hearts condemn us, God is greater than our hearts, and he knows everything" (I John 3:20). Demon possession and devil possession can be said to be the end result of an idolatrous relationship with something less than God. In commonsense nontechnical terms, such possession is one result of overinvesting life in someone or something that is alien to one's own "indwelling Christ."

"THE INABILITY TO FEEL FORGIVEN"

A sixth type of religious symptom in psychiatric patients is probably the most recurrent kind we see, particularly among Christians, both Catholics and Protestants. These are cases of the inability to get assurance of forgiveness. A strange commentary on our popular religion is that so many people are carrying the burden of feeling unforgiven. Strangely enough, also, these persons quite regularly are very active church people. They are scrupulous to a fault. In Catholic penitential literature, this group of people are said to be victims of scrupulosity. In one Protestant farmer's description of his disturbed daughter, they suffer from an "unnecessary conscience." They are usually persons who have borne heavy responsibilities in their churches. They may have been deacons, vestrymen, stewards, etc., in their churches. These persons will, in the tradition of the Great Awakening in which the revival is the central ritual of redemption, make profession of faith again and again and again and again and again. They go to innumerable pastors and evangelists seeking assurance that they are forgiven.

One of the standard expressions of this particular attitude is that the persons feel that they have committed the unpardonable sin. They will say that they have sinned against the Spirit, that they have blasphemed against the Holy Spirit, that they have fallen away from grace and committed apostasy. They will tell us in the language of Heb. 6:6 that it is impossible for them to be restored again unto repentance without crucifying Christ afresh. These patients are extremely conscientious persons. They have lived exemplary lives. Rational attempts to discover precisely what sin they may have committed are futile. Usually the therapist feels frustrated in doing so. The therapist may give them basic assurances of the goodness of God, the kindness and the forgiveness of God. A few days later, they present the same set of symptoms and again need reassurance. They will do this so often that the resident will tend to lose patience with them and become shriller and shriller in an attempt to assure them of forgiveness.

It would be helpful, therefore, for us to take another look at the difficulties of these particular patients. What can contemporary psychiatric studies of these patients present to us? Let us give an example of such a patient.

Illustrative Case Number 6: A forty-three-year-old woman who was an assembly line worker in an electronics company, a high school graduate who had completed one year of college, married a man her own age. He was an auto mechanic, given to periodic times of drunkenness that interrupted his work and at times resulted in his losing his job. They had no children, because they lost their first child fourteen years ago by a premature birth. She could not have any more children. They lived in a house for which they were paying, but the bills were paid from the wife's income. Both husband and wife were Protestant but belonged to different denominations. Hers was a very strict denomination concerning attendance at movies, dancing, drinking, and smoking. His religious group was much more flexible about these things. In her own words she said: "I can be in church and get fearful, almost like I'm leaping over something, like I'm thinking or trying to think evil and bad thoughts for which God can never forgive me. The first time it happened most severely was during the Lord's Supper. I was afraid to drink and afraid not to drink the Lord's Supper. I remembered what the Bible says about eating and drinking damnation to yourself and I felt I would die before I got out of there if I did the wrong thing. I've felt this way at funerals and in church. I'm so afraid that I'll think blasphemous thoughts, I get beside myself and I stay depressed for days, crying much of the time."

The therapist can look into the longer-term history of this woman. For three years after her birth, the patient lived with her parents. She had one younger sister and when she was three her mother divorced her father because of the father's alcoholism. Each parent went to a parental home, taking one of the children for the grandparent to raise. The patient went with the father to the paternal grandparents.

The grandmother was in her sixties. She was a very pious woman who used religious beliefs about the end of the world, or the unforgiving nature of God, to discipline the patient as a child. As the patient became older, she worked and prepared all year round for excellence in her church. Yet she had a constant fear that she was not forgiven and that she could not stand in the presence of God. She said that she memorized the little saying: "Go nowhere you wouldn't want to be found when Jesus comes. Say nothing you wouldn't want to be saying when Jesus comes. Do nothing you wouldn't want to be doing when Jesus comes." She blames the fact that she could not have any children in adulthood on the fact that she is an unforgiven sinner. She has made repeated professions of faith in revival meetings. She struggles with thoughts of cursing God for which she cannot feel that God will forgive her. This patient is a classical example of a lifelong compulsive-obsessive way of life.

An acute depression brought her to the hospital. The depression grew out of her severe conflict with her alcoholic husband, who was reminiscent of her father. Underneath that depression was her lifelong compulsive-obsessive religious attitude. While she was in the hospital, conventional psychiatric treatment of chemotherapy and shock therapy removed the depression. Upon leaving the hospital, she perseveratively held religious ideas that she could not be forgiven. These symptoms serve to get the warmth and kindness and understanding of pastors who will meet these dependent needs. As long as a pastor, a Sunday school teacher, or a psychiatrist treats this kind of person as something of a child and gives reassurance each day, then the person tends to move along fairly well. One of the treatments of choice that we established was that, after she left the hospital, she would be under one particular pastoral counselor. He saw her in his office once every other week for an hour's conversation about her feelings, her life situation, and her needs. This sustained her over a period of five or six years. However, when this particular pastoral counselor moved out of her territory, the dependency was broken and she became depressed again. She went to a psychiatrist who dealt with both the depression and the compulsive obsession in longer-term psychotherapy.

In more recent cases of the treatment of such patients, this appears to be a form of addictive thinking just as a person is addicted to drugs or addicted to that popular drug, alcohol, or addicted to work, or whatever else. This kind of person is addicted to obsessive thinking. It is possible to deal with the thinking on a habit reconditioning approach or a behavioral modification approach. The aim is to challenge dependence upon psychiatrists, pastors, etc., and to build an adequate life support system of additional people around the patient. Thus, the patient is not overly dependent upon any one person. Rather, the patient has a group of people upon whom to depend and rely. If the person can become a part of a continuing group that sustains and encourages at the same time that it confronts, he or she has a guarded opportunity to recover from this particular kind of habitual or religious malaise. Therefore, we suggest some of the more recent findings in behaviorial and thought modifications which are very helpful in dealing with this particular set of symptoms. Probably every veteran psychiatrist and pastoral counselor has met this particular kind of person just often enough to have best efforts defied.

"The Spirit of God Has Left Me"

The seventh type of religious symptom cluster found in psychiatric patients concerns persons who feel that the Spirit of God has left them or that they can no longer communicate with God. Symptomatically these persons are Saul-like personalities. Saul, in the Old Testament, when the Spirit left him, felt a spirit of weakness take over in his life. Tragically he ended his own life. Patients who feel that the Spirit of God has left them tend, quite often, to be very desperate people. The suicidal risk is fairly high. People who feel that they have committed the unpardonable sin may be struggling with an unconscious temptation, a semiconscious temptation, or a conscious temptation to kill themselves. They would feel that this is something of which they could not later repent and, therefore, there would be no forgiveness for them if they did succeed in killing themselves. These are very dynamic and dangerous ideas. These persons who feel that the Spirit of God has left them tend to have a life history that shows signs of having been abandoned. That abandonment may have come very early in life through the death, the divorce, or the desertion of one or both parents. That abandonment may have come later in life through the progressive abandonment of people with whom they attempted to form love relationships, such as a boyfriend or a girlfriend, a husband or a wife, or an associate at work. That abandonment may also be a part of the post-divorce bereavement of a person who has lost someone by divorce. This sense of abandonment has been studied by John Bowlby in his series of books on attachment and loss in which he says that it moves through three phases: protest, despair, and detachment. We usually find these persons in the last stage, detachment, when they have experienced loss after loss after loss. They refuse to commit themselves to anyone or to anything. Life is a suspended animation because these patients cannot commit themselves to any durable relationship because of having been abandoned so often and so deeply. In other words, they seem to be suffering from a long series of broken relationships. They initially experienced a great deal of protest. Then they experienced a depression and despair. Now they are living their lives in a time of detachment and uncommitment.

This kind of patient appears in a pastor's study more often than in a hospital. They quite often are hardworking, productive on the job, and Mr. or Mrs. or Miss Faithful in the church. These persons nevertheless plod from day to day and do not feel that there is any positive feedback from the world around them. They seem to be hungering for affection. When the counselor listens very carefully to their life story, they reveal that they are mourning for persons who have left them, for they did not get to express their grief fully. There will be persons who have died to whom they did not get to tell good-by. The persons who have left them are to them irreplaceable. They tend to worship them. They are basically bereft persons. Yet they have heavy responsibilities. In order to carry out those responsibilities on their job, and in their home or wherever, and to meet the needs of a large number of persons who depend upon them, they simply have to put their own feelings on ice, i.e., freeze them. In doing so they freeze their relationship to God as well. They can no more feel the warmth and closeness of God than they can feel the warmth and closeness of anyone else. Once they have seen that this is a case of their having placed their feelings on ice, the issue in patient care is one of taking these feelings out and letting them "thaw" with the passage of time in a warm relationship to a therapist. But this is a very delicate thing for them to do. They fear the pain that will return when they start feeling those feelings again. The therapist's own human dependability and consistency awakens these feelings with kindness. Old denied feelings are found and sensitized. Gradually, over a period of time, these persons begin to feel a return of the kindness and goodness of God. They begin to feel that God is a person with whom they can converse warmly as a friend.

Illustrative Case Number 7: One person in particular lost her husband by divorce. She was unable to pray. She felt that God was extremely far from her. She felt that the Spirit of God had left her. She was told that it could well be that all she was saying about God were things she could just as easily say about her husband. She was asked whether she had in fact been worshiping her husband or whether by his leaving her she concluded that God had left her. She was advised, "Think about that; don't answer me; think about it, and I will see you again tomorrow." On her return the next day, she said: "I think you are wrong. I do not think that I have been worshiping my husband, because I have long since felt that I had lost him. To the contrary, I think I have been worshiping the institution of marriage. My status as a married person now being gone has caused me to be a nobody, a nothing. Unless I am a married woman I have no place, no standing before God or people."

In a real sense there was a kind of idolatry going on here. It was a freeing insight for this particular patient to see that the institution of marriage, as Jesus said, is a distinctly human institution. "In the resurrection they neither marry nor are given in marriage." Just as "the sabbath was made for man, not man for the sabbath," so also marriage was made for man and woman—man and woman were not made for marriage.

Once she began to see this particular insight, her relationship to God became closer and warmer. Then she began to say, "I have trouble putting my prayer into words." A pastoral counselor practiced with her in saying, "If you were talking with God and told God exactly what you have thought, what would you say?" He said: "Suppose we practice that now, and you just tell me what you would say to God if you were talking with him. Act as if you are talking to God." Alfred Adler called this the "language of hypothesis," of living *as if.* She began to say exactly how she felt about God and what she wanted to say to God. Then the pastor said to her: "God hears you, and this *is* your prayer. Talk with God just as you did right then, because God is with you and hears you as you think and as you speak." She became less bound up and a little freer in expressing her prayers to God. Sometimes a pastoral consultant can teach such patients to pray. But she had to give up her "Little Miss Goody Two-shoes" conception of what it means to be a Christian before she could tell God what she was thinking. The Biblical psalms are very helpful to patients who express this particular feeling that God has left them or that the Spirit has left them. The psalms will help them to put into words what they really are feeling. In fact, the psalms have the diagnostic value of a Rorschach or Thematic Apperception test for identifying the inner attitude of patients.

CONCLUSION

These have been rehearsals of recurrent religious symptom pictures of psychiatric patients. The degree of cultural difference in symptom presentation will vary from one geographical area to another according to the secularization in a given area. The themes of conflict between religious and psychiatric sanctions will be less intense in highly secularized cultures. The themes of the quest for identity, the feeling of being controlled by external forces, the feeling of being unforgiven, and the sense of having been abandoned will persist in any culture, it seems to us, but the symptomatic vehicles of expression will vary. The underlying existential struggles, however, are the stuff of which both healthy and unhealthy religious concern tends to be made.

4

RELIGIOUS DIAGNOSIS AND ASSESSMENT OF PSYCHIATRIC PATIENTS

The religious symptom pictures presented by psychiatric patients lead the therapeutic team to the issues of diagnosis. Until the appearance of the psychoactive drugs, diagnosis of psychiatric patients was more optional than now, since medications are used as specific agents for specific disorders. The shift of psychiatry to a distinctly medical approach has prompted shifts in the responsibilities of other members of the clinical team. The pastoral counselor, for example, gathers pertinent data about the religious world view of the patient that may or may not be accessible to other team members. Therefore, the concern of this chapter is to report the beginnings of a more precise set of data collection processes in the interviewing of psychiatric patients by pastoral counselors and other team members. Thus religious ideation and affect becomes diagnostically significant.

A Brief History of Religious Diagnosis

Diagnosis has been a process known since the ancient Greeks. In classical Greek, the word "diagnosis" means distinguishing, discerning. To be able to diagnose means to have the power of discernment, to resolve, or to decide. In the Greek New Testament, diagnosis refers to medical appraisal and decision as well as to legal pronouncement. In the earlier

Christian era, precise criteria and "earmarks" for making a diagnosis of the spiritual and emotional life of a person were well known. These were not diagnoses of sickness or health ordinarily. They were estimates of the integrity and whole-heartedness, the degree of deceptiveness or authenticity in the person. The idea of sickness does appear in the early Christian documents. In the pastoral epistle I Timothy, ch. 1:10, we find a reference to the "healthful teachings." The assumption of this phrase is that right living comes from right teaching freely accepted. In I Tim. 6:3 we read about "healthful words," with a similar assumption. The conviction of the New Testament writers was that a lack of health can develop from unhealthy teaching. The diagnostic concern of the early New Testament writers was to discover the degree of sickness or health in the basic belief system and value system of the person.

Therefore, I John says: "Beloved, do not believe every spirit, but test the spirits to see whether they are of God; for many false prophets have gone out into the world" (I John 4:1). Diagnosis in the Biblical era was that of "testing" between false prophets and true prophets. The process of testing was both a self-examination of one's own being and a no-nonsense "testing" of the lives of others.

Thus, the diagnostic criteria for distinguishing between true and false prophets were as follows:

1. What was the person's attitude toward the human body? Many in the first century A.D. believed that the religious person should deny totally the reality of the human body and its needs for food, sex, etc. Some denied that Jesus Christ indeed in fact had a human body. They refused to believe that he was genuinely human. They believed that he only seemed to have had a body. Therefore, the crucial test of Christian sincerity in this era was: "Do you believe that Jesus Christ is come in the flesh?" The Christian consecration of the human body and recognition of its human needs have been distorted through the years by the heretical belief that the body and its needs are evil. Deciding that belief in the

distinctly bodily existence of Jesus Christ was the bedrock of being a healthy person led to the insistence that food, marriage, etc., were divinely ordained. They were to be consecrated with thanksgiving and prayer.

2. What was the person's attitude toward fantastic visions, disembodied spirits, and pretensions of special revelations that came to that person and to only that person? The early Christians said that "no man has ever seen God." They and their Jewish counterparts believed that no one could look upon God and live. They therefore were extremely suspicious and tested closely the pretensions of false prophets. Fantastic, imaginary, and delusional visions were out of keeping with the basic teachings concerning the majesty and "hiddenness" of God.

3. What was the person's attitude toward other persons, i.e., toward fellow human beings? Brother and sister are defined in terms of the larger family and not merely the nuclear family. The firm conviction of the early Christians was that "we know that we have passed out of death into life, because we love the brethren." God is love. The person who is truly in touch with God has a loving relationship to his brother. The question is even asked that if a person cannot love his brother whom he has seen, how then can he love God whom he has not seen?

4. How willing is this person to be reconciled with his neighbor when the neighbor and he have had a disagreement? In Matt., ch. 18, a process is outlined whereby if a person cannot get along with a fellow human being, he or she is to go to that person and see that person face-to-face and see whether or not the person can be reconciled. The phrase used is: "if he listens to you." If this does not work, he or she is to go with another person and seek to arbitrate the matter with a third person present. If this does not work, the Christian is to bring the offending person before a disciplined group of Christians and see whether or not that person will hear them. Only after this rather rigorous face-to-face interpersonal process is gone through is a person justified in "writ-

ing off" a brother or sister in Christ as being outside the Christian community.

5. In other sections of the New Testament, one finds an additional criterion for the testing of a true prophet in the matter of work. If a person will not work, neither let him eat, is the instruction of the apostle Paul (II Thess. 3:10). In a post-Biblical document called The Didache, a quaint technique of testing a false prophet is used. If a person as a stranger comes to stay with you and poses as a prophet, then he or she is a true prophet if the stay is three days and three nights. But if he or she stays longer, then the chances of that person being a false prophet are very high! Therefore, the prophet was asked to leave after three days and three nights because he or she was perceived as a false prophet. To this day, knowledgeable Christians say: "Come and visit us! We will give you a true prophet's welcome."

The processes of religious diagnosis and assessment became much more systematized by the fifth century A.D. John Cassian about this time made a careful diagnostic description of the behavioral and mental states of persons who were afflicted with what he called the "seven deadly sins." His descriptions of behavior are vivid and precise. He even uses some of the same language used in psychiatric examination manuals today. Donald Backus, in his doctoral dissertation at the University of Minnesota in 1969, devised a psychological test on the basis of the seven deadly sins. Those seven deadly sins listed are: pride, envy, anger, greed, sloth, lust, and gluttony. Backus called these seven deadly sins states of mind or attitudes and prepared a "Sin Scale" on the basis of modern criteria of psychological test construction. He attempted to use modern scientific methods, therefore, to explore the value of these ancient religious and ethical constructs. He wanted an instrument that would measure the strength of these "sin states" in given individuals. He sought to correlate these sin states with mental disorders by comparing and contrasting the "Sin Scale" results with the mental illness category set forth in the Minnesota Multiphasic Personality Inventory (MMPI). In short, he was interested in the correspondence between these ancient diagnoses of sin and contemporary diagnoses of mental illness.

When the word "sin" is used here, it is not used in the sense that a psychiatrist or a psychologist would use it, i.e., as a thing a person does for which religious people are condemned by other religious people and for which they are punished. As Backus says: "The sins are not sins in the sense dear to most legalistic moralists. That is, they are not specific actions contrary to law. . . . These are not individual deeds, not transgressions of the law for which the transgressor can be apprehended, convicted by testimony, and punished. Rather they are tendencies to behave in certain ways." (Donald Backus, *The Seven Deadly Sins: Their Meaning and Measurement*, pp. 21–22; Ann Arbor, Michigan: University Microfilms, 1969.) Similarly, the MMPI does not measure specific acts but frames of mind behind acts. For example, the deadly sin of sloth, or acedia, correlated positively in all five test groups used by Backus with five of the eight categories of the MMPI. The depression scale, the psychopathic deviant scale, the schizophrenic scale, and the manic scale of schizophrenia correlated positively in three of the test groups on five of the sin scales—pride, envy, anger, sloth, and lust.

One of the values of this "Sin Scale" is to be found in the use of terminology in a psychotherapeutic interview situation. From a semantic point of view the word "schizophrenia" is much more a mystery and a signal reaction word that blocks out clear thinking than are the words pride, envy, anger, sloth, and lust. The psychotherapist could experiment with using these words to describe certain states of mind in psychotherapy. For example, grandiosity is a psychiatric equivalent for pride. Also, sloth, or laziness, is an equivalent for the psychiatric term "passive aggressiveness." The latter includes even a touch of anger. The purpose of language is to communicate. When language ceases to communicate, then the purpose is somewhat aborted. Therefore, if Backus' sin scale of categories will help us in the process of communicating more clearly with psychiatric patients under treatment, much can be said to commend them.

The seven deadly sins were used as a penitent's handbook for self-examination and a confessor's handbook for conducting confession well into the thirteenth century. As with all repetitively used guides for understanding persons and helping them, the use of these manuals degenerated and they became tools of the political control and sadistic needs of a highly systematized religious bureaucracy. This can happen in the use of psychological tests such as the Minnesota Multiphasic Personality Inventory, especially when they are used in settings for which they were not designed. The inventory may become a means of punishing and exercising reprisals against nonconforming persons in various power structures, organizations, etc.

Such misuses of psychiatric categories of diagnosis today are reminiscent of misuses of the "catalogs of sins" in church history. On December 9, 1484, Pope Innocent VIII issued a declaration giving two preachers, Henry Krämer and James Sprenger, the right to use a manual that they themselves had prepared. It was entitled *Malleus Maleficarum.* They used it as a guide for recognizing some of the mental states that we would today identify as insanity, witchcraft, and heresy. This loosed the inquisitorial urge of Western Europe in the Dark Ages. Innumerable people were killed as being heretical or given to witchcraft on the basis of this diagnostic manual describing the anti-erotic, misogynous nature of evil. Particularly harsh were they with women. Almost a century after the publication of the *Malleus Maleficarum,* the Burgundian judge Henry Boguet could say: "The sorcerers reach everywhere by the thousands; they multiply on the earth like the caterpillars in our gardens. . . . I want them to know that if the results were to correspond to my wishes, the earth would be quickly purged because I wish they could all be united in one body so that all could be burned on one fire." (Quoted by Gregory Zilboorg and George W. Henry, *A History of*

Medical Psychology, pp. 162–163; W. W. Norton & Company, Inc., 1941.)

There seems to be a natural history to the development of diagnostic and statistical manuals: they begin with the scintillating insight of pioneers who treat people as persons. Then they become useful guides to students and new teachers who find them valuable. In no way are they sacrosanct and absolute in their authority. The authoritarian use of diagnostic categories in bureaucratic ways deletes the distinctly human values and makes the "labels" into "things-in-themselves." As one studies the classification systems of psychiatric disorders and the classification systems provided by theologians, one sees that this process can be characteristic of both but it certainly need not be so.

The Protestant revolution took place in the earliest part of the sixteenth century. However, even though massive religious and political changes occurred, the Protestant churches, such as the Lutheran, the Reformed, the Anglican, and the Presbyterian, remained state churches. They were supported and sustained by the governments in each of their regions. Quite a few radical Protestant groups rebelled against this and formed fellowships of their own. They were usually very small, highly disciplined groups of people.

One such group of persons formed the Broadmead Church of Christ in Bristol, England. With the help of Professor Hugh Wamble of Midwestern Baptist Theological Seminary, I was able to find a copy of their church record. Recorded in the minutes of their church is the story of their healing of a mentally ill person. The striking part of this story is the care with which they did two things. First, they relied upon the physicians in their community to be of as much assistance as was humanly possible; second, they developed a system of diagnosis of the particular symptoms that the patient presented. The patient was a bachelor, although they failed to tell his age. He was old enough to be a salesman who went from door to door selling his goods.

The church describes John Frye, the patient in question,

as having fallen distracted. They say that it "first came upon him in a way of despairing, that he was lost and down; then he broke out in bad language to all the brethren that came near him, calling them very bad names and immodest expressions to some women, raving and striking them that came near him to hold him and when they were forced to bind him on the bed, he would spit at some and use such vile, grievous words, it was a consternation of the spirit to all that knew him, it being so directly opposite and contrary to the whole frame of his former way and temper."

They observed his mood and temper to move from one set of symptoms to another. After having sought the help of the physician that was available to them, they added to the physician's care by praying as a community.

In doing so, they set a day aside for dealing with each new set of symptoms that he presented. They stayed with him night and day, and the first day of prayer that they set aside was to deal with the spirit of rage that took place after their assurance and prayers had relieved him of his spirit of despairing. Then another day was set aside to deal with the "spirit of fear" that overwhelmed him. After giving him some time to rest and to take nourishment, they discovered that he was filled now with a spirit of shame "after the spirit of rage and the spirit of fear had left him." This spirit of shame kept him from going near his neighbors and kept him from wanting to see any person that came in.

Therefore, they appointed another day of prayer to deal with the spirit of shame that was holding him. They were so successful that "from the very next day after this he was embolden to go forth about his business in the city, as he did formerly; yea, he went from house to house about his occasions, to his customers, for the space of four-five hours and returned." They summarized the case by saying that "thus the Lord cast, as it were, three spirits, visible, to be seen out of him; viz., a spirit of uncleanness for rage and blasphemy; secondly, a spirit of horrors and fear; and thirdly, a spirit of shame as it were, dumbness." They gave the credit for all of this to God. They concluded the record by saying that nearly three years later "he is still recovered and the Lord has kept him in his glorious frame of spirit."

This quaint record reveals a kind of realism of concerned diagnosis as related to treatment which we rarely find today in religious groups that purport to be healing groups. Yet this particular group of people did not seem to feel that this was a great and unusual thing, nor did they feel themselves in opposition to the medical profession in their efforts to heal and help their friend.

(E. B. Underhill, The Records of a Church in Christ, Broadmead, Bristol, England. No date.)

CONTEMPORARY RELIGIOUS DIAGNOSTIC AND ASSESSMENT APPROACHES

The language of religion is a language of symbolism. The capacity of persons to distinguish symbol from reality and relate symbol to reality is one index to their mental health. Psychiatrists and other members of the treatment team rightly are cautious about the use of religious language with patients. They know that mental patients think very concretely. They are unable to separate symbol from reality and to understand symbols in a commonsense way. For example, the "voice of God" is an actual, audible, sensory experience to many mental patients. However, more recently we have begun to see that the very misuse of the symbols of religion by a mentally ill patient provides a sort of "royal road" to the deeper level of problems the person is trying to solve. Thus, I am suggesting that we take these symbols seriously and not be afraid to use them. Like medication, these symbols must be used very carefully and wisely.

Regardless of what a person's religious background is, the symbols of that particular religion are psychodynamically significant. The therapist goes underground into the labyrinthine catacombs of the inner world of a mental patient who is religiously conscious and states the patient's problems in the symbols of the person's religion. Most of my training and experience has been in the Judeo-Christian tradition. Therefore I tend to take the Bible very seriously as a basis of interpreting the deeper-level problems of people. Nevertheless, let me enter a disclaimer: the particular symbols of another religion, not those of the Judeo-Christian tradition, can be used similarly by people who have been educated and reared in the culture where those symbols are alive.

The Bible can be a "royal road" to the deeper levels of the personalities of patients reared in a Judeo-Christian culture. The use of the Bible as an instrument of diagnosis therefore needs initial attention and extended study. The question needs to be asked, Does the Biblical material in the stream of speech of an emotionally disturbed person give distinct clues to the understanding of some of the dynamic causes of the person's distress?

Oskar Pfister, in his book *Christianity and Fear,* gives a positive, generalized answer when he says, "Tell me what you derive from reading St. Paul, and I will tell you what the state of your disposition towards religious fear." (Oskar Pfister, *Christianity and Fear,* tr. by W. H. Johnson, p. 269; London: George Allen & Unwin, Ltd., 1948.) Here the Bible is seen not only as a record of the revelation of God to men but as an instrument of the revelation of the personality of both the therapist and the person with whom the therapist counsels.

This concept is suggested by at least one passage in the Bible. In James 1:22–24, the writer says: "Be doers of the word, and not hearers only, deceiving yourselves. For if any one is a hearer of the word and not a doer, he is like a man who observes his natural face in a mirror; for he observes himself and goes away and at once forgets what he was like." The Bible is a mirror into which one projects one's own concept of oneself, and which in turn reflects it back with accuracy. Speaking in psychoanalytic terms, we could say that the Bible then is to many people as dream symbolism and superego function are to the psychoanalyst. The meaningful symbols and ethical realities of the Bible have direct connections with the forces that work in the less accessible areas of the personality of the patient. As a fast-moving epic of human history, the Bible itself is psychodrama of abiding fidelity to the functional laws of personality. Likewise the Bible as a book of pictorial illustration is to the religious counselor what the Thematic Apperception Test or a Rorschach is to the clinical psychologist. As Gardner Murphy describes these tests, they are based upon the principle that the individual has specific needs that occur in response to the "press" of the environmental situation. A unified expression and need are perceived out of the individual's total background of experience and projected upon art forms in a mirrorlike fashion. The object of the tests is to have a "wide diversity of individual interpretations given." (Gardner Murphy, *Personality: A Biosocial Approach to Origins and Structure*, p. 671; Harper & Brothers, 1947.) Applying this principle and objective to the use of the Bible, any member of the therapeutic team has in Biblical symbols a means of insight into the deeper problems of people. A "wide diversity of interpretations given" is no deterrent. To the contrary, the very diversity reflects the individual variations of a given patient. These interpretations will fall into about three categories:

1. Conventional or "programmed" interpretations. These are interpretations that are characteristic of the large group of which the individual patient may be a part. They are representative of ingroup teachings that have been handed from one generation to another by a particular religious subgroup.

2. The private, idiosyncratic interpretations. These are interpretations that the individual has wrought out of his or her own private meditations. They tend to be characteristic of that person alone. However, they are realistic, common sense, and faithful to a reasonable interpretation of the person's life.

3. The bizarre interpretation. These are interpretations

that are "far out," that are linked with no discernible connection in reality, and are more or less delusional and/or hallucinatory in nature.

When one separates or sorts the various responses of a patient to fit the above categories, then one already has a diagnostic leaning as to how sick or well the person is. One would be naive indeed if one did not say that separating these references requires a considerable knowledge of the Biblical background.

The acutely disturbed person in a psychiatric treatment setting is more likely to use the Bible in a self-revealing manner than other people. The more secure and mature a person is, the more capable the person is of discerning and interpreting accurately the meaning and content of the Bible. The less secure and more immature, the more likely the person will be to quote the Scripture for his or her own purposes. In these latter cases, the member of the therapeutic team can get a fairly clear cut understanding of the life situation of the person as well as a feeling for the purposive drift of the life energies of the person.

Three clinical examples of these facts demonstrate best the diagnostic use of the Bible.

Mrs. M. H. is a twenty-four-year-old woman, married, and with no children. She came to her pastor's attention when she complained of having committed the unpardonable sin, which she interpreted as "cursing God." She felt that she had called God a g—— d—— s.o.b., and that there was no forgiveness.

Later, she was admitted to a general hospital as the patient of a private psychiatrist. The psychiatrist interpreted her problem to the pastor as arising from "feelings of inadequacy in her estimate of herself as a woman, as a sexual partner, and as a social being." He diagnosed her as being severely obsessional neurotic with schizoid tendencies. The recurrent obsessive "cursing thoughts" and self-derogatory attitudes were interpreted as a sort of mental hypochondriasis.

The patient was preoccupied with Scripture verses and

constantly demanded interpretations of the following passages in the New Testament: "The Scripture verses keep worrying me, and I cannot figure my way out: 'If you repent and then continue to sin, there is no way to repent again without crucifying Christ afresh'" (a paraphrase of Heb. 6: 4–6 and 10:26–27). On the second interview, she said: "I think of myself as the wicked servant in the parable of the talents. I have taken my gifts and buried them, and I have a master who is too hard for me. I want to submit myself to him, but I just can't seem to do so fully." On the fourth interview, she repeated this parable and gave an interpretation: "I just don't seem to be able to use myself like I want to—it's myself—I just can't seem to do so."

On a fifth interview, she asked this question: "What does the Scripture mean when it says that men and women should not be married who are unequally yoked together?" (Compare this paraphrase with II Cor. 6:14, I Cor. 6:6, and Deut. 22:10 for the disparity between the historical record and the projected effect.)

The history shows that this woman was a Presbyterian before her marriage. After marriage she joined the Baptist church in her community in response to pressure from her husband and her mother-in-law. She felt guilty about having married and moved away from her mother, who had been a mental patient in a state hospital. She also felt quite inferior to her mother-in-law and incapable of "winning her husband's affections" away from his mother. In the intimacy of sexual relations she said she was frigid. She could not "use herself as she would like."

The unequalness of the life situation was accurate: the apostle Paul was specifically referring to the institution of marriage. Likewise, the "buried gifts" in this instance could indicate something of the sense of ethical necessity the woman had about being an adequate marital partner. However, the master in the drama undoubtedly was the husband, who had usurped the place of God in the woman's life. The idolatry of the "master" ended in desecration—the god in the case was an s.o.b.! And the reference to idols in II Cor., ch. 6, was entirely appropriate to her.

Miss S. R., a forty-three-year-old single woman with a high school education was a patient in a state hospital. Upon admission, she showed general loss of interest in things about her, except that she felt compelled prior to admission to visit all the neighbors in her community excessively, with no apparent reason at all and at inappropriate times. She was obsessed with the fear that something was "about to happen to her sister."

In the first interview with this patient, the chaplain learned that her father had been a lay preacher and that her father had "petted her a lot." This included taking her on his lap, sleeping with her until she was "fourteen and after." The father brought another minister to "board at the home." She and the sister both fell in love with this man. He was an older person whose first wife had died. A keen rivalry developed. The patient's sister finally succeeded in marrying the man. The patient then went to live with the sister and her new husband. The marriage between the minister and the patient's sister ended in divorce just prior to the time of the hospitalization of the patient. Less than a year later, the sister died.

This history information is exceptionally significant in the light of the use that the patient made of the Bible. Being a very religiously inclined person, she laid great store by the Bible. She referred repeatedly to the fact that she loved the story of Jacob, Rachel, and Leah better than any other part of the Bible. She was asked to tell the story. The patient said: "Leah married Jacob before Rachel did, but he and Rachel were finally married anyway and it turned out right." The patient had come to the hospital shortly after the death of her sister. Now it *was* a possibility that the husband of the deceased might be interested in the patient. Could she face the guilt of replacing her deceased sister?

The sibling rivalry situation of this patient was integrally related to the affective value attached to the Biblical story.

Rachel did finally get Leah's husband. The psychodramatic situation was reenacted in the interpretation.

"The third patient is a twenty-five-year-old woman, married, and the mother of a five-year-old daughter. She is well oriented to time, place, and situation. She is noticeably tense and a little shy. She has an eighth-grade education and belongs to a Baptist church.

"She came to the hospital because of an attempt to take the life of her child. She had entered the room while the child was sleeping, took a pair of scissors, and was standing over the child to kill her when the husband came into the room and stopped the proceedings. The patient explained that she felt called of the Lord to sacrifice the child after having heard a sermon the same evening on Abraham's sacrifice of Isaac. The minister had greatly dramatized the story.

"She expressed the fear that she had perhaps committed the unpardonable sin (not necessarily in connection with the child). The child had been begotten out of wedlock; the father had to be brought home from the army for the wedding at a rather late stage of the pregnancy. The patient was living with her parents and was the decided favorite of her father. But the father was not willing to forgive her. He sent her out of the home telling her that she was not fit to live with the other children. She could not find her way back into the affection of the father. She lived with an aunt until her husband returned from overseas two years after the marriage.

"The husband had selected the child as the center of his affection, leaving the patient greatly isolated. He did things for the child, forgetting his wife on almost every occasion. He seemed to have no respect or love for her.

"The woman frequently said she could not understand her own behavior, since she insisted, weeping, that she loved the child. She came gradually, however, to see that she had some unbridled aggressiveness toward the child. This aggression seemed to revolve about the fact that the child had actually been the casual agent in separating her from her father's affection and from that of her husband.

"The sermon on Abraham served as a precipitating point in the attempt to discharge her aggression under the guise of a sacrifice to God. Indications were that the earthly father was the god in this case, and the child became a sacrifice or peace offering. The patient appeared to be attempting to remove the cause of the original isolation in getting rid of the child. She was out of fellowship with her god, the father, and it was of such long duration that she wondered if the unpardonable sin against him had not been committed.

"The patient gradually came to see who her god was and took responsibility for her aggression toward the child. She was able to make a fairly good adjustment at home." (Myron C. Madden, "The Contribution of Søren Kierkegaard to a Christian Psychology"; unpublished thesis, Southern Baptist Theological Seminary, 1950.) The latter case was recorded before the use of psychoactive drugs.

In no sense are these cases quoted in a "proof text" way. They are simply illustrative of the integral relationship between the dynamic causes of the patient's illness and the use they make of the Biblical material. These patients were acutely disturbed. A bold connection is easily seen between their problems and their expression of Biblical material.

Furthermore, it is evident that to argue with these patients over their interpretations would only serve to seal off insight and lucid religious thinking, rather than convince them. Again it is obvious that the patients herein described were persons who attached great feeling to religion as such. They were not like a vast majority of people in the secular culture —Biblical illiterates.

This creates the need for further exploration of the use of the Bible in the convalescent reeducation of a disturbed person. A warning, however, is that the diagnostic and therapeutic uses of the Bible involve as much danger as they promise help in the diagnostic and therapeutic processes. Any instrument is no safer than it is dangerous. But this is no justification for ignoring the Bible, taking the Bible away from patients, or depreciating the importance of the ideas to them.

To the contrary, it points to a "prescriptive" use of the Bible in which decisions are made about the patients' use of the Bible much in the same way they are made about the patients' use of medication. Some medicines will be dangerous to a patient and others will not. Some effects are to be noted in any prescription. Similarly, the prescription analogy applies in that the pastoral counselor should be a person who knows the pharmacopoeia of the Scripture as well as the medical doctor knows the standard medicines that are used which have been approved by the Federal Drug Administration.

The pastoral counselor on the therapeutic team knows in comprehensive detail the dramatic story, the historical context, the principles of exegesis, and the psychology of the Bible. Here is where the pastoral counselor's expertise either exists or does not exist. He or she needs the benefit of disciplined experience in clinical counseling relationships with large numbers of persons who seek his or her help. The pastoral counselor must be acquainted with the living human documents of patients as well as with the ancient Scriptures and their meaning.

In 1965, an exceptionally interesting and useful article on the diagnostic value of religious ideation was published by a group of psychiatrists. Edgar Draper, M.D., was the leader of the team of psychiatrists who studied systematically the diagnostic value of religious ideation. The team had formulated a pilot study in 1960 designed to examine the ways in which patients individualized their religious views no matter what their formal religious background, if any, may have been. They concluded that details of patients' interpretations of religion not only fit with their diagnostic picture but also offer clues to diagnosis at the clinical, developmental, and psychodynamic levels. Their methodology was essentially a double-blind study in which they developed a semistructured religious interview that could be conducted in thirty to forty-five minutes by the psychiatrically trained members of their team. The responses of the patients concerning their religion or personal philosophy were recorded verbatim, without other diagnostic tools being used, such as the standard mental status examination. Information sought included the religious history of the patient and of the patient's family, changes in religious activity or affiliation, and religiously influential persons or experiences in the patient's life.

Draper randomly selected psychiatric patients from both the inpatient and outpatient sections of the University of Chicago clinics and hospitals. These patients were seen in a religious interview. This was done concurrently with, but completely independent of, traditional psychiatric evaluations by other members of the staff not related to the research team. The findings of the research team were laid down alongside the findings of the routine psychiatric examinations made by those who were not on the research team in order to compare and contrast the double-blind results. In terms of assessing the patient, the team that used purely religious categories for diagnostic purposes reached a 92 percent correlation with the team that used conventional psychiatric categories. Draper and his team found that religious data enlivened the psychodynamic formulations. They offered keys to understanding the patient's current conflicts that were not easily grasped from other available clinical data. He says, "A number of patients who might be called 'unpsychologically minded' whose communications in the psychiatric interview were stilted and guarded, talked with interest, eagerness, and enlivened affect of their philosophical and religious views." Draper enters several disclaimers: He does not see this as a potentially useful projective test. He does not recommend that religious inquiry be routinely incorporated into clinical diagnostic investigations of every patient. He concludes that a patient's religious and philosophical views present as useful an avenue for psychiatric diagnosis as any other personal facet of the patient's life. The rich resource that religious material offers dynamically qualifies it as another "royal road to the unconscious."

It will be useful to include at this point the list of questions that the Draper team used:

1. What is your earliest memory of a religious experience or belief?
2. What is your favorite Bible story? Why?
3. What is your favorite Bible verse? Why?
4. Who is your favorite Bible character? Why?
5. What does prayer mean to you? If you pray, what do you pray about?
6. A. What does religion mean to you?
   B. How does God function in your personal life?
7. A. In what way is God meaningful to other people besides yourself?
   B. How is God meaningful to father or mother?
8. What religious idea or concept is most important to you now?
9. What is the most religious act one can perform?
10. What do you consider the greatest sin one could commit?
11. What do you think of evil in the world?
12. What are your ideas of an afterlife?
13. If God could grant you any three wishes, what would they be?

In addition to these questions, I would add the following questions:

1. What is your greatest temptation as you feel it now?
2. Who has been the most important religious person in your life?

(Edgar Draper, M.D., George G. Meyer, M.D., Zane Perzen, M.D., and Gene Samuelson, M.D., B.D., Chicago, "On the Diagnostic Value of Religious Ideation," *Archives of General Psychiatry,* Vol. 13, Sept. 1965, pp. 202–207.)

Further research could be done with the material that Draper has presented. For example, the kinds of responses of a given patient could be classified in the three categories mentioned earlier:

1. Conventional or "programmed" responses
2. Personal and idiosyncratic responses
3. Bizarre responses

It seems to me that using these three categories in a systematic way produces a further body of research that will be useful in sorting out and developing a meaningful diagnostic picture of the patient.

Likewise this set of categories can become very useful in teaching members of the psychiatric team how to be more precise in their evaluation of religious ideas that patients present routinely. This will enable the psychiatric team to be considerably more sophisticated in assessing the validity and nonvalidity of the religious thought of a person. Having worked for a considerable time in psychiatric units, I have been impressed by the way in which psychiatric team members will tend to "lump" all religious responses into one category regardless of its psychodynamic significance to the internal frame of reference of the particular patient. Such a classification system would tend to offset this "lumping" procedure

Another important distinction to make concerning the diagnostic approach to the religious ideation of patients is that patients from different religious cultures will respond differently to any given religious idea. For example, I personally am a Protestant and come from a religious culture in which the Bible is a focal emphasis. However, as one interviews Catholic patients, one notices that additional vehicles of religious expression become prominent. For example, instead of asking them who their favorite Bible character would be, one can ask who their favorite saint would be. I have found that some Catholic patients rely very heavily upon their knowledge of saints. The virtues of these saints provide models for the growth of the human person. Discussing religious concerns with Jewish patients reveals that the various seasons of Judaism tend to become far more significant to them than the choice of specific Bible verses, such as Rosh Hashanah, Yom Kippur, Hanukkah, and the Passover. However, they too will have specific Biblical characters out of the Old Testament that are very important to them. Similarly, some of the stories, the sagas, and other events described in the Old Testament become useful to them in symbolizing their inner concerns with life.

A philosophical issue appears relevant to this discussion of diagnosis and assessment. Religious diagnosis and assessment of patients, through their ideas and language, is one more positive example of the importance of symbolism and language. The writings of Sigmund Freud, Carl G. Jung, Erich Fromm, and Harry Stack Sullivan show the meticulous care with which they attended to language and symbolism. They have been experts in symbolic representation and in language analysis. The training of the psychiatric team is incomplete unless it involves discipline in structures and meanings of symbolism and language. Erich Kahler says that a "genetic line" can be traced "from the *symptom* (undirected sign) through the *signal* (the made sign and the stabilized sign) to the fixed sign, the actual inception of the *symbol.*" (Erich Kahler, "The Nature of the Symbol," in *Symbolism in Religion and Literature,* ed. by Rollo May, p. 57; George Braziller, Inc., 1960.) Dream symbols always move toward a human partner, even if it is one's own self to whom a message may be carried. In the therapeutic relationship, the therapist therefore can move from the symbol to the signal to the symptom and back again. The kind of communication that goes on within the person and between that person and others becomes more evident. Paul Tillich says that religious symbols have a figurative quality, a characteristic of perceptibility, and an innate power. He attaches affect and devotion to the symbol. The main force, he says, with religious symbols is their social acceptability. In a therapeutic relationship, the psychiatrists and their colleagues are interested in bringing the person into a realistic relationship to his or her environment. The goal is that the patient may function creatively. Religious symbols, it is hoped, may be another useful tool in the diagnostic and therapeutic armamentarium for bringing this to pass.

In my own interviewing of patients, I have discovered

that a more or less existential approach to the patient's being as a person, quite without regard to whether or not the person is sick or well, is a valuable way of gaining entrance into the life of the patient in such a way that a therapeutic alliance can be established in counseling. I have devised a pastoral assessment outline which I use in a somewhat *ad hoc* manner without feeling that I have to follow the outline as it is set out below in any particular order. I have found through the use of it, in groups particularly and with individuals, that this instrument is a way of moving the conversation from the trivial to the significant in enabling the patient to come to terms with the issues of his or her basic existence.

PASTORAL ASSESSMENT

A Thematic Evaluation Interview Pattern for Religious Concerns

I. In the beginning . . .
   What are your feelings about having been born?
   What sorts of blessings did those who brought you up confer upon you?
   What sorts of curses did they pronounce upon you?
   What do you think you were meant to be and to become from the beginning?

II. The way things have been . . .
   Whom of all the people you know would you most want to be like?
   Whom do you have to turn to when the going gets rough?
   Whom would you hurry to tell about something really good that happened to you?
   What are the things that people have done to you that you have the hardest time forgiving and forgetting?
   What recent things have happened to you that you would say are "the straw that broke the camel's back"?

III. The way things are now . . .
   What is the greatest injustice that you feel has happened to you?
   What keeps you from doing the things you most want to do?
   If all the hindrances were removed and you could do just

as you most wanted to do or have the thing you most
wanted, what would it be?

What is the biggest mystery to you? What do you have the
most trouble figuring out?

What appeals to your curiosity the most?

What is your greatest temptation?

Of what are you most afraid?

If you were to blame someone or a group of "someones"
for your present trouble in life, whom would you
blame?

If you pray, do you think God would understand if you
told God what your deepest angers are?

Does God want you to do what you yourself would be
happiest doing?

IV. The way things can change

Do you think there is any way that things can change?

Have you any hope that things can change?

Do things change by luck, magic, or chance?

If you were a magician and could change your whole situation, what would you change?

Have sudden and strange experiences come into your life
that changed everything?

How did you feel? What did you see, hear, smell, touch, or
taste? Did you want to tell about it? Whom did you tell
about it? What was their reaction?

V. What is God like to you?

VI. Does the church turn you on, turn you off, or leave you
cold?

Settled beliefs: What are some of the things that you believe and that you don't think will ever change in your
thinking?

This assessment outline is divided into sections on the person's attitudes about his or her origins, about his or her life
story as it was, about his or her life situation as it is, and about
his or her hopes and aspirations as he or she evaluates the
future. Two questions focus on the patient's personal relationship to God as he or she understands God and the patient's personal attitude toward the institutions of religion. A
final question with reference to the basic convictions of the

person as to what it is that he or she believes that will not be changed. Whether directly or indirectly, an assessment of the patient's values, prejudices, and hopes calls for competent wisdom in both religion and psychiatry.

As Gordon Allport, the late professor of psychology at Harvard, has said: "In a general way, we know what mental health requires. It requires that we learn to grow muscles where our injuries were. In the words of the Eighty-fourth Psalm, that man is blessed 'who going through the vale of misery, uses it for a well.' One thing we have learned is that a full discussion of mental health requires a rich bilingualism. It requires both the poetic and prophetic metaphors of religion and the precise, hard grammar of science." (Gordon Allport, "Behavioral Science, Religion, and Mental Health," in *The Person in Psychology*, p. 142; Beacon Press, Inc., 1967.)

5

THE RELIGIOUS CARE
OF THE DEPRESSED PATIENT

Depression is one of the most common illnesses to which the human being is subject. "Paradoxically, it is probably the most frequently overlooked symptom, and, even when recognized, is probably the single most incorrectly treated symptom in clinical practice. Not only are the signs and symptoms of depression multiple and complex, at any given stage of the disorder, but there are many stages and different problems in different age groups." (Alfred M. Freedman, Harold I. Kaplan, Benjamin J. Sadock, *Comprehensive Textbook of Psychiatry—II*, 2d ed., Vol. 1, p. 811; The Williams & Wilkins Co., 1975.) The term "depression" is much overworked. It is used to describe everything from temporary states of disappointment to long-term emotional states of dejection and sadness. The term is used here to describe an outright clinical syndrome of illness. Specific clinical features of persistent sleeplessness, a loss of initiative and enjoyment in life, suicidal threat, and biochemical changes comprise the depressive syndrome. By depression as an illness we mean a syndrome of symptoms that interfere with the total life function of the person in such a way that the person is disabled. This is what is called in medical circles an "endogenous" depression. It is not within the range of normal mood changes. Mood changes occur along with other impairments of the somatic and psychosocial functions of a person's life.

PRESCIENTIFIC DESCRIPTIONS OF DEPRESSION

Depression as an acute disorder of the total human life of persons is not new on the scene of human behavior. Many prescientific accounts are available that describe the depressed state of consciousness itself, its patterns of behavior, and the devastation that it can work in people's lives. Lengthy and accurate descriptions in detail of patterns of treatment for the disorder may also be found.

One of the earliest historical personalities in religious literature to be afflicted with depression was Saul, the king of Israel. One reads the story of this very interesting personality in I Samuel in the Old Testament. The Spirit of the Lord departed from Saul, and he began to be troubled by an evil spirit. A harpist, in the person of David, was required to charm away his deep melancholy. However, a therapeutic confusion occurred in that David himself became a competitor with Saul in the popularity and approval of the people of Israel. Saul became jealous of him and pursued him with relentless fury in bursts of vindictiveness. Apart from David, Saul and his armies became involved with the Philistines, who were invading the Israelite territory. Saul became depressed again. He began to feel sad forebodings of a fate that was awaiting him. He made a night's journey to visit a woman of Endor who was reputed to have the power of calling up even the dead. She gave him the evil news that he and his sons would perish in the battle that was approaching the next day. Saul himself was wounded. He asked his armorbearer to finish killing him. The man refused, whereupon the depressed and defeated Saul killed himself.

Psalm 22 captures the spirit of desolation characteristic of the depressed person. This is the psalm that Jesus repeated, the opening words of which were heard by those nearby, when he was being crucified:

My God, my God, why hast thou forsaken me?
  Why art thou so far from helping me,
    from the words of my groaning?
O my God, I cry by day, but thou dost not answer;
  and by night, but find no rest.
. . . .
. . . I am a worm, and no man;
  scorned by men, and despised by the people.
All who see me mock at me,
  they make mouths at me, they wag their heads;
"He committed his cause to the LORD; let him
    deliver him,
  let him rescue him, for he delights in him!"

The psalms are replete with such descriptions of depression. Such can be found in Ps. 130:

Out of the depths I cry to thee, O Lord!
  Lord, hear my voice!
Let thy ears be attentive
  to the voice of my supplications!

However, the book of Psalms is not *just* a book of depression. The whole spectrum of human emotions is described in this series of poems. Also, the book of Psalms speaks of recovery from depression and the healing of despair in the life of prayer. For example, in Ps. 40 we read as follows:

I waited patiently for the LORD;
  he inclined to me and heard my cry.
He drew me up from the desolate pit,
  out of the miry bog,
and set my feet upon a rock,
  making my steps secure.
He put a new song in my mouth,
  a song of praise to our God.
Many will see and fear,
  and put their trust in the LORD.

Greek literature likewise takes careful note of depression as an illness. One of the methods most frequently used by the healing temples of Greece was that of incubation. The phenomena of sleeping visions were used in sleep temples in order to restore people to a more optimistic and joyful life. The state of sadness was distinctly perceived as a sickness that needed healing. A person would go to the grove and temple of such gods as Asclepius and Trophonius to stay in certain buildings for an appointed number of days to get in touch with "the Good Spirit" and "Good Fortune." As part of his therapy the traveler bathed in the river Hercyna, and was anointed with oil. He was then taken by the priest to fountains of water. He first had to drink the waters of "forgetfulness," that he might forget all that he had been thinking hitherto. Afterward he drank the water of Memory, which caused him to remember what happened during the stay. The traveler then engaged in worship and prayer and proceeded to the oracle on the mountain beyond the grove. Upon return from this ceremonial he visited with the oracle of Trophonius. The priest seated the pilgrim upon a chair, the chair of Memory, and asked of the traveler all he had seen or learned. After debriefing the person from the journey and gaining his information, the priest entrusted him to relatives. The relatives carried the sojourner back to the building where he had lodged before with Good Fortune and the Good Spirit, to remain until he recovered all his faculties, especially the power to laugh. (Pausanias, *Description of Greece*, Vol. IV, pp. 349–355, tr. by W. H. S. Jones, The Loeb Classical Library; Harvard University Press, n.d.)

This rather detailed description of one form of therapy for depression as an illness is reported with an emphasis upon the use of sleep and water. One wonders whether perhaps contemporary uses of electrosleep therapy are more efficacious than other methods in the treatment of depression for the simple reason that they re-regulate the sleep rhythm of a person's life. Interesting is the comparison also between the degree of forgetfulness and the recovery of memory that is characteristic of contemporary shock therapy.

In the early Christian era, as among the ancient Hebrews,

depression was known as the "noonday sickness." Psalm 91 speaks of "the destruction that wastes at noonday." In the Christian era, after the institutionalization of the Christian religion, as early as A.D. 495, John Cassian identified what we call depression as "the spirit of acedia." He noticed the loss of initiative, the increase of helplessness, the agitation, the inability to work, the sleeplessness, and the feelings of hopelessness that we usually associate with the clinical syndrome of depression today.

Mark D. Altschule says that Petrarch shifted from thinking of acedia as a sin and understood it as what we today would call a psychiatric symptom. He spoke of it as a disease. Altschule says: "Petrarch himself manifested an important symptom that had never been mentioned in that connection: an almost voluptuous pleasure in one's own emotional suffering. Another aspect of the syndrome that he unwittingly manifested was delight in exhibitionistic self-revelation, as shown in the minutely detailed account of his own spiritual sufferings." (Mark D. Altschule, "Acedia—Its Evolution from Deadly Sin to Psychiatric Syndrome," *British Journal of Psychiatry,* Vol. 3, 1965, pp. 117–119.)

An ancient pattern of treatment was recommended for the recovery of a person suffering from acedia. A distinct pattern of treatment, based on the apostle Paul's teachings in I and II Thessalonians, is outlined as follows:

First, one begins with the soothing application of praise and appreciation. This is necessary to enable the depressed person's "ears to be submissive and be ready for the remedy of healing words." As this praise of the good work and achievements of the person is applied, it is generously intermixed with encouragement to continue to do as one has done in the past. There is a strong affirmation of the past pattern of life in its productivity and creativity.

Second, the depressed person is encouraged to tend to his or her own business. This is based on the assumption that a part of acedia lies in the person's feeling of inability to control the behavior of other people. In this effort to control other people's behavior, disappointment occurs and the person falls into despair. Thus, the person who accepts responsibility for doing that which is his or her "own business" is less likely to be discouraged. He or she is urged to give up trying to run other people's lives for them.

Third, the depressed person is encouraged to examine himself or herself honestly and to walk honestly in relation to other people. Thus, the person is urged to examine the accuracy of his or her perception of reality and to bring his or her thinking into keeping with things as they are and not just as they appear.

Fourth, the person is encouraged not to covet other people's goods. The ancient assessors of personality assumed that much despair arises out of the covetousness of not having achieved the things that other people have achieved. Learning to be content with that which one has was a goal of treatment. One is encouraged to prove one's own worth, to work with one's own hands, and to produce things by working with one's physical body. In fact, at one place the injunctions say that if a person will not work, neither let that person eat. In other words, if the depressed person refuses to be productive, then food deprivation is used as a form of negative reinforcement to see to it that the person does work.

And finally, the person is encouraged to cease to "gad about" among the brethren, gossiping and speaking idly of others. If indeed this pattern continues, then the community is encouraged to ignore the person and withdraw from that person. A form of "judicial neglect" is suggested.

All through these rather quaint suggestions of therapy for the depressed patient is a continuing sense of seriousness with which the suffering patient is taken by the community as a whole. This set of suggestions assumes a highly disciplined, face-to-face community of people who care specifically about what is happening to the other person. However, today, in the religious life of the average conventional religious organization, these close-knit, face-to-face communities are very, very rare. Therefore, let it be clearly under-

stood that I am simply reporting an ancient method of therapy in the Christian community as I did the ancient method
of therapy in the Greek community to indicate that not only
were there accurate descriptions of the symptomatology of
depression in ancient eras but that also there were formal
efforts of treatment with resources that the community had
at hand.

One could not review all the religious literature on depression. The above excerpts indicate something of the drift of
such literature. However, one can examine the writings of
Augustine, in his *Confessions;* Martin Luther, in his letters;
George Fox, in his journal; John Bunyan, in his book *Grace
Abounding;* Jonathan Edwards, in his *Treatise Concerning
Religious Affections;* and many other historical figures. In
these writings are to be found vivid descriptions of the clinical syndrome of depression. Outstanding contemporary authors such as Harry Emerson Fosdick, H. Wheeler Robinson,
E. Stanley Jones, and Anton Boisen are powerful religious
leaders in whose writings may be found autobiographical
reports of times of depression.

More recent forms of therapy used by contemporary religious leaders are meditation, retreat centers for stress inter-
ruption, and specific emphasis upon mystical experience.

Mystical experience has been reported by Paul C. Horton
in three cases of suicidal patients as being an "oceanic state"
which provided the patients with a reliably soothing safeguard against their overwhelming loneliness and possible
suicide. Horton recognizes as a psychiatrist the importance
of a mystical state as a transitional phenomenon that, along
with other therapies, will tend to offset the possibility of
suicide. (Paul C. Horton, M.D., "The Mystical Experience as
a Suicidal Preventive," *American Journal of Psychiatry,* Vol.
130, No. 3, March 1973, pp. 294–297.)

THEORIES OF DEPRESSION

Members of the therapeutic team, regardless of their profession, face a bewildering fragmentation of theory as to the nature and causes of depression. Similarly, the very seriousness of the disorder is interpreted from various degrees of a sense of jeopardy for the life of the patient. However, since the advent of the antidepressant drugs, there has been a remarkable revival of interest in psychiatric diagnosis emphasizing the clinical signs and symptoms in relation to the long-term life history of the patient. Dean Schuyler, M.D., presents a comprehensive review of depression in its range of emotions, its signs and symptoms, classification, theories, outcome, and treatment options. He systematizes the research in the field with what he calls a "spectrum approach." He distinguishes between a normal depression and a clinical depression and says that in normal depression, one has "the blues" and "grief reaction." To the contrary, in the pathological depression, there is the neurotic, indecisive, depressive state and the endogenous psychotic depression.

Clinicians generally agree as to the symptomatic presentations of a depressed patient. The fragmentation and controversial thinking of the field of psychiatry has a way of becoming more confusing at the points of etiology and treatment of choice. In an overview of recent research in depression, Akiskal and McKinney seek to integrate the varieties of interpretation of the cause and care of the depressed patient's condition into ten conceptual models. The conceptual models may be subdivided into the models that are proposed by *five different schools of psychiatric treatment.*

1. The psychoanalytic schools propose four different emphases in the interpretation of depression: First, the psychoanalysts propose that depression represents *anger and aggression turned inward against one's self.* This particular conception is highly relevant for the religiously inclined patient and the religious care of that patient, in that such a heavy taboo on anger and aggression is held by so many

different groups. Second, the psychoanalytic schools since Freud have made much of *object* loss as a theory of depression. This moves all the way from René Spitz's understanding of an anaclitic depression which roots back into the earliest days of a person's life when the person was abandoned to the pathological grief situation of a person who has lost someone or something and has never "worked through" the grief. This last point of view is classically set forth in Freud's article "Mourning and Melancholia." A third psychoanalytic school characterized by such persons as Erich Fromm and Karen Horney would assess depression as *loss of self-esteem, poor self-image,* etc. A fourth set of psychoanalytic theories is that of a *negative cognitive set.* This person is characterized by hopelessness and a loss of mutuality in his or her interaction with his or her environment.

2. A second classification of theories of depression is found in the behavioral school in which Martin E. P. Seligman speaks of depression as "learned helplessness," a theory that was devised in animal experimentation. The first phase of learned helplessness is exposure to a situation that is painful, combined with the conditions that prevent a person from doing anything to put the painful situation to an end. The second phase is a "giving up" phase in which the person simply accepts passively his or her helplessness. This suggests that even from earliest infancy, individuals may be classified as tending to express stress reactions either outwardly or inwardly, but not both. In terms of biogenic temperament, the work of Macfarlane suggests that there are "internalizing infants"—that is, those who show their difficulties by secondary gastrointestinal and other types of upsets, and that there are those other infants who are inclined to an overt expression of response in terms of action and behavior. Gardner Murphy says: "This is as good a hypothesis for a constitutional typology, though the problem will doubtless be restated many times before a really workable typology is found." (Gardner Murphy, *Personality: A Biosocial Approach to Origins and Structure,* p. 82.)

In the behavioral approaches of depression, a second

concept appears for which we are indebted to Wolpe. He calls this a "loss of reinforcement" view. The depression rewards the patient for losses that he or she has sustained in life.

3. A third set of theoretical models of depression has been proposed by the social psychiatrists. Social psychiatrists are not a breed apart among psychiatrists. To the contrary, they are physicians who are thoroughly trained in a broad spectrum of modalities of treatment. They consider themselves as distinct humanitarians who "as humans" maintain their respect for the dignity of the individual. They maintain awareness of the uniqueness inherent in the social situation of each patient. Ever since Freud wrote his classical work, *Civilization and Its Discontents,* the social dimension of psychiatry has been vividly present.

The social psychiatrist is likely to present a "displaced or unplaced person's" concept of depression. The patient is seen as not being able to find a place in life, or, upon finding a place in life, losing it and suffering a loss of role or status. For example, the pathologically grieving widow suffers not just the loss of her husband but also the loss of her role status as a married person. She is a single person again in a "couple-oriented society." She does not have the status of being a married person. Many of the prerogatives she and her husband shared together in clubs, churches, and other associations of the community have been taken from her, and the social groups in which she moves are usually all female. She has only a minimal contact with both sexes. This role status contributes to her depression, if it does not cause it. Similar things could be said of divorced persons, some unemployed persons, persons who have finished school, and others who have finished rearing their children. They are likely to think of themselves as being "finished."

4. A fourth group of theorists are the existentialists. Such persons as Viktor Frankl, Carl Jung, and Rollo May insist that the great dynamic of depression is the loss of meaning and existence. Radical psychiatrists like R. D. Laing have built

patterns of treatment that assume that mental illness is a "quest" for this meaning.

5. A final school that provides at least two models of depression is that of the biogenic school, which is at this time at an intense level of research and treatment. The biological approach to depression has been demonstrated somewhat conclusively. Martin Allen and others have studied affective illnesses in veteran twins and made a diagnostic review. They studied 15,909 pairs of twins born between 1917 and 1927, among whom both twins served in the United States Army. This large sample was screened for twin pairs in which one or both had received the diagnosis of psychosis on active duty. They found 156 twin pairs in which one or both had been diagnosed as having an affective illness. Although computer-listed comparisons between "single ovum" and "double ovum" twins were insignificant, chart review diagnoses demonstrated much more significance. A study of 25 pairs of identical twins found that both were diagnosed as depressed persons. Out of 53 "double ovum," or "nonidentical," twins, in none of the pairs were both affected by a depressive illness; only one of the pair was so affected. One raises questions about data like this: "If none of the nonidentical twins showed concordant diagnoses of depression, then how much less would it be characteristic of family members who were not twins at all?" "If identical twins present a highly elevated percentage of concordant diagnoses of depression, then is there something about identical twin genetics in and of themselves that needs studying rather than using these high percentages as criteria for judging the biogenetic possibilities of a whole population?" Furthermore, another question could be asked: "If 36.5 percent of identical twins suffer concordant depressions, then how is it that the other 63.5 percent of such twins did *not* present such concordance?"

However, the most active research in the biological approach to depression today is in the area of using drugs that have a psychological effect. Treatment hypotheses say that certain substances in the biochemistry of the body are depleted, causing the depressive episode. Groups of hormones known as "biogenic amines" are facilitators of several central nervous system functions. Elation, it is hypothesized, may be associated with an excess of such biochemicals. The British are moving on the hypothesis that other biochemicals are at a significantly high level and thus affect the person in such a way that he or she becomes depressed. Stress studies such as those of Peter Bourne, especially upon Vietnam veterans, suggest that certain steroids are out of balance, causing exhaustion, and that depression is one result that follows. Other research persons are working on the relationship between depressive illness and hyperglycemia or hypoglycemia. In the field of psychiatry today, a wide array of pharmaceutical studies seek to establish dependable hypotheses for the treatment of depression.

At the distinctly practical and clinical level, however, the treatment of depression moves toward an intensification of the importance of the diagnosis of the particular kind of depression. If the depression is an anxiety or neurotic depression, then the treatment tends to move in the direction of anxiety-controlling types of drugs. But if the depression is diagnosed as "endogenous," antidepressants are to be used (or chemically based). Thus diagnosis cannot be written off as irrelevant today as in the years prior to 1952, when the psychologically effective drugs had not become available.

As a theologian and pastor, I emphasize that when a counselee seems depressed or is depressed, the first line of response is to ask the person to have a thorough medical examination by a doctor of internal medicine. Then I suggest that the pastor ask for consultation with that physician and collaborate as to whether or not pastoral counseling is indicated or whether additional care is needed from a psychiatrist. If the psychiatric referral can come from a conjoint assessment by a clinically trained pastor and an internist, then the patient tends to feel that he or she is more cared for and is being taken seriously. Thus the patient is more likely to accept a psychiatric referral. The patient will know that he or she has not simply been hurried off to a psychiatrist.

If indeed a psychiatric referral is necessary, it may well be that the person needs separation from his or her environment by hospitalization. The indicators of this are: (1) the degree of disability that the person is experiencing in work, interpersonal relationships, and basic sense of somatic well-being; (2) the degree to which the patient is likely to make impulsive judgment about major issues in his or her life, such as quitting a job, confessing a long list of past sins to injudiciously selected people, spending great quantities of money unwisely, etc.; (3) the degree of suicidal risk that exists in the person. One of the dangers of pastoral counseling with depressed persons is that the pastor sees many normative states of sadness and grief that "hurt" in ways similar to depression, e.g., the loss of someone by death, divorce, defection, or alienation. Yet this may or may not be unreasoning, indefinable, and prolonged sadness. The person may "come through" quite well, depending upon the person's life support system, ego defenses, history of dealing with problems, etc.

However, a pastor may well find a person to be in a prolonged depression, have major difficulty in functioning, and unable to pull out of the state of despair. The pastor can prolong this by continuing to see the patient on pastoral counseling interviews over a long period of time when, instead, some medical intervention could alleviate the suffering much more quickly. The in-hospital treatment of a psychiatric patient by a therapeutic team that includes skilled and experienced pastoral counselors is an issue that needs attention at this point. One needs to raise the question: What are the religious dimensions of depression? Then one needs to ask: How can these dimensions be implemented in the treatment of the patient concurrent with milieu therapy, pharmacological therapy, and social work therapy that includes work at a psychotherapeutic level and at a family therapy level? It takes a smoothly working team effort. I shall attempt to answer these questions to some extent in the ensuing section.

DEPRESSION, RELIGIOUS CRISIS AND PASTORAL STRATEGIES

Let me emphasize depression as a religious "value crisis" and identify some of the dimensions of that crisis in such a way as to reflect the fact that pastoral wisdom may be strategically helpful to persons in the religious crisis presented in many depressive illnesses.

The hallmark of effective religious therapy is interpretation and the provision of meaningful patterns of understanding of what is happening in the life of a patient. These patterns of understanding must be acceptable to the patient without too much persuasion or indoctrination on the part of the therapist. Nevertheless, clinical experience has shown that sometimes a clear-cut sentence of interpretation that provides a precise meaning or key to the plight in which the person finds himself or herself becomes lastingly useful and may mark a turning point in the person's direction toward health.

The religious crisis of many depressions presents several specific facets of these mood disorders that can be approached pastorally in definable ways somewhat as follows:

The Crisis of Nostalgia and Rumination

Nostalgia is a word that was used during the Civil War to describe depression among soldiers. To them it focused on wanting to return home. An original medical definition of nostalgia was "a severe melancholia caused by protracted absence from home, as of military personnel." In brief, it means simply looking homeward, looking backward and ruminating the way things "used to be." Nostalgia becomes a crisis in people's lives in the form of depression. Subtle development crises are often neglected in the history-taking procedures with such patients. Examples help to illustrate what is meant:

First, a fifty-eight-year-old man, a widower of ten years, became unreasonably depressed, with no particular visible precipitating event. He was a very religious person who had worked both as a tool and die operator and as a minister in his community. He was able to retain his full-time job as a tool and die operator. By reason of changes in personnel and the closing of smaller churches, the church of which he was a pastor went out of existence. He was not able to find another church. He became so depressed that he simply sat on the front porch of his son's home and "moped" and ruminated about "the way things used to be." His condition became prolonged enough that his son and daughter-in-law, parents of four little children, insisted that he get medical treatment. Upon diagnosis, he was discovered to be free of any physiological disorders, with the exception of a slightly elevated blood pressure. Yet he was extremely sad, agitated, listless, without initiative, and noncommunicative. He was somewhat hypochondriacal. He wanted medication for the slightest difficulty he felt in his body.

Upon closer scrutiny, it was discovered that this man's value system grew out of his own father's value system. His father had always believed that it was the children's God-given duty to honor their parents by caring for them after they got "too old to work." The critical issue was that the father had a religious value which prompted him to think that his creative years were "over" when he got his children grown. Also, he felt that his purpose in life beyond this point was to "sit and rock" and do nothing. This attitude is not an uncommon value among blue-collar people.

The staff confronted him in psychotherapy with the fact that he had much life still left to live, and that it may well be God's calling that he dedicate that life to a new chapter in his existence. The staff suggested that he could make a new contribution by continuing his work as a tool and die operator and by getting the assistance of his church people in finding an additional place for his preaching ministry. To all this he was very resistant. He became considerably angry and his blood pressure fluctuated upward. However, he was presented with the other alternative, that if he chose his depressed state of inactivity as a chronic way of life, it would be necessary for him to be moved to a welfare type of hospital. He opposed being on welfare. He saw it as "going to the poor house." He became intensely angry. He refused any further treatment and decided to go out of the hospital against medical advice.

However, in his anger he went back to his job. He did indeed, with some assistance from the social service staff, get in touch with his church organization and find a new pastorate. He established himself as an ongoing independent person. However, his poignant remaining problem is loneliness. The life support system of his church will, it is hoped, provide him a larger family than just his son and daughter and their children. Also, it is hoped that he will meet an eligible person to become his wife. They too might form a new home in which his loneliness can be assuaged by the pleasure of the company of a new wife, inasmuch as his first wife has been dead ten years. The "odds" on such hopes are not too good, but it has happened to other people. Maybe it can happen to him.

A second example of the crisis of nostalgia as a form of depression is found in women who have suffered the loss of their first child in stillbirth or by miscarriage or by abortion. They may have gone on into a highly productive life and been privileged to raise a normal family. Nevertheless, they continue to ruminate about their "first loss."

An example of this is a forty-nine-year-old woman who had had an abortion thirty years before, at the age of nineteen. She was in an unreasonable depression. A close scrutiny of recent occurrences in her life revealed that her youngest daughter, with whom she had a close relationship, had been married just three or four months before, at the age of nineteen. This was a turning point in the patient's life and may have reactivated memories of her own youth. This mother's mind at this point was obsessed with whether or not God could forgive her for the abortion thirty years before. Both the patient's daughter and her son were apparently happily married, lived near, and were solicitous to her. Yet their words of solicitude fell with cold comfort on the mother's ears. The pastoral counseling proceeded along two lines of strong affirmation of the highly creative and productive life that the woman had lived since marrying her husband. She had apparently done a quite successful job of rearing her children. However, "the wedding over" and the "crowd having thinned out," she was faced with the necessity of reorganizing her whole routine of life. She must now reestablish her relationship with her husband in their new identity in the "empty nest" stage of family living. Yet she was exhausted by the prospects of facing these new responsibilities. Did she really want to go forward? Or did she wish to turn back and ruminate nostalgically and sentimentally over the mistakes of the past? Antidepressants were being used with this patient and she was making some progress. However, one raises the question as to how much of a compulsive obsessional type of thinking is involved in addition to the depression. How much habit remodification is going to be needed? The term "behavioral modification" does not make as much of "thought modification" as it potentially could. A few therapeutic successes I have had in the past in working with this kind of ruminative circularity of thinking are more related to thought modification built upon behavioral modification concepts than they are upon insight therapy. This is the approach that was instituted in this patient's religious care.

The Crisis of Self-Consistency

Prescott Lecky made a remarkable contribution to psychotherapy in his book *Self-consistency*. He rejected what he termed the "hydraulic analogies" of psychoanalysis. By this he meant that human feelings such as anger and sexuality are not "fluids" whose "pressures" are created by the lack of emotional outlets, drainages, etc. He assumed instead that behavior is motivated by the need for the unity of one's personal values in life. He conceived of the personality as an organization of values which are felt to be consistent with one another. Behavior expresses the effort to maintain the integrity and unity of the organization. (Prescott Lecky, *Self-consistency*, p. 152; Island Press Co-operative, Inc., 1951.) Conflict arises when a value enters the system which is inconsistent with the individual's personal integrity. Such an entry may precipitate a depression, because a person cannot assimilate an experience that is contradictory to his or her values. This particular kind of depression is often thought of as a "neurotic depression." It is characterized by indecision. The person knows what he or she should do in order to maintain his or her integrity, but is at a loss as to how to bring it off, or lacks the courage to do so.

An example of this kind of attempt at maintaining integrity is the case of a twenty-nine-year-old black woman who was admitted to an emergency psychiatric service after having taken an overdose of sleeping pills. Upon having been resuscitated, she said that she was in one "hell of a fix." She said: "I'm trying to make my mind up. I don't know what to do." Her dilemma was that she is the mother—out of wedlock— of four children. She was living with a man with whom she did not want to have any further dealings. Her children had become attached to him and did not want to leave him. They had "sided" with him. As a result, if she left him, she would lose her relationship with her children. At least she thought she would. If she stayed with her lover, she would be subjected to a relationship in which she felt that she was treated "like dirt." Thus, in the critical dilemma, she cried for help by a minimally lethal attempt at suicide. The value conflict here between maintaining her personal integrity, on the one hand, and maintaining her relationship with her children on the other hand was intense. Two approaches to her dilemma were taken. The social workers instituted family therapy with the children, the lover, and the patient. Individual pastoral counseling with the patient brought to focus her own sense of self-worth, her value as a person before God, and the kinds of ideas she wanted her children to learn from her.

From a religious point of view, maintaining one's integrity means maintaining one's sense of self-respect as a person made in the image of God. In Judaism, this is an extremely important value. In Christianity, the value of being made in the image of God is the same. Added to it is the conviction of being a person in one's own right, having been redeemed by the Lord Jesus Christ as one for whom Christ died. Yet being a person of integrity calls for the capacity to make a clear-cut decision and to stay with it. A part of the religious care of the psychiatric patients suffering from an integrity crisis is that of enabling them to learn the arts of making decisions, of reinforcing good decisions that they have made, and of staying with them and following through as they implement these decisions. The nineteenth-century Danish theologian Søren Kierkegaard had a remarkable analysis of this in his book entitled *The Sickness Unto Death*. He said that despair is the sickness unto death. That despair is the sickness in the spirit. Despair assumes a triple form. First, some persons have despair at not being aware of having a self or of the necessity of having integrity. Second, others despair at not having the courage to decide or to will to be themselves, i.e., to have integrity. Third, other persons despair at willing to be themselves, having decided to be themselves, and at the great burden of maintaining their integrity. The issue, therefore, of maintaining one's integrity lies at the root of much neurotic despair of depression. (Søren Kierkegaard, *The Sickness Unto Death*, p. 17; Princeton University Press, 1941.)

The Crisis of Power and Powerlessness in the Systems of Society

In some of the earliest myths, the desire to be in control and to have power in the system of which one is a part stands as one of the foremost needs of the human being, one of the most ambiguous dilemmas of the human being. The story of the temptation and sin of Adam and Eve in the garden reveals this need "to be as gods." The depression of Saul described in the earlier part of the chapter was an outgrowth of his sense of powerlessness in the system of which he was a part. Today, persons are involved in several systems out of which a considerable amount of depression ensues. These are the home, the work situation, and the political situation.

Some fertile sources of depression in the systems of society are unresolved bereavement and divorce, both of which are focused in the system of the home. A common temptation is overinvestment, or idolatry, which tends to focus heavily upon the home. Daniel Tucker, M.D., in private conversation, defined "reality" as "the least alterable facts in one's human existence." The loss of someone by death tends to be probably the least alterable fact in one's existence. Adjustment to a loss by death depends heavily upon the degree of overinvestment that one has made in the deceased loved one. However, one of the most common indications for the involvement of religious professionals in the care of a psychiatric patient is that of prolonged, pathological grief situations. The death of a spouse or a child very likely causes the depressive syndrome of bereavement where overinvestment or, to use a theological term, idolatry of the dead is evident.

A case in point is a thirty-eight-year-old woman who had lost her son three years before by death by cancer. She had him through his terminal illness for nearly a year. She said: "I simply cannot accept the fact that my son is dead. If I accept it, the fact that he is dead, then he would be dead." In speaking to me as a minister, she said: "How can God help me to accept the fact of my son's death?" She asked this question in a highly insistent manner, as if to "demand" a perfect answer to it. I told her that I felt that she was having a greater problem of accepting the fact that she could not control and determine obvious reality that her son had died three years before. I pointed out to her that one of the effects of her illness was that it dominated and controlled the rest of her family situation. She was in control over the rest of the family, even though she could not control the life and death matter of her son. There was a long silence in the conversation. I asked her to pose this issue with her psychiatrist, who had asked me to see her, and make this an item for their psychotherapy. In conferring with him, I suggested that this would be a vital issue to consider: i.e., pathological grief can be a refusal to live life without being in total control. In long-term chronic cases of pathological grief, I have found the factor of personal power and control of the family system to be a driving force that maintained the depression.

The work situation is a second system in which depression becomes evident in the powerlessness of the patient. In the technological and bureaucratic structures of our society, people develop institutionalized neuroses in relation to the employment structures of which they are a part. They tend to think of their organization as the whole universe itself. They are likely to think of it as "a flat earth." If one goes beyond the edge of the organization, then annihilation is the result. Bureaucratic organizations give a person some individual satisfactions over and beyond the "uses" of those for the organization itself. The enlargement of the spiritual life and personal growth of employees is an important ingredient of effective productivity, but is a low priority item in business, educational, and professional administrations. One obvious truth that a person can outgrow a job is rarely a topic of management planning.

Twenty years ago, William H. Whyte, Jr., said: "Of all the organization men, the true executive is the one who remains most suspicious of The Organization. If there is one thing that characterizes him, it is a fierce desire to control his own destiny, and deep down, he resents yielding that control to the organization, no matter how velvety its grip. He does not want to be done right by, he wants to dominate, not to be dominated." In another connection, he says: "Here lies the executive's neurosis. Some of the executive's tensions and frustrations are due to psychoses—his own and others'—and these are amenable to individual treatment. To a very large degree, however, the tensions of organization life are not personal aberrations to be eliminated by adjustment; they are inevitable consequences of the collision between the old ethic and the new." (William H. Whyte, Jr., *The Organization Man,* pp. 166–167; Doubleday & Company, Inc., Doubleday Anchor Books, 1957.) The whole system of healthy religious values indicates that an organization will "take care of its own." The average ethic is that the organization takes care of itself. Individuals are expendable.

For example, a leading executive enjoyed twenty-five years of effective service to his organization. When he came to age sixty-four, the policy concerning retirement was changed. Persons now could continue year after year, on the assumption of medically certified healthiness, until they were seventy. However, this man had been on the wrong side of a whole string of political issues that had arisen in the organization's relationship to the national government. He had opposed the chief executive of the organization much to the chief executive's displeasure. As a result, the chief executive terminated him at the age of sixty-five. Effective prevention of a depression was available for this man by providing a creative strategy for offsetting the sense of powerlessness he felt. This is a contradiction of the old maxim that therapy is a highly individual, idiosyncratic, endogenous matter. This prevention work was done on a macroscopic, systems-engineering basis in behalf of the well-being of an individual.

The rectifying of specific political situations of powerlessness in the development of new strategies and alternatives is integral to an adequate process of therapy. Otherwise, those responsible for psychiatric treatment fall into the errors of priesthoods of all types. One who is a member of the psychiatric team cannot be politically naive. Social ills exist that need some modification. If they cannot be changed, people will be broken. A therapist who ignores these will be much less effective. Examples of the sense of powerlessness in the depression of persons in systems of society appear in the "acting out" behavior of people who are in positions of power and who are depressed. The acting-out behavior has a way of ensuring that the patient gets the kind of therapy that he or she needs. A classical example of this is Representative Wilbur Mills in the tragic episodes that led him into a treatment situation and a recovery from depression and alcoholism. Such cases give cause to philosophize about powerlessness and powerfulness. Is the presence of unmanageable power, i.e., the possession of more power than one knows what to do with, a source of depression?

Does this depression lead to inadvertencies of judgment, to malfeasances of behavior, and to dramatic conversions such as that experienced by Charles Colson and many others in the Watergate tragedy?

The Crisis of Injustice

In psychiatric services, it is almost a truism that depression is internalized anger. In psychotherapeutic sessions, patients are confronted with the possibility that they are deeply angry. This confrontation doubles the resistance of distinctly religious patients. It causes them to increase the power of their denial systems. However, statistical cross-sectional studies of depression indicate that the greater the anger score, the more likely the patient is to present a depressive syndrome of a non-endogenous type. (Issy Pilowsky, M.D., and Neil T. Spence, "Hostility and Depressive Illness," *Archives of General Psychiatry*, Vol. 32, Sept. 1975, pp. 1154–1159.)

One possible definition of anger is that it is the normal reaction of a person to injustice. Therefore, a way through the resistances and denials of the distinctly religious patient as to having any "anger" is to raise the issue of injustice. Does the person feel that God has treated him or her justly or unjustly? Justice is an "okay" value for religious people. It is easy for them to discuss this. They are committed in their value systems to seeing to it that "justice is done." A consider-able portion of their anger is therefore a natural reaction to injustice.

Patients will say to a therapist that they are angry, or that they may be angry with God and that they feel very, very bad about feeling this way. One of the most helpful insights that comes from a careful reading of the Old and New Testa-ments is that anger can be expressed openly and forthrightly in prayers to God. (See Psalm 137 and Psalm 109.) One can-not, by keeping these feelings to oneself, keep a secret from God. Nor need one feel that one is going to be destroyed if one expresses real feelings to God. Therefore, a patient can be encouraged to "tell it like it is" to God with the sure certainty that God can "take it" and understand, and re-spond with justice and mercy and love. Such is the experi-ence of persons like Moses, the apostle Paul, and Jesus in their expressions of anger before God.

It would not be accurate to leave the definition of anger at simply a feeling of injustice. A considerable number of per-sons feel angry and depressed because they have basic needs that go unmet, such as sexual desire, economic opportunity, and companionship. Frustrated as they are, they become depressed because of a lack of legitimate and affirming op-portunity to express their deepest needs. In such instances, patient understanding and realistic appreciation of the poi-gnant hungers of the person have a way of letting the person know that it is also acceptable to express these feelings to God in prayer. This comes as good news and surprising news to a great many pietistic Christians.

The Crisis of Competence

One of the real confusions that arises between members of the psychiatric treatment team when considering the reli-gious treatment of mentally ill patients is the stereotypical assumption that the only set of values that the religious world represents today is "moral values." These values refer to self-condemnation for minor moral infractions, feeling sinful because of culturally imposed restrictions or taboos. However, the higher reaches of religious concern focus upon competency values. These values refer to the aspirations that people have, the hopes they hold, the goals they have been trying to achieve, and the expectations they have of themselves and that other people have of them in an achieving society such as ours. This set of distinctions is made forcefully and well by Milton Rokeach (Milton Rokeach, *The Nature of Human Values*, pp. 8–9; The Free Press, 1973.) A person tends to feel *guilty* about having violated moral taboos. However, a great sense of *shame* comes over the person who has not achieved the goals that he or she may have set for himself or herself. Helen Merrell Lynd says that Shakespeare uses shame about nine times more often than guilt. The sense of shame contrasts not with right doing nor with approval by others, but with truth and honor in one's own eyes. The wounding of one's own self-ideal and disgrace in the eyes of oneself inhere in the feeling of shame. This shame is associated with the loss of honor and of self-respect.

Therefore, it is important to consider the feelings of shame that people have when they have not demonstrated the competence they require of themselves. Depression, therefore, would arise out of such experiences as various kinds of impotence, particularly sexual impotence. Withdrawn persons are overwhelmed with a feeling of shame that they are not competent to attract the affection and care of other people. For example, a thirty-eight-year-old man with an I.Q. of 126 is a successful person in his chosen field of technical research. Moreover, he has such high ideals of perfection for his graduate dissertation that he is immobilized and incapable of completing the dissertation. This in turn limits his ability to succeed in his profession because of his needs for the doctor's degree as a "credential" for doing his work. He has been in and out of psychiatric hospitals for twelve years. When asked what the greatest loss he has sustained through his illness is, he replies: "The shame I feel because I have not achieved in my work as I should have." The situation can be the reverse also. Instead of the sense of failure being the cause of the shame, the depression itself may predate the testing situation and contribute to the failure of the candidate, in spite of the best efforts of conscientious committees. As Akiskal and McKinney say: "For instance, man who ascribes his depression to having lost his job may have in reality lost his job as a result of his depressive illness." (Hagop S. Akiskal, M.D., and William T. Kennedy, "Overview of Recent Research in Depression," *Archives of General Psychiatry*, Vol. 32, March 1975, p. 288.)

The Crisis of Self-Elevation

Ancient literature reveals a perspective of depression that is rarely found in the contemporary literature of psychiatry. These sources "finger" the degree of pride and envy involved in depression. The prophet Elijah, during one of his states of depression (which seemed to alternate with states of elation as well), said to the Lord in his prayer: "I have been very jealous for the LORD, the God of hosts; for the people of Israel have forsaken thy covenant, thrown down thy altars, and slain thy prophets with the sword; and I, even I only, am left; and they seek my life, to take it away" (I Kings 19:10). It is not uncommon, in conversing with depressed persons, to hear them remonstrate that "nobody knows the trouble I've seen," and to be told that they are unique and different in their suffering. No one could have had just the kind of suffering they have had. This theme becomes persistent enough in some patients that one gets the feeling they are proud of their plight and like to be "set apart" in uniqueness.

Similarly, depressed patients continually "suffer by comparison." They place themselves alongside other persons and compare themselves unfavorably with them to such depths and to such extent that sometimes it seems that they are envious of the other person's good fortune. This particular attitude is expressed by the psalmist in Ps. 73 when he says:

> But as for me, my feet had almost stumbled,
>> my steps had well nigh slipped.
> For I was envious of the arrogant,
>> when I saw the prosperity of the wicked.
> For they have no pangs;
>> their bodies are sound and sleek.
> They are not in trouble as other men are;
>> they are not stricken like other men.

Backus, in his comparison of the "seven deadly sins scale" with the Minnesota Multiphasic Personality Inventory, discovered that in all five of the groups he tested the persons who showed high depressive elevations on the MMPI also showed similar high elevations on the seven deadly sins scale in the pride and envy categories. Whereas they also showed the same kind of correlations on the sloth scale, the sloth scale itself is almost synonymous with the depressive scale. From a psychotherapeutic point of view, an exploration of these three subtle correlations would be helpful in changing the categories of thought and plowing new ground in the circularity of thinking with depressed patients. Psychotherapists find themselves stalemated with the ruminative thinking of the depressed person. Such a shift of semantics may in turn bring up the possibility that these patients would begin to think of themselves somewhat differently if they thought of themselves as being proud that they were suffering so badly. It can be used to interrupt the pattern of circular, ruminative thought.

Along with this pride in suffering is the perfectionism of the depressed person. Much of the lack of initiative of a depressed person rests, it seems to me, in the self-elevation of the person to the effect that whatever he or she does must be done perfectly or not at all. As a result, the patient falls back into sloth or inactivity or lack of initiative or physiological retardation, depending on how profound the changes in the behavior are. Once biochemical imbalances are corrected, the issues of psychotherapy and/or pastoral counseling are to make open agendas of the pride, envy, and self-elevation of the person.

The Crisis of Courage

Depressed patients will complain of a loss of faith. An initial response to this complaint is that of an intellectual discussion of "articles of faith" such as belief in God, belief in the goodness of God, belief in the existence of God. However, in the tradition of the Judeo-Christian teachings, faith is seen at its best as an expression of courage and adventure in the face of the unknown. Faith is defined in The Letter to the Hebrews as follows: "Now faith is the assurance of things hoped for, the conviction of things not seen" (Heb. 11:1). The critical issue in depression is the failure of nerve, the loss of courage. Margaret Mead has said in several places that the cross-cultural constant in all religion is that it generates hope. Erik Erikson at one time said that hope is generated by mutuality. The depression of the patient represents the collapse of the patient's sense of mutuality with things and persons about him or her. Hence, hope perishes.

In a psychiatric milieu, we are concerned about the life and death of patients. That concern heavily centers upon the possibility of suicide. Depressed patients are highly suspect as being suicidally potential. However, in our overconcentration upon suicide, we may neglect the clinical reality that depression itself may be a life setting conducive to massive physiological disorders that end in death. Gerald L. Engle, M.D., of Rochester, New York, has written an article entitled "A Life Setting Conducive to Illness" (*Annals of Internal Medicine,* Vol. 69, No. 2, 1968, pp. 293–300). He describes what he calls the giving up–giving in complex. He himself may be tempted to giving up. The staff, on the other hand, may be prone to give up on the patient. Five psychological characteristics which he identifies as being evident in the giving up–giving in complex are as follows: a feeling of giving up, experienced as helplessness or hopelessness; a depreciated image of the self; a sense of the loss of gratification from relationships of roles in life; a feeling of disruption of the sense of continuity between past, present, and future; and a reactivation of memories of earlier periods of giving up. These characteristics are easily identifiable as depressive symptoms. He describes how in both human beings and animals organisms simply die outright upon having had all the hope of a mutual relationship dashed.

The psychiatric liaison teams tend to see these phenomena more than inpatient psychiatric unit teams see them. These patients are found on medical, surgical, obstetrical, orthopedic, etc., wards far more than they are found on psychiatric wards. One sees these patients in coronary care and intensive care units. The more experience one has had in the open community, quite apart from hospitals, the more reports can be produced to document the collapse of courage in the face of life's heirlooms of suffering.

For example, a couple in their middle seventies had lived a long and fruitful life together as husband and wife. The wife became psychotic and dangerous to herself and other people. She had to be placed in a nursing home temporarily. After adequate psychiatric care, she found herself in remission of the symptoms of the psychotic episode and she and her husband were able to continue to live together in the nursing home. The husband saw it as his purpose in life to "see to it" that his wife was cared for until her death. He had four heart attacks between ages seventy-five and eighty-one. He rallied from each one of them and was able to do the minimal things necessary to see to it that his wife had company and care. He continued to reiterate that his purpose in life was to care for his "sweetheart" and see to it that she was not left alone in the world.

Then came the death of his wife. Ten days passed after her death. He set his business matters in order. He called for his pastor and told him that his life's work was done. He gave thanks in prayer with the pastor for having had such a long and useful life and for having been granted the privilege of caring for his wife until her death. This was at about 4:00 in the afternoon. At 6:30 that afternoon, after having eaten his dinner, he lay down on his bed and died. One wonders, in such cases, whether or not the power of decision has anything to do with the time that a person dies, without regard to the factor of suicide.

Also, one wonders if the degree of mutuality that existed between this man and his wife was not the source of hope that kept him alive, the basis of his courage to face life. If one of the purposes of religion is the generation of mutuality and community, then the discovery and creation of new alternatives for human existence—as Elton Trueblood used to call them, alternatives to futility—seems to be the card of entry that energizes the role of prophetic religion in the therapeutic care of the depressed person.

Yet young persons, seemingly with every reason to live, nevertheless become depressed and see no reason for being. As one nineteen-year-old young man told me: "I wish there was a building in this town tall enough that I could jump off and get forgiveness for committing suicide before I hit the ground." As irrational and patently untrue is the belief that suicide is unpardonably sinful; nevertheless the belief reflects the partial truth that we are really "playing God" when we decide to suicide. We take all the matters of the whole world into our hands. We rule out God and everybody else. The belief that suicide is a sin reflects our subtle awareness that we are usurping God's place. Little wonder that so many suicidal attempts represent a spectrum of indecision on the one hand and lethality on the other. Occasionally, however, self-elevation reaches the level of intensity that Friedrich Nietzsche did when he said: "There is no God. If there were, how could I stand it if I were not God!" It was he who did commit suicide. It is as if the critical issue of suicide is to accept, not the existence of God, but the reality of our new humanness.

6
THE RELIGIOUS CARE
OF THE SCHIZOPHRENIC PATIENT

The diagnostic term "schizophrenia" was first used by Eugen Bleuler. He used it to describe the splitting off of portions of the psyche which, in turn, dominate the total life of the patient. In the ancient metaphor of Plato, it is "the rising up of a portion of the soul against the whole." "Schizophrenia" has replaced the earlier term, *dementia praecox,* to describe a set of personality changes which flattens and desensitizes the affective, or "feeling," life, splits feeling away from thought, distorts thinking, and separates a person from reality. Reality in this case means the least changeable aspects of a person's life. The disorder represents a progressive and/or intermittent regression of the personality to more primitive and infantile levels of behavior.

These schizophrenic processes are often mistaken for the "three faces of Eve" or "Sybil" syndrome popular in the cinema. This latter condition is a neurotic dissociative reaction, not to be confused with schizophrenia, although the latter word literally means "splitting the mind." The neurotic dissociative reaction is a relatively rare clinical phenomenon as contrasted with the high percentage of schizophrenic disorders among the population of mental patients. Some authorities estimate that as much as or more than 50 percent of psychiatric admissions to hospitals are schizophrenic patients.

DIAGNOSTIC CRITERIA FOR SCHIZOPHRENIA

The definition of schizophrenia linguistically is not enough. Specific diagnostic criteria need to be stated. Robert L. Spitzer and others have developed the Research Diagnostic Criteria (RDC). They use these criteria to obtain a relatively homogeneous group of subjects for a common understanding among professionals as to what is meant by the serious action of diagnosing a patient with this term "schizophrenia."

Many different approaches are taken to the diagnosis of schizophrenia. The approach taken here avoids limiting the diagnosis to cases with a chronic deteriorating course. However, the criteria are designed to screen out subjects frequently given clinical diagnoses such as borderline schizophrenia, brief hysterical or situational psychoses and paranoid states. Subjects with a full depressive or manic syndrome who would otherwise meet the schizophrenia criteria are excluded and are diagnosed as having either schizo-affective disorder, major depressive disorder, or manic disorder. If the symptoms listed below occur only during periods of alcohol or drug abuse or withdrawal from them, the diagnosis should be unspecified functional psychosis.

At least two of the following characteristics (as they are defined in the RDC manual) are required for a definite diagnosis and one for a probable diagnosis of schizophrenia.

1. Thought broadcasting, insertion, or withdrawal.
2. Delusions of control, other bizarre delusions, or multiple delusions.
3. Delusions other than persecutory or jealousy, lasting at least one week.
4. Delusions of any type if accompanied by hallucinations of any type for at least one week.
5. Auditory hallucinations in which either a voice keeps up a running commentary on the subject's behaviors or

thoughts as they occur, or two or more voices converse with each other.

6. Non-affective verbal hallucinations spoken to the subject.
7. Hallucinations of any type throughout the day for several days or intermittently for at least one month.
8. Definite instances of formal thought disorder.
9. Obvious catatonic motor behavior.

A period of schizophrenic illness lasting at least two weeks.

At no time during the active period of illness being considered did the subject meet the criteria for either probable or definite manic or depressive syndrome to such a degree that it was a prominent part of the illness.

To the criteria of Spitzer should be added further insights from Bleuler's "three A's" of schizophrenia: Affect blunted, Ambivalence extreme, and Autism evident. The affect, or emotional tone, of the person is flat, toneless, and lifeless. The person is ambivalent to the extreme; he or she is regularly giving "double messages" to the people around him or her. The person is autistic in that he or she is "all wrapped up" within himself or herself, i.e., all thinking and points of reference come from within the person. Attachments to other persons are few, if not nonexistent. Furthermore, Harry Stack Sullivan's concept is applicable to the schizophrenic person: these persons do not seem to have the capacity to form and maintain long-term, durable relationships. John Bowlby's more recent research on attachment and loss would suggest that these persons are persons for whom abandonment by significant others early in life was sufficiently severe and repetitive to impair profoundly their capacity to commit themselves to other persons, ideals, etc.

Another interesting view of the religious dimensions of schizophrenia is provided by Backus (1969), who constructed the 280-item true-false test measuring inclinations to the seven deadly sins—pride, envy, anger, greed, sloth, lust, and gluttony. As has been said before, he found that all seven sins were significantly related to the presence of mental illness, as measured both by the MMPI and by the extent of current psychiatric treatment (psychiatric inpatients were more apparently sinful than outpatients, who in turn showed more sin than a control group of 70 normal people).

Of particular interest are Backus' findings about a group of 28 inpatients who were diagnosed as schizophrenic. They scored significantly higher than the 72 other inpatients on the sin of pride (17.0 to 13.9 for the other inpatients, and to 11.2 for the control group). In 64 percent of the schizophrenics, pride was ranked first or second of the seven sins, compared to only 27 percent for the other inpatients. Backus noted that of all the sins, only pride is based on a distortion of reality. The proud person and the schizophrenic both often believe that they are like God, equal to God, or have no need for God. In relation to other persons, both frequently assert that they are superior to, essentially different from, or have no need for other human beings. Such attitudes contribute to the syndrome of grandiosity noted in schizophrenics. This grandiosity presents a simple and logical explanation for the schizophrenic's severe isolation from God and from fellow human beings. This grandiosity accounts for the schizophrenic's characteristic tendency to deny or disregard the limits of his or her own mind and body. Likening themselves to God, who is all in all, schizophrenics lose sight of the boundaries between themselves and those around them (they may feel that the body is disintegrating, or that their thoughts are controlled by outside forces). Without these boundaries, schizophrenics typically compensate by erecting false boundaries (extending their territorial space, seeing everything concretely, believing that others are conspiring against them, etc.).

Although the differences were smaller than with the sin of pride, the 28 schizophrenics also scored significantly higher than the other inpatients on anger and greed (p < .05). Anger is defined not as the emotion of anger, but as the habitual coping styles of harboring a grudge and wanting vengefully to "get even." Thus the habitually angry person and the schizophrenic both refuse to let vengeance be God's. They are intolerant of being in a "one down" position. They become easily irritated at the frailties of others, which may remind them of their own clay feet. In a similar way, the schizophrenics were more greedy, in that they especially wanted to be free of the human limitations of a bank account, etc. They were easily irritated if others they perceived as less worthy than themselves were found to have more money.

So the theme of Backus' research suggests that schizophrenics tend to perceive themselves as more Godlike than human. Therefore they may behave as if they had no need for either God or human beings. Of course the biochemical aspects of schizophrenia cause severe disorganization of a person's logical concepts and trains of thought. This condition both discourages close personal relationships and enhances the imagination needed to fantasize that one is essentially like God. What remains to be seen is the extent to which these biochemical imbalances are the cause or the effect of believing that one is more like God than like human beings. (Donald Backus, *The Seven Deadly Sins: Their Meaning and Measurement.*)

RELIGIOUS ASPECTS OF CRITERIA
FOR SCHIZOPHRENIA

Psychiatric diagnostic criteria are *one* way of interpreting human behavior. They have proven useful in enabling persons to be "clothed and in their right mind." This way can be enriched and illumined by an exploration of the religious dimensions of the criteria. The religious perspective is another "angle of vision" of the same distorted thinking, affective life, and behavioral rituals of schizophrenic persons. The religious world view sees reality as ultimately expressed in God, the source of all being. The "least changeable elements in one's life"—i.e., a psychiatric definition of reality—are seen by many religious persons as "necessity," "tribulation," "suffering," "limitations," "afflictions," etc.

The Incapacity to Symbolize

The first religious criterion for assessing a person as being schizophrenic is the incapacity to symbolize. In psychiatric parlance this points to the concrete thinking of the schizophrenic person. Religious language is symbolic by nature. The mentally healthy person can distinguish between the symbol and the "things of God"—or larger reality—which the symbol represents. The religious symbol points toward the reality; it is not equatable with the reality. The schizophrenic person, however, thinks concretely, literalizes, and confuses the symbols of religious thought and that which they symbolize. In fact, the opposite word, "a sign," is often used by schizophrenic patients. The sign *is* equatable with that which it represents, such as the "one way street" sign. In the perception of a psychotic patient, the knocking of a chair being moved in the next room *is* the "movement of God" to a patient, for example. Perceptually, then, to be able to symbolize is to be able to see the accurate relationship between things and ideas. The incapacity to symbolize is to fuse and confuse the thing and the idea with each other.

Patient D.W., a twenty-three-year-old single woman, for example, had decompensated into a psychotic episode while at a Pentecostal meeting. She was terrified at the thought of Jesus "entering her heart." To her this was a literal invasion of her body. She interpreted Jesus as her enemy because of her "uncleanness." Awakening from a sound sleep when the chaplain came alongside her bed, she said she was dreaming that she was struggling to keep Jesus out of her heart.

The Incapacity to Accept Human Limitations of the Body

The second religious criterion for schizophrenia is that the person ignores, denies, opposes, or refuses to accept the limitations of the body. One criterion of mental health is the ability to accept the limitations and to use to the maximum the particular body that one has. The mystics of religious history have been aware of this struggle. Jesus of Nazareth struggled in the wilderness with the limits of human hunger, human obedience to the laws of gravity, and the testings of the limits of his physical endurance. (Luke 4:1–13.) The apostle Paul tells of a "man in Christ who fourteen years ago was caught up to the third heaven—whether in the body or out of the body I do not know, God knows" (II Cor. 12:2). Buddhist Nirvana is a transcendence of pain, of bodily confinement and restriction, into ecstasy almost equivalent to transmigration.

Yet, in both Hebrew and Christian thought the critical issue of the sanctity of the body, the realization of the fruits of the spiritual life *within* the limitations of the body, and the incarnation of the holy within the reality of the body is the mainstream of one's commitment as a person of faith. The Hebrew conception of the soul as the "breath" of the human body, and the Christian conception of the revelation of God in the humanness of Jesus of Nazareth are in marked contrast to the schizophrenic kind of mystical flight from the bounds of the habitation of the body. The earliest heresies of the Christian era were Gnostic heresies, which denied the reality of the bodily existence of Jesus as a man.

A psychiatric patient, a twenty-eight-year-old man, was hospitalized repeatedly over a four-year period. Upon each admission he was possessed with the idea that he was the Christ, that the limits imposed upon him of having to be one sex or the other were transcended in his Christlike state. On his third remission of his psychotic state, he asked the author: "What am I going to do if I should get outside the hospital and begin to think again that I am becoming the Christ?" I replied: "The real Jesus of Nazareth was completely committed to accepting the limits of the human body and becoming fully human. We are the reverse. We are ambitious to become God and Christ. The real Christ accepted his human body, even to the point of dying. He did not ask to be exempt. Are you avoiding the normal limits of your body when you get these ideas?"

Another case in point was that of a twenty-three-year-old white mother of two boys, recently divorced from her husband. She was born on December 22 and wondered what it would be like to be called by God to be the mother of the Christ-child. She said, however, that men have been running her life, and they are made in the image of God. When asked if women also are made in the image of God she began to sputter and stammer and have difficulty admitting that women are in God's image as well.

In the demands of the human body, reality has a way of crowding in upon the schizophrenic and making itself known. Coming to terms with these demands of the body and learning to live within the bounds of its habitation is a concrete way of communicating a kind of religious faith to a schizophrenic person that can be a form of self-therapy. Better still, the realistic communication of a kind of religious faith "that is not too bright or too good for human nature's daily food" is a down-to-earth way of being pastorally helpful to the schizophrenic. To declare as heresy those forms of religious teaching that would deny, distort, or confuse a person about the human body itself is as good a place as any to begin reconstructing the religious world view of anyone, but especially the schizophrenic person. In fact, the history of the schizophrenic patient is often a long saga of dreadfully distorted teaching and the wretched exploitation of the body.

The Incapacity for Commitment and Blunted Affect

The flat, listless, and toneless affect of the schizophrenic patient is also accompanied by a poverty of language. The autistic lack of attachment to persons on any durable basis is not unrelated, it seems to me, to the tonelessness of affect. One particular patient in our case group stated it this way: "If I cannot trust anyone, then I must not let myself feel affection; I must not respond to any binding commitment to anyone else; I must not feel anything even if I am grieved." Our student group identified this as a phenomenon of noncommitment in an observation about the sequence of interviews they had with different schizophrenic patients. They would find little or no *continuity* of relationship from one interview to the next. They would have to *start over* almost as if they had not met the patient before. It was not a matter of the patient not recognizing them, or of the patient being so far out of contact with reality as to be oblivious to the presence of the student chaplain. It was a matter of *forming a bond of friendship* with the patient that carried over from one day to the next. It was as if the student when "out of sight" of the patient was "out of mind" of the patient. The student *existed* only when there with the patient. When this began to change, the students felt that (*a*) the patient was becoming less psychotic, (*b*) the patient was beginning to form some kind of trusting relationship ever so slowly, and (*c*) the cumulative record of a personal commitment, even if it were ever so faint, was beginning to form. An excellent example of this process is found in the record included at the end of this chapter.

The theoretical foundation for this understanding of the schizophrenic process can be found in Bowlby's insistence that severe noncommitment is the result of unformed or broken attachments occurring again and again until the growing person ceases to commit. Erikson's concept of basic trust describes basic trust as the psychological equivalent of faith for which there is no substitute. To say that the schizophrenic person is forever doomed to be incapable of such trust and commitment is a kind of "psychiatric predestinationism" that reflects as much about the therapist as it does the patient. However, to be a theoretical optimist and assume that the schizophrenic person does *easily* form attachments, commitments, and durable relationships reflects the same kind of doctrinaire attitude.

The demand that schizophrenic persons make upon the commitment of the therapist is for a long-term, consistent, even commitment of time and attention in literally reparenting them. In other words, such results do not just happen.

Herbert Wagemaker, M.D., in personal conversation, has said that at the core of the being of the schizophrenic is warmth and deep feeling. If we are willing to take the time, we can connect up with it meaningfully. This is one of the wiser things said about the schizophrenic person. Taking the time is "the rub." Who has it?

The understanding of a religious factor in schizophrenia as a disruption of the basic capacity to make commitments goes beyond the idea of religion as the substance of the hallucinatory or delusional content of the person. This can vary from one generation to another, from one culture to another, and even from one area of the country to another. The disruption of the basic capacity to trust, however, tends to be cross-culturally constant.

Schizophrenia and the Ascetic Life

Another religious criterion for assessing schizophrenic reactions is the patient's ascetic tendencies. Asceticism is a basic attitude of separation from "the world." Asceticism may take a highly individualistic form—as in the "eremitic" or "desert" asceticism of hermits. Or it may take a communal form, as in the case of the ascetic orders of the Eastern Orthodox, Catholic, and Anglo-Catholic faiths. These are known as "cenobitic" forms of asceticism. The individual and communal forms of asceticism are seen in Protestantism in such groups as the Shakers of an earlier time. Modified forms of asceticism that do not include celibacy are those of the Quakers, the Mennonites, and the Hutterites.

The earliest forms of asceticism were responses to the hope that the world as we know it would end in the lifetime of the persons then living. A quotation from Hippolytus, the bishop of Rome, in the second century A.D. states the situation well: "A bishop, who was a pious and modest man but who placed too much trust in his visions, had had three dreams and began to prophesy: 'Know, brethren, that the Last Judgment will take place within one year. If what I tell you does not come to pass, have no more faith in the Scriptures and do as you please.' At the end of the year, nothing had happened; he was abashed, the brethren were shocked, the virgins got married, and those who had sold all their possessions were reduced to beggary." (Quoted by Jacques Lacarrière, *The God-Possessed*, p. 23; London: George Allen & Unwin, Ltd., 1964.)

When this hope for the immediate coming of a new world faded, then the church began more and more to be conformed to the political shape of the Roman Empire. Corruption and cynicism took over. Discipline ceased. Affluence took the place of poverty. Asceticism in its many forms arose as a spiritual reaction formation or protest against these excesses. In turn, the ascetics developed excesses in self-denial, self-mortification, and separation from the world. These persons made a radical break with the realities of the world as they knew it. A case history of one of these ascetics, Anthony of the Desert, gives a clearer perspective than didactic descriptions. (These case notes are taken from Lacarrière, *The God-Possessed*, pp. 51–63. They are not quoted verbatim but present a case summary paraphrase of the data. When Athanasius' *Life of Anthony* is quoted, the exact wording is cited.)

Anthony was born about A.D. 251 in a village of middle Egypt named Coma. He was born into a wealthy Christian family. When he was in church one day, at the age of twenty, he heard the voice of Jesus say: "If thou wilt be perfect, go and sell that thou hast, . . . and come and follow me." His parents had died shortly before this. Therefore, he sold all his possessions, distributed his wealth among the poor, keeping only a small sum for his young sister, and turned his back upon the world.

Anthony then placed himself under obedience to an old man who lived in a nearby village and practiced the ascetic life. He had not completely broken with the world about him. The devil prodded him with ideas of his earthly responsibilities, such as "the possessions he had left behind, the care he should have shown his sister, pride of race and love of riches, the pleasurable sensations to be found in life. Moreover, he drew his attention to the immense difficulties and hardships to be experienced in the exercise of virtue, to the weakness of the flesh and the many years he had to live; in short, he created as it were a dust-cloud of thought in his mind" (*Life of Anthony,* by Athanasius).

Thereupon Anthony decided to leave the old ascetic and to plunge into the desert. To him the desert meant a place peopled by creatures other than men—angels and demons. No person could live there without the constant attacks of the devil and the ever-present help of God in the face of temptation. Anthony made arrangements with a friend to bring him bread at long intervals. He entered a sepulcher there, closed the door behind him and stayed there alone. Here he was deprived of all contact with persons. He never ate more than once a day and often on alternate days. Then his diet was bread, salt, and water. He rested very little, most often lying on the naked ground.

Anthony's experience during his stay in the tomb is described by Athanasius: "An infernal band of creatures worked up a massive noise. He saw the tomb sides open and crowds of demons clambered in. They assumed the shapes of wild beasts and snakes, the figures of lions and bears, leopards and bulls, asps, scorpions and other reptiles. . . . The appearance of each of these creatures was as cruel as it was fierce and their hissing and crying were horrible to hear. Anthony stayed several months there and his attacks were so violent that he felt his body was beaten black and blue. He lay unconscious on the ground hours at a time."

Anthony left this tomb after several months and went to a fort in the desert. He stayed at the fort for twenty years alone beneath a scorching sun and exposed to the cold of the night. He saw apparitions and he had trouble distinguishing good from bad among them. He spent twenty years in an experiment to discipline himself in making a distinction between the real and the illusory. The good angel from God did not need a great crowd around him, whereas the evil demons came in great crowds. This was his criterion for distinguishing the real from the illusory.

At the end of this twenty years, he felt that he had sufficiently tested himself in solitariness. Then he was ready to see people and to choose disciples to form a community of ascetics.

When they saw him they were astonished to find that he was robust in health, neither stout nor having lost weight. His face was the same and he had a calm and pleasant manner. He was neither depressed nor elated. He seemed well balanced and quite natural.

Asceticism today has become institutionalized. The roots of the spiritual life that nourish such forms of behavior are not institutionalized. The classical form of asceticism requires vows or decisions to be celibate, to accept poverty, and to be obedient to the authority or rule of the order. Throughout the history of religions there has been a recurrent emphasis upon asceticism, both solitary and communal, as a way of dealing with the issue of separating the real from the illusory and becoming creatively related to the real.

The schizophrenic way of life represents, in my opinion, the *attempt* to solve these same problems in the cases of a considerable number of patients seen in clinics and hospitals today. What is real and worthy of commitment and what is unreal and unworthy of commitment? Furthermore, the ascetic way of life in its classical forms contained ingredients that are missing in the schizophrenic way of life in the cases that find their way to the hospital and clinic. The hypothesis can be posed that *some*—not all—schizophrenic patients are committed to celibacy and to poverty. They seem to be exceptionally nonchalant about getting into the family life cycle of marriage and parenthood. They are indifferent to getting into the competitive whirl of earning money and becoming affluent. Yet they have a "truncated" asceticism in that they have not "worked through" the issue of the true authority in their lives as did Anthony in his twenty or more years of struggle to decide to whom to listen, i.e., whom to follow and to whom to surrender in commitment.

The contemporary counterculture has reasserted the issues of asceticism as well as those of schizophrenia as a way of life. The counterculture movement of the '60s still perdures in certain values among young persons,.particularly those from affluent families, as was Anthony. These young persons reject the values of the establishment, which are those of competitive affluence, role-oriented work performance, and the "square" interpretations of the nuclear family. They dedicate themselves to a kind of poverty and beggary and resist the closures of the traditional marriage. Hallucinogens are used to go "out of this world." As Levinson says, joining a counterculture or hippie group and using marijuana sometimes help a patient to "block out reality" and raise his or her self-esteem. (Peritz Levinson, "Religious Delusions in Counter-Culture Patients," *American Journal of Psychiatry*, Vol. 130, No. 11, Nov. 1973, p. 1267.)

From an observation of six such young men between the ages of eighteen and twenty-five, we discovered a recurrent pattern of an "abortive asceticism." The pattern moved through the following phases:

1. The person came from an affluent family. The family had supplied all the material needs of the young person and his only task was going to school. The family were formally religious and attended church as a regular and socially expected ritual. Yet their development of an inner mystical appreciation and personal involvement with religious realities at an existential level was nonexistent. The patient as a child was required to attend church because it was "good for him." Religious experience was not discussed in the home. It was a taboo subject.

2. In middle adolescence, around the ages of fifteen to seventeen, the young person dropped out of the formalities of church attendance. The parents no longer could force him to follow these rituals. At or about the same time, the young person began to adopt the hippie life-style: drug use, long

hair, characteristic costuming, rock music, and vegetarian-ism. Universal camaraderie on a first-name basis with all persons, the pursuit of pleasure, free and easy sexual standards, and a passive way of expressing anger became their "thing."

3. Toward the years of late adolescence, the young person began to lose interest in and to be bored with the way of life of the hard-core hippie. The inability to form and maintain durable relationships, so characteristic of the schizophrenic way of life, was aided and abetted by the hippie life-style. However, the restlessness and boredom as well as the loneliness and isolation prompted the young person to seek something else new. A subtle dropping out of the hippie culture was then marked by a sudden encounter with and embracing of an ecstatic form of religion. Sometimes this would be a form of Eastern religion, as reported by Levinson and others. In the particular culture of Kentucky and Indiana, the form this took was that of the Pentecostal groups indigenous to the culture. The person would begin "speaking in tongues," have experiences of "receiving the Holy Spirit," etc. The particularly inadequate personalities of those patients was matched in the Pentecostal group by the overpowering persuasion of a strong leader of the group.

Ascetic commitments were then required of the young person. He was expected to "lay off" drugs and depend on the Lord for his ecstasy. He was expected to become chaste and sexually abstinent. He was expected to have done with all expressions of anger and to "love everybody."

4. At this point in time, the patient decompensated into a florid psychotic episode. The hospital itself became the community of the newly pledged ascetic. Similarly, conflict was introduced in that psychotropic drugs were used in treating psychosis. They were seen as antithetical to the newfound religious commitment, i.e., to take drugs of any kind was a sign of lost faith in God.

Psychodynamically, these young persons had much in common with St. Anthony. They came from affluent families. At the stage of industry inferiority, they were chilled by the competitive existence of their parents. All these patients were men. They chose not to learn from their fathers the art of making a living, known as work. Their fathers were successful persons in the sense of being able to amass monetary wealth. Hence, the inadequacy of the son at the earliest stage of industry inferiority, described by Erikson, resulted in incompetence at basic survival ability. In turn they were overdependent upon the parents for financial support. As one young man said in his family conference with his parents and the psychiatrist: "You know you can afford to pay for my having an apartment of my own!" Furthermore, these young men had a revulsion for "the world," in common with St. Anthony. Their world was pervaded by the indecision of the Vietnam War and the cynicism of Watergate. Their "good-morning–starshine" idealism depicted in *Hair* came crashing down around their heads in the tragedies of the Kent State killings by the National Guard. Thus, in their words, they *"split* from the scene."

The vows of asceticism, as we have seen, are chastity, poverty, and obedience. These young persons entered a religious experience associated with a psychotic break and embraced chastity and poverty at a cognitive, "heady" level. However, when observed behaviorally their sexual mores remained somewhat untouched. Their poverty was more apparent than real. They readily relied upon their parents to "foot the bill" for their itinerant way of life and religious indulgences. When the vow of obedience was an issue, the whole life-style went out of order because the center of authority at more than a blind obedience level was missing. One such person said: "I myself have tried to be God. When I couldn't make it, nothing was worth anything." As another patient said to the staff: "All of you are just like specks of sand on a beach. You don't amount to anything. All of us will be dead in a little while and nothing will matter then anyhow." When the nihilism of such thinking took over, the life tended to fly apart in a schizophrenic break.

Levinson again identifies the principal features of the schizophrenic delusions as "the belief in one's own omnipotence and omniscience, the avoidance of affect-laden experiences and thoughts, the pursuit of ascetcism, the experience of exalted mystical states, and the tendency to form symbiotic relationships that are devoid of emotional investment." (Peritz Levinson, M.D., "Religious Delusions in Counter-Culture Patients," *American Journal of Psychiatry*, Vol. 130, No. 11, Nov. 1973, p. 1265.)

These schizophrenic states call for considerable differential diagnosis as to how much desperation and concern is involved in them. The presence of acute concern may point to the possibility that they are transitional states rather than endogenous biogenic states. We are accustomed to thinking of depressions as being differentiated from each other as to which is an anxiety depression and which is an endogenous one. Rarely have I found the literature speaking of the difference between a transitional schizophrenic state and an endogenous one. The presence of an active family history of schizophrenia, the history of a previous schizophrenic break, and a careful assessment of traumatic stresses in the precipitating situation of the patient will help make these differentiations. More specifically, the *survival value* of the religious ideas themselves will help clarify the kind of schizophrenic episode with which one is dealing. For example, Paul C. Horton, M.D., found that patients directly experiencing an "oceanic state of mystical consciousness provided several patients with a soothing safeguard against their overwhelming loneliness and possible suicide." He describes one of his cases:

An eighteen-year-old girl, the fifth of six children, had been deprived too early in life of a symbiotic attachment to her mother. Her insecurity was evident in her thumb-sucking and bed-wetting, which continued until she was twelve years old. Stuffed animals, pets, a blanket, and other transitional objects were in prominent usage until the patient was well into her teens. An additional instance of her transitional mode of existence is suggested in her description of her early religious training:

"I was brought up on what was a good dose of 'religion.'

Church and Sunday school every Sunday, youth group once a week, religious instruction classes during grade school, Bible school in the summertime, Bible drills at home—I even taught Sunday school during my high school years, and I went to a Bible-centered college."

She enrolled at a distant college and began decompensating "out of sheer loneliness." She sought refuge in hallucinogens, which merely exacerbated her confusion and sense of loneliness:

"A major turning point came in my life January 15, 1969, when I mixed LSD-25 with alcohol. Bingo! I flipped out fast; it was hellish. . . . I even went so far as to try to kill myself. The only truth I knew was that I was, indeed, in a hopeless situation. Every other thought in my head was utterly distorted and warped."

A psychiatrist was unable to help her, and other suicide attempts followed. She said:

"Just to give you an idea how utterly alone I was in the madness of my mind, even since recovering I still can't find a human being who has or could feel the pain, the fear, the hopelessness, nor aloneness I felt then."

It was then that she experienced her "conversion": "I remember looking around at the moment I understood I was forgiven past, present, and future, and saying, is that what it is? Oh, is that what it is? How did I feel? Like a huge knot had been untied inside my head. For the first time in two months, I slept soundly and peacefully; without fear; I was filled with warmth and love for a living God."

In the subsequent two and a half years the patient has been a productive member of a campus religious organization and has made no further attempts on her life. Though still quite discouraged, she appears to be continuously improving her life situation.

When one compares and contrasts the abortive kind of asceticism found in schizophrenia with the asceticism of St. Anthony and his classical successors, one observes that some vital elements are missing in the subcultures such as the

counterculture of today. The element of a culture sanction-
ing of "desert experiences" is missing. Erik Erikson, for example, suggests the need for a *"psychosocial moratorium*
during which the young adult through free role experimentation may find a niche in some section of his society, a niche
which is firmly defined and yet seems to be uniquely made
for him." This moratorium "is a period of delay granted to
somebody who is not ready to meet an obligation or . . .
should give himself time. . . . For the most part, these mora-
toria coincide with apprenticeships and adventures that are
in line with society's values. The moratorium may be a time
for horse stealing and vision-quests, a time for Wanderschaft
or for work 'out West' or 'down under,' a time for 'lost youth'
or academic life, a time for self-sacrifice or for pranks—and
today, often a time for patienthood and delinquency." (Erik
Erikson, *Identity: Youth and Crisis,* pp. 156–157; W. W. Norton & Company, Inc., 1968.)

If indeed the episodes of schizophrenia in some late and
delayed adolescents are transitional and not endogenous in
nature, then one could say that the regimen of milieu therapy, behavioral modification techniques, token economies,
and the drug therapies may indeed provide the communal
expression of a secularized kind of asceticism for such patients. The time spent in patienthood or as an outcast of
society in delinquency may become the "desert" into
which young people enter today. Anton Boisen certainly
thought of his illness as a "wilderness of the lost." Yet if the
religious culture placed as much emphasis upon solitude
and meditation as it does upon gregariousness and conform-
ity, then the individuality of a young person could be expressed in a culturally developed way. It would not do as
much damage to the young person and cause as much confusion in the minds of the parents as their offspring pulls
away from them to work out his or her own salvation with
"fear and trembling."

SPECIFIC PASTORAL STRATEGIES
FOR CARING FOR SCHIZOPHRENIC PATIENTS

The concluding section of this chapter needs to be specific about the kinds of things a pastoral counselor and teacher can do in relation to the schizophrenic patient. Several things need to be detailed.

Pastoral Presence at the Hypocenter of the Psychotic Break

We naturally assume that the pastor is doing all that is possible to create a community of faith, hope, and love in which neurotic and psychotic coping mechanisms are not needed and certainly in which they are not prescribed. Yet with the best of communal efforts, the psychotic breaks do occur. If the pastor is present at the time a person breaks into florid psychotic symptoms, then a basic relationship can be established with the family in the process of the hospitalization of the person. This is why theological students in our treatment center are given their first education in the care of the mental patient in an emergency psychiatric center. The degree of learning that takes place in the issues of voluntary and involuntary treatment, the process of persuasion of a violent or otherwise disturbed patient, the ways of assessing the mental status of a person, the gathering of a pertinent anamnesis or social history, and the care of a distraught and frightened family grouping, etc.—the degree of learning, to repeat, is greater in an emergency psychiatric treatment center. Pastors who have this kind of education are in a better position, later in the pastorate, to decide how to go about preventing such difficulties with adequate community life support systems, etc. Likewise, that pastor is more disciplined in detecting early storm warnings of such behavior and getting the person into therapy earlier. Basically, however, in relation to a given schizophrenic patient, being present at the hypocenter of the break gives the patient a sense of good news about the care being provided. It enables the pastor to get the fullest possible input from the psychiatric staff in the development of a later ministry to the patient. Optimally the continuing presence of a minister as a member of the psychiatric team plus the presence of a teaching team of psychiatric supervisors is the best way to provide a weight of care to the patient.

The Maintenance of Human Rights of the Patient

The best of psychiatric treatment is characterized by a refusal to sanction dishonest, underhanded, sentimental, and devious approaches to a mental patient. The minister as a member of a psychiatric team works at maintaining honesty and openness with the patient. His or her aim is to keep the patient's self-determination capacities as intact as humanly possible. As a team member, the minister is doubly cautious not to substitute his or her judgment for the patient's except in the most immediate, temporary matters that concern the life and safety of the patient and others. We speak of crimes without victims. We need to speak also of symptoms without victims. Is the thought or behavior of the person as a patient hurting anyone, including the patient? The minister is an ethicist by training and social expectation. Therefore, to maintain the human rights of the patient through suggestion, persuasion, action, and even confrontation is the responsible opportunity of the pastor as a member of the psychiatric team.

For example, a patient who was a bus driver for a church school became psychotic. He was hospitalized at his own request in order to keep from killing himself. In the process of diagnosis, it was discovered that the way he had thought of killing himself was to take an overdose of Dilantin, a medicine used in the treatment of epilepsy. He had a long history of epilepsy. The question of his being dismissed from the hospital was an issue in the staff meeting. The relationship of epileptic seizures to the kind of work the man was doing was raised as an ethical issue. Exploration of a job that was not hazardous to himself or to others became a part of the treatment of the patient.

Continuity of Care for Basically Human Needs of Patient

The schizophrenic patient has the same kinds of possibilities that every other human being has of things both celebrative and sorrowing in nature happening during his or her illness. A patient may have a birthday while in the hospital. The patient's son or daughter may graduate from a school while the patient is hospitalized. A patient may become a parent while in a psychiatric hospital. In the instance of a mother, the double psychiatric and obstetrical treatment pattern is obvious, but the need of the patient to have her child blessed, baptized, etc., may not be considered by anyone but the chaplain. If the patient becomes a father while in the hospital, the need to see the baby, to converse about the meaning of the event, is just as great or greater than in the case of a person who is not mentally ill. These are times of mingled emotions and the specifically religious context is provided by the minister.

Conversely, times of sorrow come to the patient while he or she is hospitalized. A beloved relative or friend may die. A courtship is broken. A divorce is instituted or finalized. The religious and ethical needs that arise are intense, in any event. The event occurring in the context of the hospitalization of the person is all the more intense.

Use of Religious Ideation Inventory to Chart Patient's Progress

The religious ideas of a patient change while he or she is undergoing psychiatric treatment. By this I do not mean that the patient totally reverses his or her religious stance toward life. This rarely happens, although many people fear it.

Rather, I mean that the religious ideas change their degree of symbolization while the patient is in the process of treatment. For example, one patient whom we followed presented this sequence of changes in her idea of the devil. On Day 1, the devil was in her room, roaming around, and scratching her. He was the "old Scratch." On Day 2, the devil was still the same as Day 1. On Day 3, the patient was sleeping most of the day. On Day 4, the patient thought of the devil and God together as being in a huge war with each mother and that the Battle of Armageddon was being fought. On Day 6, the patient thought of the devil as a "demon" within her and asked for an exorcist. On Day 11, the patient thought of the devil as a tempter who presented her with the opportunity to do evil. On Day 14, the patient thought of the devil as God's fallen angel who works against God in the world and is the evil side of human conscience.

This particular patient's capacity to symbolize changed as her psychotic state was improved with the use of powerful psychotropic drugs and as her perception was clarified. The empirical charting of the progress of religious ideation changes or of the regression of religious ideation changes is of valuable service in appreciating the patient's situation. One of the most important changes to note is the patient's religious ideation about suicide. When a patient says on an outpatient visit that he or she has contemplated suicide but feels that God would not approve of this, then the control mechanisms seem to be in place. However, when the patient calls in an emergency and says that he or she has been praying and that God has removed every hindrance to his or her committing suicide, the lethality of the suicidal threat has increased.

The Development of a Post-Psychotic Bereavement Care System

Regardless of the particular theory as to the genesis of schizophrenia, discouragement overwhelms the patient who has recovered, whose psychosis is in remission. A job may have been lost, a mate may have given up and sued for divorce, even church members look askance at a person who has been hospitalized. These situations may produce what could be seen as normal bereavement symptoms. Some physicians have identified what are called "post-psychotic depression" syndromes. Bowers and Astrachan identified thirty-six patients who were unequivocally diagnosed as schizophrenic upon discharge. They said that half of them were seriously depressed while in the hospital after acute symptoms had been controlled by phenothiazines. ("Depression in Schizophrenics," *American Journal of Psychiatry,* Vol. 123, 1967, pp. 976–979.) McGlashan and Carpenter say that post-psychotic depression can be identified following schizophrenic psychosis but is not ubiquitous. They roughly estimate the frequency at 25 percent of the cases. ("Post-Psychotic Depression in Schizophrenia," *Archives of General Psychiatry,* Vol. 33, Feb. 1976, pp. 231–239.)

From the point of view of pastoral care and counseling, one would ask what the life support system and sustaining belief system of these persons are that will stabilize them in recovery. In the absence of such, will isolation and despair overwhelm them with helplessness, loneliness, and hopelessness as they face responsible living outside a hospital setting again? An adequate post-psychotic bereavement care system by pastors can provide group support. Debriefing kinds of follow-up care and social recovery through employment and family counseling has only begun to be developed in churches. When we get into this dimension of the care of schizophrenics, we begin to discover something of the necessity and nature of a spiritual community. It is suggestive also of the observation of many watchers of the counterculture that the successful expressions of the counterculture have gone on and developed forms of community that are self-sustaining and not parasitic, care-centered and not drug-centered, hope-centered and not nihilistic in outlook.

Assimilation of the "Sense Residual"
  of the Schizophrenic's Thought Processes

When we define reality as the "least alterable facts in one's day-to-day existence," we settle for a "least common denominator" of understanding reality. Minimal necessities for existence is what the practice of psychiatry for the masses asks of the world. Patients require this least common denominator for reality testing; pastoral understandings require a larger understanding of reality. If pastoral counselors and psychiatrists have any philosophical concern at all, they often can interpret the schizophrenic patient's symptoms as protests against the social order in which we live. The schizophrenic patient's nonchalance about earning a living is mute criticism of the businessman's confessed "dog eat dog" view of competition. The ethereal religiosity of the schizophrenic patient is the same mute protest against the shallowness of the formal religion of his or her milieu. In short, the schizophrenic patient may be severely ill, but is not severely ill at *all* moments, nor are his or her ideas of *no* substance at all.

The pastoral task, therefore, is to assume that the patient's illness has an economy of its own, a sense within the nonsense, a touch here and there with reality that may be "so far out" that more mundane folk do not see it. Out of this kind of conviction the so-called "radical psychiatry" has arisen, itself filled with important half-truths looking for their counterparts. However, the pastoral counselor, and for that matter any other philosophically concerned member of the psychiatric team, is interested in finding the "sense residual" in the patient's world view. The objective is to build upon it with the patient for a new life that captures what sense the illness did have in it. Thus, expression may be found for that sense in ways that do not call for illness as a way of life. Martin Buber, the Jewish existentialist, called this effort "walking the narrow ridge." The member of the therapeutic team in outpatient dialogue with recovered schizophrenic patients will find himself or herself walking a narrow ridge between affirming the sense residual in the patient's thinking, on the one hand, and in not reinforcing the patterns of irresponsibility that nudge and shove the patient into another psychotic episode, on the other hand.

This is best done by conversing with the patient *in the past tense* about the "then and there" events surrounding the psychotic episode. For example, a patient may talk about the time that he or she thought the devil was literally scratching and clawing the skin to the point of bleeding. The "here and now" issue about the kinds of temptations the person experiences captures some of the sense residual of the conscience struggle without depending upon the literalism and concreteness of a horned and tailed devil that scratches. Some of the more recent therapeutic suggestions of Lawrence Kohlberg about the development of conscience may be a source of instruction to those patients who are given to reading. (See *Moral Reasoning: The Value of Life;* American Education Publications, Education Center, Columbus, Ohio 43216.)

Such an approach gives the patient subtle assurance that the member of the therapeutic team is taking seriously what the patient thinks and and is not "writing off" or discounting everything the patient says as "crazy." As one patient told two of us, a minister and a psychiatrist, this was the first time a minister had ever sat down with him as an individual and conversed at all about the meaning of life. Regardless of what kind of minister one is—a physician, a clergyman, a social worker, a psychologist, a nurse, or a ward attendant—to miss this opportunity of conversing with patients about the meaning of life is to drain lives of meaning. To take advantage of it is to form a lasting relationship of trust and worth with the patient.

Inpatient Treatment Process

Randy was a twenty-five-year-old single white male, who was admitted to the Psychiatric Ward on a Mental Inquest

Warrant. This action was taken by his parents because of his threats of self-mutilation, late-night walks on the streets, hoarding of dangerous tools in his room, and comments about receiving instructions from God. The patient was in a rage on admission, verbally but not physically abusive. His orientation was: "This is a jail . . . Doctors are torturers . . . They're trying to destroy my faith." This was his sixth psychiatric admission.

During his first week as an inpatient, Randy was medicated with Thorazine, and he slept a lot; his auditory hallucinations and threats of self-mutilation also disappeared. I first talked with him in his second week of hospitalization. Introducing myself, I found Randy to be distant and cautious, but willing to converse. He was well groomed, big-boned with broad features, and he carried himself with a sense of power and aloofness.

Randy felt that the staff threatened his faith, and I wanted to help reduce these fears. I set out to be guileless and supportive in my approach, but as he condemned the "godless" psychiatrists, I soon found myself defending the personal religion of our clinical director. Randy quickly began turning his anger and distrust of doctors toward me. The lesson learned was that one need not defend the rest of the helping team when one has only an initial rapport with a paranoid patient. Starting again to build a relationship with Randy, I sought to be more open to his internal frame of reference.

Randy interpreted the Bible literally. In quoting Isa. 53:5, "and with his stripes we are healed," he concluded that there was no need for doctors or medicine, but only the miracle of healing from Jesus. Never far from his Bible, Randy was often quoting or reading from Jeremiah or Ezekiel. Finding expression and justification for himself, he identified with the prophets in their social isolation, their prophecies of destruction and judgment (a release for his anger), and in their righteous relationships with God. All his friends were like Job's friends: he felt they poured salt on his wounds.

We needed to learn of Randy's support system and of possible resources to persuade him to take his medicine voluntarily. His most recent religious involvement had been with a charismatic sect, and he had been particularly close to a lay minister named Elmer. We asked Elmer to join us in a conference to learn more of Randy's religious support and orientation. We found their theology to be similar in regard to healing: a strong enough faith in God was all that was necessary. Elmer did confront Randy about his anger toward his parents, and told Randy that he should respect those in authority, even doctors in hospitals. Randy's later interpretation of this was that he would take his medicine only while we were his "jailers," but after discharge would not.

There was always a tension in my relationship with Randy. He would offer a tentative friendship and warmth, but this could be quickly replaced by righteous rage if he felt his faith to be challenged in the least. I spoke with him confessionally about my faith and religious views. This was my way of responding to such issues with Randy. Thus, I could gently confront him with other perspectives and deepen our relationship by sharing myself. We managed to keep our friendship despite our differences by agreeing to disagree. One of our ongoing themes of discussion dealt with interpersonal openness versus closedness. Randy confessed that he was afraid to reach out to people for fear they would hurt him. He spoke of the walls he kept around himself which had drawbridges that could be tentatively lowered if he felt safe enough with someone. When questioned about what Jesus would have him do with his walls, Randy decided to start breaking some down.

Two conferences with Randy's family were held during this time; arguments erupted in both. In the second conference, Randy and his father began yelling at each other. Randy stood up and angrily proclaimed that he did not need his medicine, or his father or mother, the doctors, or any of the rest of us. He used repetitive phrasing for additional force, as a prophet would, in expressing his anger and autonomy. After finishing his oration, he strode powerfully out of the conference room and returned to the ward.

His parents seemed shaken, and yet resigned. Venting their frustrations and sorrows, they shared with me many of Randy's setbacks from the past six years. Their grief seemed chronic, and unresolved as Randy continued to alternate between times of remission and times of acute psychosis. His parents felt ambivalent about religion. They prayed for Randy's healing, but could find nothing in the church that related to or helped them deal with Randy's illness. Religion was often associated for them with *sickness*, for whenever Randy became psychotic, his religious thinking would intensify and become bizarre.

Within a few days after the family conference, Randy was showing improvement. He was relating and expressing warmth to almost everyone on the ward. He was less rigid and defensive about his faith, and his anger did not seem as intense. Subtly, however, his improvement ceased; he began to deteriorate, becoming tense, withdrawn, and argumentative again. Randy then spent a whole night without sleep, barricading his door with the room furniture. He was then pulled out by the security guards. Amidst his shouting and crying, he was put in restraints in the seclusion room and given his medicine by injection. He confessed that he had not been swallowing his medicine, but merely pretending to and then spitting it out.

Within two days of this event, Randy told me that he needed to have the medication, no matter what the Bible said. As a result of his own experiment, he had decided he needed the medicine. From the change in his thinking induced by the medicine and from his own experience, Randy decided it was unwise to take the Bible literally. He showed an increasing interest in the message of forgiveness and hope in the New Testament and was more flexible in accepting the ambiguities of the Bible. He decided that after discharge he would attend a more "middle of the road" church.

As Randy became more open theologically, he also became

more open interpersonally. With these improvements and with Randy's agreement to come back to the outpatient clinic while continuing to take his medicine, he was discharged. Before he left, Randy, his social worker, his doctor, and I joined hands for prayer. I led this prayer, giving thanks to God for his gifts of healing, for what we learned from one another, for what we learned about ourselves during this time, and asking for God's support for each of us in the tasks and changes that faced us.

Outpatient Process

Since discharge, Randy has returned every Wednesday to the outpatient clinic, and has been regularly taking his medicine. His religious perspective has continued to change. When discharged, Randy was doing some light Bible study in the New Testament, through which he became interested in some constructive devotional material. Currently he is looking at secular self-help books as resources in keeping his reality perspective healthy.

Since his discharge, Randy has not gone to church. He fears that he might be swayed into some unhealthy thinking if he were to become involved again. He now perceives his previous church as being manipulative, as not respecting individual differences, and as using a person's guilt to keep one in line. Randy still professes his Christian faith, but is so cautious about finding an appropriate expression for it that he has found none.

Family and social relationships have changed dramatically for Randy. Carrying on a conversation with his father and actually having something to say is a new phenomenon for him. He states that for the first time the deep rage he had for his parents is no longer there. He has developed social relationship and a reawakened interest in the opposite sex. Feelings of awkwardness and shyness still complicate many of his romantic attempts. Randy is having to make up for the growth he could have made if he had not been sick. Although he is twenty-five years old, he is developmentally in his late adolescence.

Randy is currently trying to integrate his past identity as a patient with his more recent healthy self. He is also dealing with the conflicting feelings of fear and attraction in regard to psychosis. Psychosis is potentially attractive to him because it provides him with a familiar escape from his new-found responsibilities and pressures. As both chaplain and friend to Randy, I am seeking to help him pour out his need for freedom from some of his pressures, to share with that which gives him joy and meaning, and to be a consistently personal link in the outpatient psychiatric treatment of his illness. Randy has now started college.

For reflection upon this case, the reader or a group of readers might consider the following questions:

1. Can a trust relationship be built with a person who is in an open psychotic state?

2. Can medical doctors automatically assume credibility with a patient just because they are doctors? Can ministers do so as well? What are the hazards and responsibilities involved in "transferring credibility" back and forth?

3. Should changing a patient's belief system to aid medical treatment be done?

4. To what extent was isolation a characteristic of both Randy's illness and his religion?

5. How desperate do you think Randy was? Would this patient likely commit suicide, especially if his belief system were shattered?

The reader will do well to assume that anyone who writes anything on the subject of schizophrenia tends to leave the subject shrouded in mystery because of the vast amount that is not yet known about the processes of life that produce such states of consciousness and ways of existence. The chapter we are now concluding is no exception to this. Let it be said here, however, that the pastors, social workers, psychologists, and psychiatrists who take the mystery of schizophrenia seriously will find that many other problems in the work, play, worship, and love life of people will be simplified by what they discover. They will be rewarded with a fresh angle of vision on whatever they read and hear. The fact that we prophesy in part and know in part need not be a deterrent to both prophesying and learning.

7

SOME INDICATIONS AND
CONTRAINDICATIONS FOR
REFERRAL FOR PASTORAL COUNSELING

The various members of the psychiatric team ask what are the situations in which pastoral counseling can be useful and those situations in which pastoral counseling is not indicated. The pastoral counselor needs to be specific and precise rather than general in the prescription of pastoral counseling. This precision calls for the religious assessment of patients as to whether they are merely superficially religious or whether their religion is a profound part of their life development and purpose. The pastoral counselor needs genuine triage ability, "triage" meaning the ability to "sort out" the most pressing needs of patients from the needs that can be deferred in time. Pastoral counseling is no panacea: it is indicated in some instances and not indicated in others.

SOME INDICATIONS FOR PASTORAL COUNSELING

Routine Pastoral Assessment

One of the most effective ways of regularizing the religious care of psychiatric patients is to establish a policy that all patients will be seen routinely for a standard religious assessment by a pastoral counselor. This assessment is *not* a psychiatric examination. A religious assessment deals specifically with the religious history, religious education, religious peak and low experiences, religious delusions, religious beliefs, knowledge about the particular sacred writing of a given group with which the patient is affiliated, the kinds of emotional and spiritual support available to the patients, and the degree of pathology in the patient's religious world views.

The following outline may be used by pastoral counselors in a facility where a routine religious assessment of all patients is done by pastoral counselors.

Date:
Patient's Name:_____ Age:_____ Sex:_____
Marital Status: _____ Parental Status: _____
Occupation: _____ Religious Affiliation: _____
Length of Religious Affiliation: _____
Changes in Religious Affiliation:_____
1. Religious Experiences, Both "Peak" and "Desolating"

2. Significant Religious Influences & Sources of Support

3. Quality and Depth of Religious Concern
              _____None
              _____Superficial
              _____Compulsive Obsessional
              _____Sociopathic and/or Manipulative
              _____Profound and Authentic
              _____Hostile and Alienated
4. Beliefs of Diagnostic & Therapeutic Significance

5. Pastoral Impressions & Recommendations

Obviously this procedure calls for a teaching program in which the student can both learn and provide the personnel for such evaluations and assessments. Indications *for* referral are as follow:

Bereavement

Psychiatric patients are no exception to significant personal losses by death and other means of separation, such as abandonment, divorce, and alienation. Psychiatric patients get considerable help from conversing with a pastoral counselor about the loss of someone who is very significant to them, because these desolating experiences often make them aware of God. This loss may not be "someone" but "something." For example, a person in the middle years may have lost a very significant job.

Bereavement may be *acute*, as in the case of a thirty-year-old mother whose nine-year-old son, with no premonition, simply dropped dead from a cardiovascular accident as he was walking home from school one afternoon. Bereavement may be *chronic*, as in the case of an aging man who had to sell his home and move many miles away in order to be with his only daughter and her family after the death of his wife. Bereavement may be *pathological*, as in the case of the man who, when his son was killed in an automobile accident, chose not to bury the body but to entomb it in a glass-topped casket in a room in his home. He encircled the room with all sorts of religious symbols. He sought to create a chapel there. He expected people to come there and worship. The pathological grief became blatantly psychotic when he began to develop elaborate plans for finding and killing the person who was driving the car that struck the car of his son.

A considerable portion of the training of a pastor has been in the thoroughgoing study of death and dying, of bereavement, and of the follow-up care of bereft persons. Therefore, the amount of work and the nature of the problems can be shared by referring to a pastoral counselor the patients who have either acute, chronic, or pathological grief.

Terminal Illness

Psychiatric patients quite often are suffering from additional disorders other than those of a psychotic or neurotic nature. One of the recurring disorders is that of the presence of a terminal kind of illness, such as leukemia, malignant tumors, etc. Another disorder may be chronic alcoholism. One may find, as I did recently, a patient in whom all three of these conditions exist at the same time: terminal malignancy, alcoholism, and a bizarre psychosis. The pastoral counselor is especially equipped to care for people facing the realistic threat of death. This is not to say that a referral should be made quickly and automatically. The timing of the entry of the pastoral counselor into the therapeutic milieu of a patient is of the utmost importance. It is to say, however, that, given the right kind of timing to the particular patient's needs, pastoral counseling can be exceptionally helpful as a person moves through the critical phases of a terminal illness.

Reality-based Guilt

Some of the acts that a patient has committed are such as to cause the person to feel directly responsible to God. The patient's own perception of sin or wrongdoing is what must be considered, not the particular concepts of the pastoral counselor or the other psychiatric team members. Historically, "disburdening," or confession, has been an important part of therapy. Catharsis can result in abreaction. The pastoral counselor takes seriously the ministry of confession and intercession. For example, patients quite often suffer more of a burden of guilt over things they have not done but are tempted to do than they do over things they have actually done. Therefore, the pastoral counselor can be exceptionally helpful in enabling the person to get past a feeling of self-condemnation to a feeling of injustice, anger, frustration, and the accumulated temptations that these present. Assurance of forgiveness by God is an ultimate form of acceptance.

In the confessional ministry one occasionally finds that the patient has a long-standing and chronic sense of combined grief and guilt—sin for some deed committed many years ago. For example, one may discover persons in their middle years who experienced an abortion during their late teens or early twenties. One must bear in mind that when that particular event occurred, such an act was not only felt to be sin but actually a criminal act. The compulsive obsessional preoccupation with this particular, in some cases, may be accompanied by a severe depression. The depression arises out of biochemical changes, age changes, value crises, station-in-life changes, or a plexus of these and many other changes. The depression may be cleared up, but the compulsive obsessional preoccupation with the "wrongdoing" of the past persists. Close teamwork between the psychotherapist and the pastoral counselor is intensely needed with such patients.

Patients with character disorders may present an anesthesia, a numbness, or an absence of feeling about specific wrongdoing. The psychiatrist quite often is heavily preoccupied with coping with the problems of the authentically psychotic, neurotic, and organically disordered thinking of patients. The use of his or her time with character disorders is not the primary devotion of a considerable number of psychiatrists. Similarly, pastoral counselors tend to be less challenged by the morally obtuse persons usually found in the categories of character disorders. Psychiatric theory has tended to relate aberrations of religious consciousness to schizophrenic, depressive, and neurotic types of disorder. Rarely does one find psychiatric theory focusing on religious pathology in the character disorders. Yet character disorders run rife among persons who use religion as a means of base gain, as a means of avoiding responsibility, and as a means of exploiting other people. In such instances reality-oriented pastoral counseling can be a helpful resource. However, if the pastoral counselor is timid about representing reality to the patient, it may well be that he or she is as ineffectual as anyone else. To the contrary, some patient records are extant which point to the effective role of religion and quasi-religious influences in changing behavior patterns of persons with basic character disorders. Not the least among these successful ventures is Alcoholics Anonymous and similar reality-oriented group approaches to caring for persons who have severe personality disorders.

Vocational Confusion and Lack of Direction

Psychiatric patients struggle with a sense of "calling", the decision or the compulsion to enter religious work, to leave religious work, or to change work. Underneath this vocational confusion lies the heavy threat of the meaninglessness and purposelessness of life. Mingled with it is the often overlooked loss of curiosity and exaggerated boredom in the life of many psychiatric patients. Such persons are often helped considerably by pastoral counseling. There is a distinct "vocational heart" to the work of the effective pastoral counselor. The life and work of the minister moves on a motivation of "mission" or "call," even as does that of the other members of the therapeutic team. Pastoral counseling at its best represents a disciplined study of the work adjustment of persons, the varieties of careers of persons, and the important parameters of actualizing the "gifts," "talents," and aptitudes of a person.

In the case of psychotic persons, the sense of mission or call may be far out of touch with reality. In these instances pastoral counselors are equipped to represent the realities involved in the day-to-day work of religious leaders. For example, a patient uproots his family of four, moves his place of work to a city seven hundred miles away, and becomes absorbed completely in all-day work with a particular church and all-night work on a menial job that does not support his family. His wife in turn has to work and supply three fourths of the family budget. The children begin having all sorts of difficulties by reason of their resistance to the move. The family come into a psychiatric outpatient clinic on the assumption (*a*) that one of the children is mentally retarded and (*b*) the wife is mentally ill. These are "diagnoses" of the father. The underlying conflict of the family with the father over his religious call is a more ample explanation of the family stress than either the inability of a child in school or the understandable despair of the wife and mother. Yet the religious defenses of the father were such as to fend off any approaches of the other members of the therapeutic team. Hence, a pastoral counselor was asked to become a part of the family therapy of this particular family unit. The hope that the distinctly pastoral relationship would reduce the resistances of the father also failed.

A large range of personal struggle in terms of the vocational commitment of people appears in the care of emotionally ill pastors, priests, and other religious workers. Routinely these persons are made more productive in the treatment situation when pastoral counselors are involved either as cotherapists or parallel consultants in the process. This is a specific indication for the value of the inclusion of a pastoral counselor in a patient's therapy.

Religious Conflicts Between Family Members

A considerable amount of alienation occurs between family members over denominational differences. Sometimes we find that one or the other person of a marital partnership will become intensely interested in a new kind of religion in an attempt to handle the insoluble stress in the family. For example, a woman may feel keenly that she as a wife does not have any personal freedom of her own. Her liberation may take the form of an interest in a religious group that is far apart from the rather routine habitual religious interest and behavior of her husband. Or, in another case, a husband may feel that he does not get the sense of warm approval, emotional support, and tender solicitude from his wife that he is due. Thus, he may become hyperactively involved in the life of the church to the neglect of all his relationships in the home. In the church, he is "somebody." In turn, he may use his religious concern as an excuse for expressing his anger covertly toward his wife for what he perceives to be her neglect of his deep needs for appreciation. Such religious overzealousness has some rather mundane and "earthy" psychological roots. The denial and defense system of such a husband or wife is sufficiently encased in religious materials that the pastoral counselor becomes a person who can "meet them on their own ground." Other members of the psychiatric team, regardless of their emotional commitment as religious persons, may be "written off" by the patient.

Biblical Interpretation

The language of the Bible is not by any means a universal language in contemporary secular culture. However, in a considerable portion of the population, Biblical passages often become issues of confusion, debate, conflict, and emotional infection. In the process of treatment some psychiatric patients will repeatedly present Biblical teachings on such matters as forgiveness, divorce, adultery, anger, murder. Much of the catalog of virtues and sins that the patient has collected from a random reading of the Bible is taken out of the context of the basic meaning of the Scripture. Consequently, in a culture that is dominated by Judeo-Christian teachings, persons who have been profoundly trained in the study of the whole teaching of the whole Bible on any particular subject can be of remarkable help in putting the attitudes of the patient into the right context. The pastoral counselor is a person who has had such training and equipment. In the close-at-hand operation of a psychiatric team, this responsibility for accurate and thoroughgoing interpretation of the Bible is an indication for referral to a pastoral counselor. Upon receiving such a referral, the pastoral counselor focuses forthrightly upon that teaching and deals with it in as profound and emotional a way as possible without either the pastor or the patient getting into such defenses as intellectualization, rationalization, and reaction formation.

Religious Support of Psychiatric Treatment

Many patients will resist psychiatric treatment on religious grounds. For example, they may feel that it is a lack of faith to have medication for emotional problems. They may feel that to consult a psychiatrist is in and of itself a demonstration of religious weakness. They may condemn themselves and feel that if they were good Christians, they would not need psychiatric treatment. Therefore, they are likely to want to "redouble their efforts" religiously in order to offset the need for psychiatric treatment.

In such instances pastoral counselors can be interpreters of psychiatric treatment as a part of the creative forces of the universe to bring wholeness and health to the person and to make him or her a more effective religious person. Similarly a considerable portion of religious teaching is focused on the idea that a person who is religious is not supposed to have any problems or sufferings. This is pure superstition. The effective pastoral counselor can work directly at challenging this particular set of ideas. He or she can teach that suffering is a characteristic of all humanity. One of the purposes of suffering is to learn from the suffering in order to be able to be instructive to others who are caught in such problems.

The need for pastoral counseling for a patient resisting psychiatric treatment is especially imperative in the case of a mental inquest patient who is being forced to take psychiatric treatment to which he or she objects on explicit religious grounds. The issue of the religious freedom of the patient is at stake. For example, there is a legal ground for such resistance and the legalities of psychiatric treatment against a patient's religious objections, especially when a patient is involuntarily committed and yet has not been adjudicated incompetent. D. S. Cohen cites a legal case in which it was ruled that such a patient may "refuse treatment on the basis of his/her First Amendment right of free exercise of religion." (D. S. Cohen, "Recent Decisions," *Brooklyn Law Review,* Vol. 38, 1971, pp. 211–222.)

Post-Psychotic Convalescent Care

The point at which the pastoral counselor can be of exceptional assistance is as the patient prepares to reenter the community after a psychiatric illness. For example, psychiatric literature points to the kind of post-psychotic depression that many patients experience after having reconstituted from a schizophrenic break. Facing the task of rebuilding their lives overwhelms them. The patient often feels incapable of any form of relatedness other than being "sat with silently." It is a sort of impasse in which the patient "seems to have one purpose in mind—that of preserving the status quo." (T. H. McGlashan, M.D., and William T. Carpenter, M.D., "Post-Psychotic Depression in Schizophrenia," *Archives of General Psychiatry,* Vol. 33, Feb. 1976, pp. 231–239.) It is estimated that one out of four such post-psychotic depressions occurs in schizophrenic patients. The collaboration of a pastoral counselor with the psychiatric team does two things: the psychiatric team becomes discouraged with such patients and the pastoral counselor can be a "morale officer" for the group. Also, the pastoral counselor can be a source of quiet hope for the patient.

The pastoral counselor can be a "bridge" personality, involved both in the process of treatment and in the process of rehabilitation, both in the hospital community and in the larger community of which the church is a part. Effectively working at the development of a religious support system can be a part of the collaboration of a pastoral counselor with the social worker who is also involved in the community reconstitution of the life of the patient. The pastoral counselor who has been in a given community a considerable length of time knows a "grapevine" of helpful persons. An inherently helpful person can be accurately empathetic,

nonpossessively warm, and genuine in working with a con-
valescing psychiatric patient. The pastoral counselor who is
personally acquainted with such helping persons and can
relate the patient to them is in a particularly useful position
in the post-psychotic care of a patient.

The Pastoral Care of the Family of a Patient

Members of the family undergo massive confusion, shock,
and conflicting emotions in their responses to the psychiatric
illness of their family member. For the most healthily motivated ones of them the experience is a grief situation characterized by much helplessness and plaintive concern. The
grief they bear is not easily socialized and tends to isolate
them. They quite often are so omnivorous in their need for
time and attention by professionals that "all hands need to be
on deck" in caring for them. The pastoral counselor can be
assigned the continuing care of certain family members.
When patients are under the care of a private psychiatrist,
the physician does not have the resources of a social work
team to add to his or her own care of the patient. Therefore,
for practical purposes, an effective pastoral counselor focuses
on the needs of the family in much the same way that a social
worker would if present.

In some instances, the family may have unusually rigid
religious objections, skepticism, and religiously reinforced
lack of cooperation with the rest of the psychiatric team in
the care of a family member. Therefore, the pastoral counselor must be extremely canny and aware of the possibility
of the family member "pitting" the other members of the
psychiatric team against the pastoral counselor and vice
versa. Thus, a given member of the family may divide the
team and sabotage the whole treatment process.

Premature Psychiatric Referral

A psychiatric referral is not as easily made as even the general physician often suspects. A poorly made psychiatric referral quite often assures that the patient will not get to the psychiatrist. In the face of poorly made psychiatric referrals, quite often the pastoral counselor gets the patient on "the rebound." Regardless of the condition of the patient, the pastoral counselor may be the only professionally trained person to whom the patient will talk. Access is the essence of care in this and many other instances. There are instances when the pastoral counselor may be coached by other members of the psychiatric team as he or she carries the whole responsibility for the immediate critical needs of patients who simply will not under any circumstances go to a psychiatrist. For example, patients may have had many and negative experiences with different psychiatrists. The patients may vow that they will "cut their throat" before they will go to another psychiatrist. Therefore, these patients find a pastoral counselor and begin to converse with him or her about these emotional needs. Or, the pastoral counselor may visit patients who have never seen a psychiatrist. The pastoral counselor needs to take several interviews before the patients themselves come to the awareness that they really need to get medical care. Consequently, the function of the pastoral counselor becomes similar to that of the "point men" on a military patrol. The pastoral counselor is where the most danger is, i.e., the open community. The rest of the team is moving carefully along behind, supporting, coaching, and advising. The pastoral counselor carries the responsibility until the patient is willing to include the rest of the team in the treatment process. Furthermore, the pastoral counselor has none of the controls of hospital walls, drugs, legal authority, etc. He or she works in the open community. Hazards are high.

These are simply a few of the indications for the need of pastoral counseling in the treatment situation. Now let us turn to some of the contraindications, those situations in which a patient should not be sent to a pastoral counselor or have a pastor come to the patient for consultation.

SOME CONTRAINDICATIONS FOR PASTORAL COUNSELING

Total Patient Rejection

The personal wishes of a patient not to see a pastoral counselor should be respected. A considerable number of psychiatric patients see the pastoral counselor as a "public" person. They are made extremely uncomfortable at the thought of a pastoral counselor conversing with them. They fear that their plight as a disturbed patient will become public knowledge. Other patients feel extremely uncomfortable at the idea of discussing their religious life, because these feelings are so inarticulate that they cannot find words to describe them. Other patients will feel that they would like to see a pastoral counselor later but not now. The timing is off. Even other patients will perceive themselves as totally hostile to the idea of religion, religious personages, and religious organizations. They may have had too many negative encounters with the church to hazard another. Therefore, they do not want to see a pastoral counselor. A considerable number of psychiatric patients have had painful rejection from previous pastors. They do not want to run that risk again. For whatever reason the patient does not want to see a pastoral counselor, my conviction is that those reasons should be respected.

"Substitute" Psychiatrist

Occasionally a patient will want to talk with a pastoral counselor as a substitute for the psychiatrist. Basic medical issues of a neurological and biochemical nature may be obvious even to the nonmedical observer. A contraindication for pastoral counseling is when a patient is seeking "to use" a pastoral counselor as a substitute for admitting the need for psychiatric treatment. As has been stated before in this book, the patient may also insist upon having a "Christian" psychiatrist and set this as a stipulation for any collaboration with psychiatric treatment. In this instance the psychiatrist is a "substitute pastor." Whichever way the resistance goes, it should be dealt with forthrightly and honestly as a means of developing an authentic and trustworthy therapeutic relationship. If a referral to a pastoral counselor is made when essentially a psychiatric treatment is indicated, this in itself may be a form of deception.

Rejection of Psychiatry by Other Medical Specialists

It is no secret that many physicians who are not psychiatrists reject the whole specialty. As a pastoral counselor, I have had blatantly psychotic patients referred to me for counseling by such physicians. These patients were persons whose mental status was so completely disorganized that their lives were in shambles. They were referred to me by surgeons, general practitioners, and other specialists in the medical profession who rejected psychiatry as a legitimate expression of the medical profession. I have no need at this point to delve into the intricacies of this kind of intraprofessional tension. Nevertheless such referrals to pastoral counselors in lieu of a psychiatrist are contraindicated. A pastoral counselor may, after careful assessment, use his or her own expertise as a pastoral counselor to bridge the patient's relationship to a psychiatrist who can give the specialized attention that is needed.

Therapeutic "Dilution"

Pastoral counseling is no exception to the general contraindication of more than one therapist talking to a patient when to do so is to "dilute" the patient's relationship to the therapist who is most likely to be doing the patient the most good. This therapist may be a psychiatrist, a social worker, a nurse, or the family physician, etc. One of the common characteristics of anxiety-ridden patients is that they will flit from one counselor to another indiscriminately without regard to the particular professional competence of the person. In doing so, they will alleviate their anxiety temporarily, then break the relationship and move to another counselor. The pastoral counselor is no exception to this. A referral to a pastoral counselor that dilutes the intensity and direction of an already existing counseling relationship by another counselor is contraindicated.

Religion as a Manipulative Tool

Another contraindication for referral to a pastoral counselor is when the patient's religion is assessed by any member of the therapeutic team, and especially by the pastoral counselor, to be superficial, to be a ruse, to be a tool of manipulation in the hands of the patient. For example, such patients may use a superficial flurry of religion as a means of getting certain privileges on the ward, shortening their stay in the hospital, or making a show of "normality." Careful observation of these patients in a hospital setting by the nursing staff and the psychiatric aides has a way of providing an outside reading on the genuineness of the religious concern of the patient. When it is seen that the pastoral counselor is a tool for the manipulative patient, then judicial neglect or forthright confrontation of the patient may, after careful consultation with physicians and nurses, be indicated.

The Psychiatric Vacuum

A psychiatric vacuum is created in the lives of many psychiatric patients when there are not enough psychiatrists to meet the basic psychiatric needs of the patients in a given hospital setting. Furthermore, there may be an abundance of psychiatrists in numbers, but certain psychiatrists themselves may see no point at all in conversing in depth with their patients. When this happens, for whatever reason, a vacuum is created. When a patient is validated by three or four responsible members of the staff as "not having seen the doctor in eight days," then the pastoral counselor who is on the service may well be drawn into the vacuum created by such neglect. In essence, this kind of pastoral counseling is contraindicated because the patient is being deprived of his or her right to adequate attention by the psychiatrist in charge. This is not an uncommon phenomenon in private, well-supported psychiatric facilities. It is a widespread occurrence in state hospitals. If a psychiatrist or a psychiatric resident is too impatient, too busy, too rejecting, or too out of tune with the idea of conversing with patients, then the referral of the patient to a pastoral counselor is a ditching of responsibility rather than a responsible referral for distinctly religious care.

Social Involvement

In unique situations, a given pastoral counselor may be so socially involved with the patient and the patient's family in an ongoing, semifamily relationship that pastoral counseling by that particular pastor is contraindicated. The need for sufficient detachment from the social circle of the continuing life of the patient is just as real in pastoral counseling as it is in other types of counseling and/or psychotherapy. For example, if I as a professor have a student who is emotionally ill, it is more important that I remain an effective teacher and friend over the long pull of the person's life than it is that I do pastoral counseling. I usually see pastoral counseling under such conditions as a contraindication. Therefore, I seek to enlist the assistance of someone other than myself if distinctly pastoral counseling is indicated. This keeps the relationship from becoming a confused, anxiety-ridden one.

Other contraindications of pastoral counseling could be

identified, but these are the most recurrent. As has been said before, pastoral counseling is *one* of the resources for the care of psychiatric patients. It is not a panacea; nor, as is occasionally inferred, is it a pernicious influence that should be avoided in all instances. The important issue is carefully to assess the lifelong pattern of the patient. In what ways have religious experience and community been the cohesive forces in the person's life? Have they provided support when all other sources of support have failed? Such a careful assessment of the lifelong history of the patient will reveal to what extent the religious concern of the person has been a liability and a threat or an asset and a support to the integrity of the patient's functioning as a human being. On the basis of such an assessment, a "prescriptive" approach to the use of pastoral counseling can be made, rather than either thinking of it as a "patent medicine" that should be peddled over the counter indiscriminately to any and all patients at any and all times, or being banned by psychiatric authority as always poisonous.

CONCLUSION

As my colleague, Conrado Weller, M.D., says, "pastoral counseling deals with belief systems." As such, it may even be thought of as one "among many psychotherapies." For many years, I have restricted the use of the term "psychotherapy" to apply to that which a physician does in longer-term kinds of uncovering "depth" therapies. The time is here, however, when a considerable number of pastoral counselors are thoroughly educated in such depth psychotherapy. With the increased preoccupation of psychiatrists with the somatic therapies, the pastoral counselor as a psychotherapist in his or her own right is a reality at hand. Heavy caution must be observed, however, to consider the amounts of time this takes and the quality and extent of education under supervision which it implies, and the legal and financial problems involved. No shortcut to excellence is available here. Furthermore, the pastor can become a gnostic, denying the reality of the body, if he or she is not quick to seek a thorough medical examination of a counselee undergoing longer-term kinds of pastoral counseling. He or she does well to get an interdisciplinary assessment of the person concurrent with a pastoral counseling relationship. Personally, I am appreciative of the ways in which much that I do as a pastoral counselor corresponds with what is called psychotherapy. However, I prefer to give the name "pastoral counseling" to what I do. Thus, I will be sure that I am not ignorant of my true identity and source of answerability to God. Also, I feel more authentic, clear, and unpretentious about what I am doing.

The unique character of the pastoral counselor's concerns becomes more vivid in the following chapter in which a dialogue between a clinical psychologist and a pastor "gets down to brass tacks" about the content and process of the religious care of persons through a discussion of psychotherapy and pastoral counseling.

8
PSYCHOTHERAPY
AND PASTORAL COUNSELING:
A DIALOGUE

CURTIS L. BARRETT, PH.D.,* and WAYNE E. OATES, TH.D.

The format of this chapter is that of a dialogue. Curtis Barrett presents the first section as a clinical psychologist. Wayne Oates responds in the second section as a pastoral counselor.

CURTIS BARRETT:

When my respected friend and colleague, Wayne Oates, asked me to participate in this dialogue, I accepted without hesitation. "After all," said I to me, "he is only asking that you talk about psychotherapy and psychotherapy research." That was a mistake. Anyone who knows Wayne Oates knows, without his saying it, that he is asking for something of yourself. So it has been that for the past several weeks I have been asking what of myself I might present rather than the cold statistics of psychotherapy research alone. The decision of what of myself to give has been made, and in another article I would like also to say where I think we are in psychotherapy and psychotherapy research.

A while back, I took a short vacation and was staying at the home of my mother-in-law in the southwestern Indiana town where I grew up. I have a program of maintaining personal

*Dr. Barrett is Director of Adult Psychological Services and Associate Professor of Psychiatry and Behavorial Sciences, School of Medicine, University of Louisville.

fitness that I use, among other things, to help me deny my mortality and prolong my life. Without comment on that illusion, let me say that I decided to continue the program while on vacation. To do so, I needed to map out a course of about five miles to jog. Since I was familiar with the area, I estimated the distance from my mother-in-law's home to a relative's at about six or seven miles. The relative lived close to the now-changed neighborhood in which I had lived most of my first eighteen years. As luck would have it, my jogging clothes had been left at the relative's, so I had to drive out there and let my wife drive back. But that also enabled me to clock the distance accurately.

The result of that clocking triggered what I am talking with you about concerning psychotherapy and pastoral counseling. What I estimated at six miles was a bare two and a half! The shock that I felt is difficult to communicate. I responded by testing my environment again—just as behavioral scientists would predict. This time, it was the distance past where I used to live and to my old grade school. Barely a mile! At that point, I was into the experience, despite my shock and disorientation. I clocked five miles and began the jog. Come with me as I have that experience.

I jogged past "the corner," a typical rural phenomenon where the grocery store, mailboxes, and a tavern were concentrated. It brought back memories of so many human experiences. There was mutual trust and sense of community in the relationship of grocer and customer. It was so clearly reflected in the bill books with the families' last names on them—there was community knowledge of which families were financially sound and which were not. And evidence, too, of what it meant, in terms of self-esteem, for a family to have to ask for credit when illness, death, or unemployment visited their home. I mused that this little corner would have done well in an episode of the television series *The Waltons.*

On "the corner," too, I remembered learning what it feels like inside to be manipulated and violated for someone else's profit. It happened when the bakery truck salesman handed out sample doughnuts and urged the gathered children to go home and tell their parents to buy a fresh dozen right away before they were gone. I did it and, on my word, I was given money to buy some. What joy to bring them home! And what hurt to be told that the salesman had unloaded his leftover, stale doughnuts on me.

The corner also taught us, as children, about the world of the grown-ups. They could enter the tavern, but we could not, even with our parents, because our tender eyes would have seen a bar. So it was that we took our money to the side door, patiently waited until we were recognized, and then bought our "Double Cola." Right now I can't remember whether, as a twelve-year-old, I went to the side door and waited on the night my father died and I ran up there to find someone who would help us. But I suppose that I did, because the corner taught us well about the distinction between children and grown-ups.

Across the street from the corner lived three women who were refugees from Czechoslovakia. Through them we experienced the meaning of cultural differences. Their customs, dress, and accents always defined them as different. But strangely, as we came to know them, we found that they were human beings just like the rest of us.

Near the corner also, I jogged by the home of a woman, long since dead, who helped me understand the meaning of middle-aged divorce. She and her husband divorced when their last daughter entered high school. He gave her no further support. Alone, untrained, with no work experience and in her fifties, she had to start over again. It was a long time before I realized what meaning it had to her to have a teenaged boy stop by in the evening to share her cake and just talk.

A little farther down the road I recalled my personal reference experience on the distinctions between acting in (depression), acting out (expressing a conflict through action), and acting up. It often comes to me when I sit in on the psychiatric staffing of an adolescent. Every year, the owner of the house I was passing planted a full quarter acre of watermelons. They were free to anyone who came along, but none of us could accept that. It was much more fun to crawl on our bellies through the cornfield to get into the watermelon patch at night and steal a bunch! That's acting up—doing it for the sheer thrill of it.

During the jog it wasn't hard to find referents for the psychoanalytic pillars of sex and aggression. There were enough fights that reflected pure aggression. Many more resulted from territorial rights, Machiavellian manipulations behind the scenes to provoke others to fight, and the ritual of establishing one's manhood. For me, those events put me in touch with my own fear of pain and death and the extent to which I will go to avoid such trouble if my wits can serve. Worse, I came to know of my own capacity to maim and to kill when angry. Living with that knowledge of one's self leads to questioning the essential rationality of man as a basis for society.

The sexual lessons came early and I openly grinned as I jogged. Some of the memories I'll censor, you can be sure. But I'll report that I recalled seeing the mother of my third-grade classmate already working hard to provide her daughter with boyfriends. The games were the classics, of course —Post Office and Spin the Bottle. But the message was clear: "Like me, like my daughter."

Another related memory. I remembered seeing a neighbor, whom I respected very much, beat his wife. I wondered how it could be that this fine, gentle person could behave like that. Later I could understand, I think, what had happened. He loved her very much. She loved her son. The symbolic expression of loving, of giving oneself, was where this lack of feeling for him had hurt him the most. She experienced no joy in sex and there was no sexual relationship in the marriage. But frigidity in his wife would never have provoked such anger in this man. Nor would frustrated male sex drive have done it. What did it was the manipulative use of sex. Sex as a weapon. Sex to control. The man's rage was in response to a violation of his integrity as a person. That violation had occurred in what he so clearly expected to be the human experience of sharing physical intimacy.

As I jogged on, I recalled using that experience of rage in the psychotherapy of a woman best labeled a hysterical personality. She was terrified by the rage that she saw in her usually calm, collected new husband. Though I knew at the theoretical level, I think, what the interaction that she reported had meant, I would have failed her at a critical point in psychotherapy if I had not experienced the intensity of such response firsthand in a person who was otherwise well known to me. It helped to tell her about the vector that results when one provokes a combination of raw instinctual expression and a sense of violation.

Down the road a piece I approached my old grade school. It was hard to recognize such a large school as my own, since, when I was there, it had one room for each of eight grades. Even then it was much larger than the one-room Hoosier school in which I began first grade. But the specific memory was tied to a time when what I jogged by was a muddy cornfield. I thought about a classmate and about the image of him that I carried for some thirty years. He was the son of what we called a wealthy farmer in the area, a man whose financial success came during the war in which he lost his oldest son. Every summer John was allowed to work in the business with his father, and by his high school days he had accumulated a good bit of personal money for himself. I was always aware that while I considered John lucky and was envious of him, he never seemed really happy. Only recently did I come to understand the struggle that he had had. For all these years, I didn't know that John's father was illiterate and that the boy's every move through academia—high school, college, an M.D., and a Ph.D.!—was regarded as direct defiance and rejection of his father. Where academic achievement brought most developing children years of positive reinforcement, affirmation of self, prestige, or even joy, this boy found rejection and conflict.

There was a lesson for this psychotherapist in that memory. If I could be unaware of the true struggle of a person whom I knew so well for so long, how vulnerable am I to overlooking what is most significant in my patient? How often do I assume the usual and not consider the opposite reaction?

Next to the school was our community's church. We never really made the distinction between the two, as I recall. The school sometimes held classes in the church and the church sometimes did things in the school. Separation of church and state didn't seem to be of much concern. I did recall the experience of being an outsider or an intruder in an established group to which I did not belong. It was embarrassing to be asked to come along on a church picnic each year when I hadn't contributed to church all through the year. I wonder how often the resistance that I see when I attempt to have recently divorced persons reenter their church setting comes from similar negatively conditioned covert responses. Do I explore for that?

As I turned the corner I saw several black children who apparently lived in houses that had been built recently. What a difference! My memory called back a crisis in our area. The school boundary was going to be changed in that mid-forties year and we might be sent to a poverty area school that, unlike the rest of the township schools, had black kids in it. There was an uproar, and old allegiance to the Ku Klux Klan was talked about. So were guns and transfers to, of all things, Catholic schools. There was no change in school boundary after all, and I and all my neighbors were relieved back then. But my memory today includes a feeling of being deprived, through all of my school years, of any human relationship outside my own race. There are no childhood experiences to use as references, no sense of sharing, no intuitive sense of understanding. In a sense, we won *and* lost the battle of the school boundaries back then.

Thinking of that experience as I jogged reminded me of how well I felt that I understood the panic of white parents in Louisville when busing was ordered. I was not surprised to see "desegregation" coded as "court-ordered forced busing." I also understood the intense rage that resulted in riots in areas that used to cheer law and order candidates. That understanding was useful when parents of phobic children called me to see if their child could be exempted from busing. I knew better than to try to confront them with the inconsistency of moving from a neighborhood school where their children would be bused for two years to county schools where they would be bused for twelve years and doing this in order to avoid busing.

Jogging on, I felt the flood of memory after memory detailing the human experience right by where I was passing. Birth and death memories. War memories. The weak and the strong. Memories of winning and losing, of fire and flood, succeeding and failing, pride and shame, guilt, relief, anxiety, fear, the new rich and the new poor, and more. Each, I realized, was organized around some personal experience, vicarious or actual, of facing situations and coping with them. Many came to me along with a more recent memory of how I had conceptualized some other person's experience of facing an analogous experience and used it in therapy. Much of what I remembered reminded me of how my own frailties —anger, hurt, resentment, hostility, stereotyping, loss, and more—had crept into the therapy I was conducting. Never had the concept of countertransference had a more profound meaning to me!

At five miles I slowed to a walk. It was hard to believe where I was. I was exactly in front of my high school. How could it be? High school for us was a distant, far-off, remote place, and certainly not a part of the neighborhood. Going there symbolized growing up, leaving home. Yet here I was, barely breathing hard, having run much more than from my home to my high school.

My plan was to walk a few minutes and then to run leisurely a mile or two more, or at least the distance to my mother-in-law's house to complete the circuit. Soon I realized that I was set up for yet another human experience. In minutes I was almost to where I started by car and then it hit me. I had jogged some five miles. But the straight-line distance from the home in which I grew up to the home of the woman I married was barely three miles. Despite the fact that we met while attending separate colleges more than a hundred miles away and a hundred miles from each other, we did just what sociologists would have predicted. A *statistic!* The lesson was clear: one deviates from base rate or actuarial predictions only with great caution in dealing with human behavior patterns. *Psychotherapy* is a human behavior pattern!

By now I knew that I had been doing psychotherapy for these years with a completely distorted concept of time and personal space. I wondered—and still wonder—how often I have misunderstood what has been said to me because of this distortion. How often have I been unable to relate to someone because of it?

Here I hope it is clear what of myself I want to share. Really it is quite simple and perhaps even too simple. What I have chosen to say is that those of us who are psychotherapists bear a special burden that we must not lay aside or fail to recognize. It is the burden of being unable simply to have the human experience as it comes to us hour by hour. No, we have to formulate that experience and to integrate it into the organized body of knowledge which we use to help people who are hurting. As you can see, I could not even escape this while off on a leisurely jog.

But then, I suppose I always knew that and intuitively did it. What I didn't know, besides my distortions, and still find hard to believe, is that so many of the reference experiences that I use in therapy occurred in an area only about one mile square. A square mile's perimeter that is but an easy jog around.

At this point, of course, I have revealed a great deal about myself and about my orientations toward therapy. But that is not, as I said before, all of my intention. I intend to point to the psychotherapist's burden of formulating his or her own personal experiences and integrating them into his or her psychotherapeutic approach. And let me be clear about my feeling that it is a welcome burden and not one to be shunned. But how do we proceed when there is such chaos in the field of psychotherapy?

My stand is that we should *unabashedly* formulate on the basis of whatever organized body of knowledge we are said by credentials to have mastered. For me, of course, that body of knowledge is Clinical Psychology, which, with all its overlaps with other fields, proceeds from areas such as learning, perception, cognition, statistical analysis, psychometrics, personality theory and so on. For psychotherapists who are psychiatric physicians, I think that body of knowledge should be the medical arts and sciences such as medical history, biochemistry, psychiatry, physiology. For social workers who are inclined toward conducting psychotherapy, the organized body of knowledge is a combination of sociology, clinical casework, and anthropology, as far as I can tell.

Out of deference to this audience's expertise and my own ignorance of the field, I have put pastoral counseling last. I do not know what organized body of knowledge this group would argue is its anchor and its source of legitimacy in conducting psychotherapy. However, I do have a very strong bias. Wayne Oates says in his book *Pastoral Counseling* (1974, p. 64):

> My own encounter with the Old and New Testaments began after I was twenty years of age. Consequently, the Bible has never been a book of magic to me, but a reservoir for my becoming a "man of understanding."

I share that experience, and I'll illustrate it with the following anecdote. As a Navy midshipman in the summer of 1957 I arrived in Norfolk, Virginia, a day too early to report to my assigned destroyer. The YMCA, the only lodging I could have afforded, was full but we were permitted to "sack out" on the concrete lobby floor. It was hard to sleep, so I spent most of the night reading the "freebie" literature available from the various Norfolk churches and other organizations. Since I was a political science and psychology student, I became intrigued with how easy it was to relate to the literature independent of any assumption that what I was reading was divinely inspired. Later, aboardship, I communicated this to the senior watch officer one midwatch when things were quiet. He invited me to organize and present my views at the next ecumenical service held aboard the U.S.S. *Wilson.* I did, under the title "The Bible as the Accumulated Wisdom of Man." Now perhaps you can understand what I felt when, years later, I stumbled across the strikingly similar view of the Bible expressed in Wayne Oates's book!

Wayne Oates comments, in the same chapter, on the problem that pastoral counselors, like all psychotherapists, face, namely, the rise and fall of the fads—and those who are politically committed to them—in psychotherapy. He points to the tension that a pastor who would be a psychotherapist too must face. That tension he identified as being between the historical-theological method of inquiry and the psychological approach to human need. He urges acceptance of the tension and the interaction of psychotherapeutic wisdom to theological wisdom to make each more meaningful. Surely, if nothing else, theological wisdom must suggest that little is really new under the sun and the psychotherapist who commits to technique—be it transactional analysis, systematic desensitization, or psychoanalysis—rather than to people has sacrificed his or her identity and integrity. With those, I believe, the psychotherapist has lost the ability to help.

No matter what fads, facts, and theories one integrates into one's organized body of knowledge and uses to understand and, therefore, to help people in psychotherapy, perhaps there is a common thread. It is that the psychotherapist practice the study of himself first, and accepting the developmental view of personality, study himself continuously. This rejects the concept of personal therapy as a rite of passage, heads it off as an interminable form of mental masturbation, and places self-knowledge and self-awareness—via personal psychotherapy or other means—as the primary form of continuing education for the psychotherapist. (Wayne E. Oates, *Pastoral Counseling;* The Westminster Press, 1974.)

WAYNE OATES:

Curtis Barrett's remarkable "parable of the jogger" is reminiscent of Lewis J. Sherrill's analogies of differing life-styles —the saga, or life as a battle, a story of *Mein Kampf,* my battle; the treadmill, or life as a constant repetition of the same patterned and monotonous behavior, working hard but getting nowhere; or the pilgrimage, or life as an unfolding search for new meanings of old experiences and for new adventures in the present. In speaking of the "emerging dynamic self," Sherrill identifies each stage of personality development with a Biblical metaphor or symbol. The life of faith moves through phases, according to Sherrill, and each phase in order is given a Biblical meaning.

Barrett's "parable of the jogger" prompts me to take him at his word when he asks that pastoral counselors *"unabashedly* formulate on the basis of whatever organized body of knowledge we are said by credentials to have mastered" our legitimacy as counselors and psychotherapists. His strong bias is that the expertise of the pastoral counselor lies in the knowledge of the Bible as the royal road to the knowledge and understanding of man, especially of our counselees. I concur in this bias.

I have emphasized Barrett's word "unabashedly," because we as pastoral counselors are often timid about our own body of knowledge in which we have spent from three to seven years becoming expert. There is something as dead about the teaching and learning of the Bible in theological schools as there is about the teaching and learning of anatomy in medical schools. People *assume* that we know the Bible in the same way they *assume* a doctor knows the human anatomy. In both instances, however, the learning took place for the doctor on a seemingly *dead corpus.* In anatomy, it was the corpse of a human being; for the pastor in theology, it was the corpus of the Bible—sixty-six separate documents written by a variety of authors at different times and places over a period of fifteen hundred years. Yet when, in practice, the physician and the pastoral counselor "go about" relating to "live human beings" as "living documents," they are likely to be abashed and insecure about these bodies of knowledge in which they are said by certification to have mastered.

Therefore, as a *pastoral* counselor I would like unabashedly to take Curtis Barrett's parable of the jogger and relate my own expertise in Biblical wisdom to it. In such a way, the understanding of the pilgrimage of "Barrett's jogging" may be seen Biblically and life may be understood better as a result. I do not jog, because I am lazy, because I have been restricted by a painful back injury, and because I talk too much and exercise too little. However, I do walk a considerable amount each day and I like to stop at various stations along the way where there are people whom I know. Therefore, I can identify with the parable of the jogger. In imagination, therefore, I as a pastoral counselor would like to walk along and stop at each of the places Curtis Barrett identifies on his jogging tour and "think out loud" with him about what this and that situation brings to mind from the Biblical stories and teachings. We can draw on that reservoir for our becoming "persons of understanding."

Mothers-in-Law

At two points Curtis Barrett mentions just a potential mother-in-law. She, even when he was in the third grade, sought to involve him with her daughter! What memories of my own childhood do the games Post Office and Spin the Bottle conjure! This was his *potential* mother-in-law. Now, many years later, it was at his real mother-in-law's home where they chose to stay. His own mother, apparently, lived a few blocks away. There is a drama! One could ask: Why did they choose to stay at *her* mother's house and not at his? We would be on dynamic territory to ask this.

Both the Old and the New Testament attest to the dramas of the mother-in-law. The whole book of Ruth is the story of a mother-in-law and her daughter-in-law, both of whom had lost their husbands and sons and were widows. They were of different kinship groups. Ruth, a Moabitess, the daughter-in-law, had married Naomi's son, Mahlon, an Israelite. To her, both Naomi and her husband, Mahlon, were "outsiders," "foreigners," sojourners." Now that her husband was dead, *she,* Ruth, was the foreigner if she went back to Israel—even Bethlehem, the reported birthplace of Jesus of Nazareth—where her mother-in-law had lived and to which she was now returning. Ruth was a Moabitess, a descendant of Lot's incestuous relations with one of his daughters after he and his two daughters fled to the hills before the destruction of Sodom and Gomorrah. The daughter bore a son named Moab, the ancestor of Ruth. Therefore, a cloud hung over the ancestry of Ruth, yet Naomi, an Israelite, loved Ruth, who decided to return to Israel with Naomi, her mother-in-law. It was Ruth who said to Naomi:

> Entreat me not to leave you or to return from following you; for where you go I will go, and where you lodge I will lodge; your people shall be my people, and your God my God; where you die I will die, and there will I be buried. May the LORD do so to me and more also if even death parts me from you. (Ruth 1:16–17)

They returned to Bethlehem and Naomi became the gentle "coach" for Ruth as she worked in the fields of Boaz, an Israelite and kinsman of Naomi. Boaz protected her from molestation and provided food for her and her mother-in-law. Ruth, on Naomi's instruction to "go and uncover his feet and lie down" after he had finished working, eating, and drinking and lay down, did as Naomi instructed. When Boaz awoke and found Ruth at his feet, he decided to protect her honor, negotiate with her "next of kin" for the right to marry her, and then married her! They bore children, and Ruth, a foreigner, became the great-grandmother of King David. She is listed as a progenitor in the family tree of Jesus of Nazareth (Matt. 1:5). Mothers-in-law *do* have influence!

In Jesus' life and teachings, the mother-in-law is present. In the house of Simon Peter and Andrew, Jesus found Peter's mother-in-law sick with a fever and healed her (Mark 1:29–31). It seems that when he went into a household, the personal well-being of each person present concerned him. He did not have a bias against mothers-in-law. They are persons, too. Yet Jesus was not naive; he was aware that the position of commitment a person took toward him and his teachings could produce conflict. He said:

> Do you think that I have come to give peace on earth? No, I tell you, but rather division; for henceforth in one house there will be five divided, three against two and two against three; they will be divided, father against son and son against father, mother against daughter and daughter against her mother, mother-in-law against her daughter-in-law and daughter-in-law against her mother-in-law. (Luke 12:51–53)

Religious persuasions often are the basis or the facade (or both) for enmity between in-laws. The serious exploration of these religious conflicts in psychotherapy reveals in-fighting between family members and often provides a paradigm for what Aldrich calls "the power structure of the politics of the family." Curtis Barrett's reference to mothers-in-law—potential and actual—triggered these responses from a Biblically expert pastoral counselor.

The Shortness of Life

Barrett jogs as a part of a physical fitness program. He says that he uses this among other things to help "him" deny "his" mortality and prolong "his" life. It seems to be one way of handling his anxiety over the brevity or shortness of life. Yet in marking out the task of jogging, he shrewdly measured the miles, lest he overdo a good thing. His anxiety had not gotten the best of him. He seems to live comfortably with running five miles. He has no anxiety or ambition to be the world's champion long-distance runner at his age. To the contrary, in this respect at least, he has judiciously set limits for himself and is aware of his need to live as long as possible. Yet if his anxiety made running a compulsion for him which enslaved him from all other important concerns, one would ask as Jesus did: "Which of you by being anxious can add one cubit [a foot and a half] to his span of life?" (Matt. 6:27). Yet, as Barrett marks out the beginning and end of his jogging journey, he is aware of his own finitude, as was the author of Ps. 39:5:

> Behold, thou hast made my days a few handbreadths,
>   and my lifetime is as nothing in thy sight.

And, in line with his comment about the pastoral counselor being a person of understanding, he can resonate with the author of Ps. 90:12:

> So teach us to number our days
>   that we may get a heart of wisdom.

In conceptualizing about psychotherapy, Curtis Barrett rejects the concept of personal therapy as "an interminable form of mental masturbation." I rather think that his concept of the brevity of his own life feeds into an awareness of how valuable the time of his client is. He marks out the length of psychotherapy to fit the client's need and not the preconceived lack of an end found in some forms of psychotherapy. Otto Rank likened anxiety of any kind to the time of fulfillment of a fetus in human birth. Anxiety was set by the termini of life, i.e., birth and death. Therefore, we are to "set ends" *with* the patient as to *when* he or she perceives himself or herself as "getting through" the process. As Curtis Barrett measured out the five miles, Rank would take the reality of the brevity of life and structure it into the process of therapy as a form of "will therapy," on the assumption that the patient *can* decide his or her own destiny.

Memory's Distortions

Barrett refers to the spatial distortion through his *memory* of distances: "What I estimated at six miles was a bare two and a half!" Space is distorted through memory. Time is distorted through memory. Using Barrett's measurement of miles as a parable, we could also say that human relationships are distorted. Just as two and a half miles seemed like six, so also the people we knew as children were distorted all out of proportion. People we considered to be "giants" as children turn out to be five feet eleven inches! Their importance was also distorted. Father, mother, brother, sister may become *all* determinative. Curtis Barrett recalls going to the side door of the tavern to get help the night his father died. What a towering memory! It is reminiscent of James Agee's book, *A Death in the Family.* Jogging by that tavern brings alive again a storehouse of memories kept quiet by adult responsibilities as a father himself.

What does the Bible say about the distortions of important relationships such as that of father and mother? The creation story—in Gen. 2:24—says of men and women as husbands and wives: "Therefore a man leaves his father and his mother and cleaves to his wife, and they become one flesh." (It goes further to say that man and woman as husband and wife can be naked and not be ashamed!) The "one flesh" passage is repeated by Jesus (Matt. 19:5) and by the apostle Paul (Eph. 5:31). Maturity in marriage calls for "leaving" parents.

Similarly, Jesus taught that maturity as a Christian calls for a subordination of one's loyalty to parents to loyalty to the Kingdom of God (Matt. 19:16–30). At the same time he warned against neglecting and dishonoring the real needs of one's parents on the excuse of serving God (Mark 7:10). The demand for emotional maturity is put most sternly when Jesus says: "Call no man your father on earth, for you have one Father, who is in heaven" (Matt. 23:9). The paradox of honoring one's parents and at the same time not deifying them is the tension of maturity. At heart, the New Testament

teaching points toward accepting the humanity and rejecting the all-controlling deity of parents. Jesus himself rejected
the deification of his mother. Yet he showed tenderness toward her when he was dying.

In essence, seeing our parents for their real and not their
distorted stature amounts to Erikson's definition of maturity.
Maturity happens when one comes to the point that one
accepts his or her parents as they are and as being non-
renegotiable. Freud gave a positive definition of the rightful
place in the development of personality. He said:

> Apart from pathological considerations, it [religion]
> places restraints upon a child's sexual tendencies by
> affording them a sublimation and safe mooring. It lowers
> the importance of his family relationships, and thus pro-
> tects him from the threat of isolation by giving him ac-
> cess to the great community of mankind." (Sigmund
> Freud, "The History of an Infantile Neurosis," 1908, *The
> Standard Edition of the Complete Psychological Works
> of Sigmund Freud,* Vol. IX, pp. 177–204)

The process of psychotherapy and pastoral counseling is
most active at the interchanges of the interactions between
the family of origin, the nuclear family, and the larger family.
The psychotherapist and/or the pastoral counselor is a
"bridge" over the troubled waters between these "accesses"
to an increasing larger sense of family to include male and
female, bond and free, Jew and Gentile, black and white, rich
and poor, intellectual and untutored, friend and stranger.

On Being in Debt to the Store

Curtis Barrett jogged past the general store. He recalled
how a record was kept of the credit rating of the people of
the neighborhood. No computer here; just the signed slips of
purchase with the name at the top, clipped into separate
little holders with a mousetrap-like lever. I can remember
this, too! Yet, the question always arose as to what happens

when you *can't* pay your debts. The whole issue of being helplessly in debt, of not having any hope, of having that self-esteem of one who is in "sound" condition, financially or otherwise, is an issue of integrity. The sense of being acceptable as a person in an established community is symbolized here. Essentially, the forgiveness of an unpayable debt is what the psychotherapist struggles with in treating the compulsive obsessional neurotic and many depressed persons. The issue has been dealt with by theologians in large concepts such as "redemption" and "salvation." Yet the teachings of Jesus call it forgiveness. The Lord's Prayer says: "Forgive us our debts, as we also have forgiven our debtors" (Matt. 6:12). Jesus told a parable that relates forgiveness and gratitude for forgiveness. To comment on the parable is to dilute it. Here it is:

> Therefore the kingdom of heaven may be compared to a king who wished to settle accounts with his servants. When he began the reckoning, one was brought to him who owed him ten thousand talents; and as he could not pay, his lord ordered him to be sold, with his wife and children and all that he had, and payment to be made. So the servant fell on his knees, imploring him, "Lord, have patience with me, and I will pay you everything." And out of pity for him the lord of that servant released him and forgave him the debt. But that same servant, as he went out, came upon one of his fellow servants who owed him a hundred denarii; and seizing him by the throat he said, "Pay what you owe." So his fellow servant fell down and besought him, "Have patience with me, and I will pay you." He refused and went and put him in prison till he should pay the debt. When his fellow servants saw what had taken place, they were greatly distressed, and they went and reported to their lord all that had taken place. Then his lord summoned him and said to him, "You wicked servant! I forgave you all that debt because you besought me; and should not you have

had mercy on your fellow servant, as I had mercy on you?" And in anger his lord delivered him to the jailers, till he should pay all his debt. So also my heavenly Father will do to every one of you, if you do not forgive your brother from your heart. (Matt. 18:23–35)

The key to forgiveness seems to be being able to forgive. Then, over whom is the compulsive obsessional and the depressed person holding a debt? Can he or she in turn forgive some of the people who have taken from him or her? Or are his or her symptoms a luring reproach to those who have offended him or her?

Anger at Exploitation

Curtis Barrett recalls having been exploited by a salesman who "unloaded his stale doughnuts" on Curtis and his friends as children. The dismay and anger at this kind of exploitation suggest an old saying that we are too soon old and too late smart. Jesus told his disciples that the world was not at all inclined to be concerned about their welfare. He said that "the sons of this world are more shrewd in dealing with their own generation than the sons of light" (Luke 16:8). He commends this worldly-wiseness and, in another passage, says that his followers are to be "wise as serpents and innocent as doves." He represents the wisdom of the Jewish race in never depreciating human intelligence nor underestimating the ruthlessness of human guile. His anger burst forth when exploitation for money was rampant right in the Temple among "religious" people. "He entered the temple and began to drive out those who sold, saying to them, 'It is written, "My house shall be a house of prayer"; but you have made it a den of robbers.' " (Luke 19:45–46.) He reached back to Isaiah, the prophet, who said, "My house shall be called a house of prayer for all peoples" (Isa. 56:7). He combined this with the saying of Jeremiah, another prophet, who said, "Has this house, which is called by my name, become a den of robbers in your eyes?" (Jer. 7:11). One of the ways to "temper" one's anger, to mobilize it accurately toward targets that are most worthy of one's anger, is to test it by the wisdom of others who are our predecessors and were prophetic in their own times. Thus, we have a kind of wisdom that is greater than one generation can provide. Jesus' historical grasp of the Scriptures of his day enabled him to do just that. He always got angry on purpose, by design, and not simply because he himself could stand it no longer.

On Appreciating Foreigners

Curtis Barrett jogged past the home of three Czechoslovakian women who were refugees. What a refreshing open window in an otherwise closed community! Barrett's ever-present curiosity made him "get to know them" until he experienced them as genuine human beings, even though they were foreigners.

Jesus went back to his hometown of Nazareth and spoke in the synagogue where he had grown up as a Jewish boy. He had been away and came back home. As long as he was saying things they were accustomed to hearing, the people were pleased and were amazed at his words. When he began to say what did *not* please them they ran him out of the place. What was it he said? Again he referred to prophets, Elijah and Elisha. Elijah had helped feed a foreign widow and her family and had cared for her sick son. Elisha had healed the leprosy of a foreign soldier from Syria. The Jews who heard Jesus say this were convinced that *only* the Jews were to be cared for by God. Yet this young Jew was saying otherwise. Jesus himself was called upon to heal the daughter of the woman from Syrophoenicia. (Mark 7:26.) Her manifest faith in him seems to have enlarged his own sense of mission to include "all people" and not just a chosen race, class, or association of people. The Syrophoenician woman was a pagan, a Gentile, a person many Jews considered as a "dog." Jesus experienced her as "human just like the rest of us," as Curtis Barrett experienced the Czechoslovakian women.

Divorced Persons

At two places, Barrett mentions divorced persons. He speaks of the middle-aged divorced woman who was alone, untrained, and unsupported at fifty-plus years of age. He speaks of the meaning of his visits and conversations with her.

Then again, as Curtis jogged along, he came to the church. He speaks of the "negatively conditioned covert responses of divorced persons" whom he has, as a psychotherapist, attempted to have reenter their churches.

In both instances Barrett speaks of divorced persons, not of divorce in the abstract. Jesus' teachings concerning divorced persons are both difficult to interpret and very easy to misinterpret. Yet the church has given us the interpretations and the misinterpretations. The questions and ambiguities that Barrett poses cause me as a pastoral counselor to ask: Can a church change its attitude toward divorced persons upon direct, faithful contact with them? The early church described in the New Testament demonstrates that a church *can* change and move toward the Spirit of Jesus' words that gives life and away from the letter of Jesus' words that can kill as easily as the letter of anyone's words can kill. Let me demonstrate what I mean.

The earliest document we have of Jesus' teachings is Mark. Mark 10:10–12 categorically states that whereas divorce is a reality to be reckoned with, a divorced person cannot remarry without participating in and causing adultery. Thus the issue shifts from divorce to remarriage to adultery, settling down upon adultery. Is remarriage a permanent state of adultery for which there is no forgiveness? Read by the letter, the answer is yes. Read by the Spirit of life, the answer is at least very ambiguous. The latter was the experience of the early church.

Therefore, they asked the question: "What if one's mate commits adultery with someone else, then is one not justified in both divorce and remarriage?" The Gospel of Matthew was written later than Mark. By this time, the church had encountered exceptional human situations of divorce. The teachings of the church recorded in Matt. 19:3–12 answer the question by attributing to Jesus' own words a revised version and insert "except for unchastity." Furthermore, in the same passage, the disciples question Jesus closely: "If such is the case of a man with his wife, it is not expedient to marry." Then Jesus says: "Not all men can receive this saying, but only those to whom it is given." One wonders whether Jesus speaks to the issue of divorce and adultery, or to the issue of not marrying at all. I would assume that it is both. The teaching about divorce applies to those who are consciously and voluntarily within the Christian hope and faith. Only those who have been gifted to do so can stay free of marriage and/or sexual union.

Yet the church had not yet dealt with the problem of forgiveness of adultery. It also interpreted adultery as a *woman's* problem and not a man's. Jesus took up the cause of women and took his stand with even adulterous women. Those who remembered him knew this. Therefore, the continuing experience of the early church brought back to their remembrance other experiences of Jesus that speak both forcefully and directly about Jesus' attitude toward adultery. The Fourth Gospel, The Gospel According to John, was written near the close of the first century. It speaks of the rule of the Spirit which God sends as a Counselor, Teacher, and Comforter. The Spirit brings back the teachings of Jesus, and those who worship God do so in spirit and truth, not in a particular temple. In this Gospel, one finds accounts of actions of Jesus not found in the first three Gospels. Two of them speak to the problem of remarriage and adultery—is it forgivable?

The first is the story of the Samaritan woman at the well in John 4:7–39. This woman had had *five* husbands, and the man she was living with was not her husband. Yet she experienced redemption, hope, and renewal of life through faith in Jesus as the Christ.

The second is the account in John 8:1–11. (Some manuscripts of the New Testament provide the story at this point and others after Luke 21:38.) This is the story of the harsh and unforgiving scribes and Pharisees bringing a woman who had been "caught in adultery." They wanted to stone her. Jesus asked that the person among them who was without sin cast the first stone to kill her. Adultery was punishable by death in Jewish law: "If a man commits adultery with the wife of his neighbor, both the adulterer and the adulteress shall be put to death" (Lev. 20:10). By the time of Jesus this law had been interpreted to mean only women. Jesus asked these men if *they* had sinned; if not, then they were to cast the first stone. When they heard this, they left one by one, beginning with the eldest, until Jesus was left alone with the woman. He asked her where they were, and who condemned her. She said, "No one, Lord." He said, "Neither do I condemn you; go, and do not sin again." This story and its advice to the woman are relevant, it seems to me, to the problem of divorce and remarriage. Such a conclusion does not please many Biblicists, because it directly contradicts a specific teaching of Jesus in Mark 10:10–12. However, the Biblicist seems to be defending a literalistic, word-for-word doctrine of the Bible rather than to be trying to discover the Spirit of Jesus. Yet when one sees the Bible as the record of the experience of other Christians in the early church seeking to apply justly, lovingly, and mercifully the teachings of the whole New testament, then one can be even more faithful to the Scriptures and, in doing so, profit from their wisdom in seeking to be a "person of understanding" in caring for other people who are about to be stoned to death by overzealous religionists. Adultery is of the heart, Jesus said in Matt. 5:28. None of us is without sin. I hope the churches in Curtis Barrett's and my hometown can learn and grow as much as did the churches of the century in which Jesus lived.

The Testing of the Powers That Be!

Curtis Barrett continues down the road and comes to the place where he and his chums swiped watermelons. He experienced the fun of forbidden fruit. The emerging conscience of the adolescent needs permission to do just this if a mature conscience is to emerge. Professor Lawrence Kohlberg of Harvard, building upon Jean Piaget's concepts, says that moral judgment has a pre-conventional level, a conventional level, and a level of independent moral judgment. The conventional level of the developing conscience involves conforming to the will of the group and obeying the rules of law and order for their own sakes. If one is to move beyond conventional morality, one must find out for oneself by experience a pattern of ethical principles that apply to all persons everywhere. In order to discover this, one must have permission to test the conventional morality of the powers that be. (Lawrence Kohlberg, "The Child as a Moral Philosopher," *Psychology Today,* Sept. 1968.)

As I test this concept against the teachings of Jesus, I find that he gave a parable that probes it even further:

> "What do you think? A man had two sons; and he went to the first and said, 'Son, go and work in the vineyard today.' And he answered, 'I will not'; but afterward he repented and went. And he went to the second and said the same; and he answered, 'I go, sir,' but did not go. Which of the two did the will of his father?" They said, "The first." Jesus said to them, "Truly, I say to you, the tax collectors and the harlots go into the kingdom of God before you. For John came to you in the way of righteousness, and you did not believe him, but the tax collectors and the harlots believed him; and even when you saw it, you did not afterward repent and believe him." (Matt. 21:28–32)

Clinical observation often reveals persons who have rejected thoroughly the verbally stated beliefs of parents and home community but *behave* more consistently than those who make the noisiest verbal preachments. I suppose stealing watermelons itself had to be *almost* as much fun for the owner, who thereby was able to relive his own adolescence. The studies of the Hutterites by Eaton point out that whereas this strict group of religious people prescribes a narrow path for its people, nevertheless they provide "a partial amnesty on 'sin' during adolescence. . . . The hope is that after going through a period of being 'wild,' he will settle down and become a good member." (Joseph W. Eaton, "Adolescence in a Communal Society," *Mental Hygiene,* Vol. 48, No. 1, Jan. 1964, pp. 66–73.)

The Manipulative Use of Sex

Barrett's jogging took him by the home of a wife beater who was otherwise a fine, gentle person. He does not condone brutality but relates the rage to the man's response to being manipulated and goaded by his wife to control and maneuver him, as a way of fighting rather than a way of sharing.

This reference takes us into the epistles of Paul and into the pastoral epistle of I Peter. Husbands are enjoined in I Peter 3:7 to "live considerately" with their wives. On the other hand, the apostle Paul discusses this considerateness with specific reference to sexual intercourse. In I Cor. 7:5, he says that neither husband nor wife is to refuse the other the experience of sexual relations for any but the specific reason to engage in prayer. Then, even, this is to be for a very short time, unless great temptation overtake one or the other partner. Prayer itself can be a weapon of retaliation after a short time of deliberate sexual neglect or refusal of one's husband or wife. Rarely do psychotherapists, overexposed to harsh misinterpretations of the Bible by their sick patients, have the chance to learn that nowhere in the Bible does it condone or encourage men and women in marriage to avoid each other sexually for manipulative and hostile reasons.

The "Successful Prodigal Son"

The classmate of Curtis Barrett whose academic achievement and professional success were rejected by his father presents a new "role and guide" in interpreting the story of the prodigal son found in Luke, ch. 15. In the Biblical story, the estrangement between father and son was followed by the son's waste of his part of the family inheritance in riotous living. In Barrett's story, the estrangement was because the son worked just as hard in ways other than his father. In the Biblical instance, the father was accepting, forgiving, and affirming upon the son's return. In Barrett's classmate's experience, the father was cold, rejecting, and irreconcilable. What in human nature made the difference? It was probably the inability of the father to learn from his son and his resulting inferiority. The dividing crest in the father-son relationship seems to appear when the son passes the level of education of the father. The struggle for identity is softened if the father and son can ease into an adult-to-adult relationship of caring for each other by learning from each other. This is harder for farmers who have sons who have M.D.'s and Ph.D's!

Yet a word seems in order on behalf of the father. To what extent is much more required of a person to whom much has been given? Jesus said: "Every one to whom much is given, of him will much be required; and of him to whom men commit much they will demand the more" (Luke 12:48). An M.D. and a Ph.D. is *much.* To what extent has the academic pursuit of the son been one of heritage-denying and seeking a put-down relationship to the father? If this young son were in psychotherapy, then would it be too much to pursue his understanding of his father, a softening of his own feelings of hurt, a mellowing of his more subtle rejection of his father in his effort to gain his father's approval? The son's M.D. and Ph.D. then become functional wisdom with which he can reassimilate his heritage rather than a means of disassociating himself completely from it. Being a pastor and having heard both fathers and sons of the kind described by Barrett have caused me to see religion as symbolic of the underlying tension. If some ground of spiritual-value congruence between father and son can be found, the tension might be relieved considerably.

Learning to Relate to Strangers Who Are Different

Curtis Barrett talks about the segregation and integration of schools. School is an experience of the stranger. One moves from the hearthstone similarities of the nuclear family, and the shared compatibilities of the extended family of the church, to the larger family of mankind in the school. This is why the public school is the battleground of human character in a way that the home and the church only run a close—and sometimes distant—second and third. The child meets persons of a different and strange color, creed, clothing, food habits, and social class in the public school.

As I project this reality on the screen of the New Testament, as well as the Old Testament, I discover that the ultimate tests of our faith in God come when we are confronted with strangers who are different from us. The Jewish people saw themselves as strangers and sojourners in Egypt and later in Babylonia. In confrontation with others who were strange and different, they learned that God is not restricted to the land of Palestine. In the laws of the Sabbath, the stranger was included in rest and respite from work for a day of rest. The "sojourner" was included in many more laws.

Jesus spoke of the faithful servant of the Kingdom who has the capacity to see him as the resurrected Christ in the "stranger" who needs a home (Matt. 25:35). The disciples on the road to Emmaus experienced the Christ as "a stranger" to Jerusalem. They invited him to stay at their home. In eating with him they discovered him to be the risen Christ (Luke 24:18, 28–31). The pastoral epistle, I Tim. 5:10, measures the sincerity of an older widow by the kind of hospitality she has shown to strangers. The revelation of God's own character comes to us through strangers. We are to be careful how we entertain strangers, for we may thereby be entertaining messengers of God without knowing it (Heb. 13:2). The apostle Peter was sent to a Gentile, Cornelius the centurion. He was "inwardly perplexed" by this mission, he being a Jew. The encounter was such that he said: "You yourselves know how unlawful it is for a Jew to associate with or to visit any one of another nation; but God has shown me that I should not call any man common or unclean. . . . Truly I perceive that God shows no partiality, but in every nation any one who fears him and does what is right is acceptable to him" (Acts 10:28, 34–35). The social situation of our treatment of ourselves is at stake in the conflict-ridden public schools of Louisville. More than that, the very character of God waits revelation in the different paradoxes of meeting people who are different from us.

Thus, I have walked as a pastoral counselor along the path of Barrett's jogging. The objective has been to approach his memories as a person who by credentials is said to be expert in Biblical literature and ethical wisdom drawn from that literature.

The Making of the Psychotherapist and/or Pastoral Counselor

The methodology Barrett has used speaks to the central issue of the making of the psychotherapist and/or pastoral counselor: the indispensable necessity of walking or jogging around in our own heritage long enough and seriously enough to be *enabled* to approach our own expertise *unabashedly.* The absence of such sweaty self-appraisal in relation to our counselees or clients leaves us out of touch with ourselves. Hence, we approach our work with some sort of insecure abashment or shame.

This objective of becoming a psychotherapist or pastoral counselor requires, however, in doing so that we not become entangled again in the bondages of our past. Effective professional education of psychotherapists and pastoral counselors by necessity includes both getting in touch with the strengths and becoming liberated from the provincialisms of our upbringing. It requires by necessity laying hold of and implementing the unique strengths of our heritage without shame or apology.

Furthermore, these objectives of effective professional education are both compatible with and inherent in a prophetic understanding of faith. I say "prophetic" advisedly because the spirit of the Hebrew prophets, or Jesus, and the apostles was always at work in affirming the ambiguous power of one's heritage both to vitalize life and/or to enslave one's life in idolatry of the forms of religion all the while denying the essence of faith.

The Hypothesis of a Formulated Body of Knowledge

Curtis Barrett's hypothesis is based on a conviction of his about psychotherapy which I share about pastoral counseling, i.e., that we have to formulate human experience hour by hour into an organized body of knowledge which we use to help people who are hurting. The body of knowledge in which we by certification are said to be competent differs from profession to profession, but the responsibility is the same. Furthermore, this body of knowledge is mastered as data, but it is inwardly appropriated through experiences such as those that Barrett experienced while jogging. By "body of knowledge" we do not mean a predigested conglomeration of cold facts. A thing can be a fact and be trivial. The greatness of a fact lies in its tissue connection with an organized view of the whole of things. We mean a cogent and persuasive organization of our field of expertise that hour by hour and patient by patient can be focused on different and unique human situations. We mean a body of knowledge that in turn is increased through contact with persons who are in need. For example, a Biblical interpretation grows and is enriched by contact with and feedback from persons whose needs are often much deeper than our interpretations have ever encompassed. New problems thrust us back upon our "body of data" and test its adequacy. We grow and learn more through clinical seriousness with patients.

Finally, let me say that Curtis Barrett's parable of jogging and his hypothesis of a formulated body of knowledge focused upon people who are hurting provide an effective antidote for superficiality and boredom for psychotherapists and pastoral counselors. He has thrust us back upon our basic expertise. Serious thought about that expertise can only result in a better grasp of the expertise and a deeper security in it. Such security on the part of the various professionals enables us to transcend the status problems involved in interprofessional competition. We have a more functional or operational concern which focuses on the competence of various team members rather than the "roles" and "territorial rights" of each. Responsibility for dealing with needs of patients is tied to decisions as to who has the most authentic "weight of being" in relationship to the patient. Combined with the need for expertise is a given body of data to implement it. This may be called a "transdisciplinary approach," a topic deserving of a separate discussion. This makes the members of whole treatment team more appreciative of one another and more effective with patients.

Barrett's challenge of me has, for example, prompted me to do one full week of concentrated Biblical study and reflection. That is a massive accomplishment—for a clinical psychologist to get a pastoral counselor to study his Bible that closely!

9

SOME CHARACTERISTICS
OF A HEALTHY RELIGIOUS FAITH

When one comes to the last chapter of a book on the religious care of the psychiatric patient, it is possible that he or she wonders what the author considers to be the "health goals" of the religious care of the patient. The cases in the preceding pages demonstrate how during a mental illness the religious beliefs and practices of persons are caricatured. The haunting wonder is: Is there any such thing as healthy religious faith? If so, what is it like? Any informed person would readily and accurately say that the mental patients have caricatures of religion and ask: What is an undistorted picture of religious faith? The answers to such questions lie along the line of distinguishing the genuine article of religious faith from the phony, inauthentic ones. This can be done without going into the realm of religious dogmatics, although dogma review is usually the route taken. Consequently, the purpose of this chapter is to identify some of the characteristics of what I consider to be a healthy religious faith.

An honest person lives in paradox and ambiguity when he or she attempts to speak of a "healthy religious faith." As Paul Tillich says: "The presence of true religion is generally hidden. It becomes manifest 'now and then' in the form of the great mystical or prophetic reactions against mere religion. The degree to which religion is open to such reactions determines its relative rank. Absolute religion is never an objective fact, but rather a momentary and vital breakthrough of the Unconditional. God demonstrates what absoluteness is by shattering the claim of religion to absoluteness, not through skepticism or the history of religion, but by revealing God's unconditionality, before which all religion is nothing." (Paul Tillich, *What Is Religion?* tr. by James Luther Adams, pp. 147–148; Harper & Row, Publishers, Inc., 1969.)

Yet, when we face the truth of what Tillich says and realize that religion is always under scrutiny of its own claims to absoluteness, infallibility, and perfection, we still look for those cross-cultural constants that characterize healthy religious living regardless of where we find it, regardless of our particular religious tradition, regardless of our varied cultural forms, and regardless of our statements of religious orthodoxy. What are the common factors in all religious living that tend to enable persons to maintain health and unity in community regardless of our particular tradition? The literal meaning of the word "religion" is "to bind together." What are the binding factors in all forms of religious faith that enable us to arrive at what John Dewey called "a common faith"?

CROSS-CULTURAL CONSTANTS IN HEALTHY RELIGION

Suffering

Whether one takes the position that suffering is inherent in human life or whether one assumes, as many religions do, that suffering is an illusion, the fact of suffering itself is dealt with one way or another in all living faiths. A faith that lives and lives long presupposes and deals with human suffering. Suffering can bind people together or it can tear them apart. One of the great tragedies of the Vietnam War was that our leaders led a nation torn asunder in dissension over a war 13,000 miles away. Yet World War II was borne with a sense of community sacrifice in that all were involved. When a tornado strikes a community, one experiences a catastrophic kind of stress that unifies those who are struck in a continuing sense of community. When one works in an emergency room in a hospital, a coronary care unit, a tumor clinic, an emergency psychiatric clinic, one sees "instant groups" form in the family rooms where friends and relatives meet. When suffering does not create a community in a psychiatric clinic, then often the professional treatment of choice is to create a temporary community of fellow sufferers. Binding people together in a fellowship of suffering lowers the stigma, destroys the isolation, and creates interpenetrating learning. One of the standard assumptions of a considerable number of religious faiths is that our faith produces a kind of comfort that becomes a tool with which we can become "wounded healers" to comfort other people who are in similar afflictions to those we have experienced. This concept is portrayed by the apostle Paul in the New Testament.

> "Praise be to the God and Father of our Lord Jesus Christ, the all-merciful Father, the God whose consolation never fails us! He comforts us in all our troubles, so that we in turn may be able to comfort others in any trouble of theirs and to share with them the consolation we ourselves receive from God. As Christ's cup of suffering overflows, and we suffer with him, so also through Christ our consolation overflows. If distress be our lot, it is the price we pay for your consolation, for your salvation; if our lot be consolation, it is to help us to bring you comfort, and strength to face with fortitude the same sufferings we now endure. And our hope for you is firmly grounded; for we know that if you have part in the suffering, you have part also in the divine consolation." (II Cor. 1:3–7, NEB)

'Pain makes you think, thought makes you wise, and wisdom makes pain bearable," says the Oriental proverb. The desire for companionship in that pain is an unquenchable source of religious community.

Hope

Margaret Mead has said that the common factor that binds all religions together is hope. We know that suicide is rising to epidemic proportions. Even young people in increasing numbers seem to be "half in love with death," as Flanders Dunbar used to put it. Suffering produces hope, and a hope that does not disappoint is the kind of hope that is sought. The source of hope is in the revelation of new alternatives for human existence and the growth of mutuality between human beings. Suicide is the reduction of life to one resolution of the stresses of life: death. A genuinely healthy faith is generative in the constant search for new and additional alternatives to hopelessness in death. In the face of hopelessness which today is being legitimized by Oriental attitudes toward suicide, easy answers by euthanasia enthusiasts, and the smiling deletion of the reality of natural death from our consciousness, the phenomenon of hope deserves psychological, psychiatric, and theological reexamination. Does one, as Alcoholics Anonymous puts it, necessarily have to "hit bottom" in order to sense or to experience any need for "a Power greater than oneself"?

Furthermore, mutuality is the source of hope, and the depersonalization of American society produces helplessness characteristic of the depressed patient. People, on an epidemic scale, feel that they are controlled by outside forces beyond their own initiative. There is "nothing they can do" but "give up and give in," because they do not have a mutual participation in deciding the course of their lives. The very absence of hope points toward the indispensability of hope in breaking the impasse of the person who not only feels forsaken but feels forsaken unto despair.

Basic Trust

Erik Erikson says that the "impairment of basic trust . . . characterizes individuals who withdraw into themselves in particular ways when at odds with themselves and with others." He says that "individual trust must become a common faith and individual mistrust a commonly formulated evil, while the individual's need for restoration must become a part of the ritual practice of many, and must become a sign of trustworthiness in the community." (Erik Erikson, *Identity and the Life Cycle*, Psychological Issues Monograph, Vol. I, No. 1, pp. 56, 65; International Universities Press, Inc., 1959.) Inherent in Erikson's statement about basic trust is the issue of the credibility of people in power in religious groups. The "ritual practices" of religious communities have a tremendous binding power because they tend to be built around the natural events of stress and transition, of separation and reunion in the developmental cycle of human families. The test of the credibility of the religious leadership and community is in the *follow-up* of these rituals. For example, after a funeral, does the community "stay in touch" with the bereft? After a wedding, does the community develop a continuing relationship of encouragement and shared wisdom with the couple? Does the community follow through with the development of a new pattern of meaning in the writing of a new chapter in the life of a retired person? These are times of renewal and restoration; or they are times of threat and destruction in a person's basic confidence in the trustworthiness of his or her universe, in the trustworthiness of the people of God, in the trustworthiness of God. If the church and synagogue can provide a credible basic trust in people at such times, then that trust is sustained by the exercise of love, attention, considerateness, and care on a follow-up basis between the times of the great ritual practices of religion.

Curiosity

Another binding force of a healthy faith is that of curiosity. The individual who has lost all curiosity capitulates to hopelessness and suspicion. If boredom is a way of life for a person, then the amount of demand that the person can absorb is foreshortened. Religious faith begins to lose its vitality when the community of faith has decided that it has all the answers to life's dilemmas and needs only to be obeyed and followed. Then people tend to be driven apart and the community itself is rent by inner schism and division. More positively, the force that keeps people moving toward each other in openness to learning is curiosity and teachableness. It is the opposite of what the New Testament calls "hardness of heart." An example of the creative force of curiosity in human life is found in something that Jack Nicklaus says about golf. He says: "Utter predictability on a golf course to me spells blindness and blindess spells dullness. If I never missed a fairway or green, never got a bad bounce, always got a level lie, I might make a lot more money, but I would be bored silly doing it. Obviously, the game's greatest thrill lies in planning and executing perfect shots, but I believe that recovering skillfully from poor shots and bad breaks offers a great challenge, and an additional dimension of satisfaction when you do succeed."

The wellsprings of a genuine religious faith seem to me to be renewed again and again by curiosity. The words of Moses are the stuff of which curiosity and religion are made: "I will turn aside and see this great sight, why this bush is not burnt" (Ex. 3:3). Similarly, curiosity is an amazing combination of the sense of worship and the scientific spirit. Rudolf Otto said that religious experience is composed of the sense of the tremendous mystery of God and creation and the sense of tremendous fascination and eagerness to learn of the Eternal and the created order. The reverent person is open to any evidence of new knowledge. He or she knows in part and prophesies in part. The genuinely scientific person cannot become irreverent because of the vastness of the unknown. As Einstein said to Martin Buber, "We physicists strive to draw God's lines to God." At the end of his formal education, he said: "I was suddenly abandoned, standing at a loss on the threshold of life." Yet he could prove the "loss" and conclude: "An academic career compels a young man to scientific production, and only strong character can resist the temptation of superficial analysis." (Quoted from Ronald W. Clark, *Einstein: The Life and Times,* pp. 18, 40, 51; The World Publishing Company, 1971.)

A sense of awe and a sense of curiosity wed themselves in a healthy religious faith and creative scientific research. The Spirit of a living God holds them in a stressful tension with each other. This is one of the reasons that the dynamic interplay between psychiatry and religion has been one productive source of renewed vitality in the life of both psychiatry and religion. The creative tension between worship and curiosity is productive of a healthier sense of faith and a less arrogant science.

Having observed some of the cross-cultural constants of vital religions everywhere, we now need to consider some psychological characteristics of a genuinely healthy faith.

Some Psychological Characteristics of a Healthy Religious Faith

Comprehensiveness

In order to be healthy a religious faith must be comprehensive enough to look steadily and honestly at the facts of life that are the most inescapable and unchangeable. In order to be wholehearted, one needs a sense of faith that is comprehensive in its affections and loyalties. This poses all sorts of dilemmas for the mature individual. He or she faces the dilemma of being an individual and yet maintaining relationship to those persons who are of different faiths and different likenesses. He or she is called upon to stay in touch with and recognize his or her own religious heritage and at the same time to go beyond the "household gods" of his or her particular provincial culture. Religious faith amounts to the investment of oneself in durable values which will outdistance time and circumstance. As Gordon Allport has said: "Often the religious sentiment is merely rudimentary in the personality that arises at the core of the life and is directed toward the infinite. It is the region of the life that has the longest-range intention, and for this reason is capable of conferring marked integration upon personality, engendering meaning and peace in the face of the tragedy and confusion of life." Allport continues to say that "religion is man's ultimate attempt to enlarge and complete his own personality by finding the supreme context in which he rightly belongs." (Gordon Allport, *The Individual and His Religion,* p. 142; The Macmillan Company, 1950.)

From a pathological point of view, one of the most recurrent problems of the mentally ill is the overinvestment of their lives in one set of human relationships. A patient has a continuing battle with a parent, a sibling, a husband, a wife, a son or a daughter. Allport describes such an instance in his book entitled *Letters from Jenny,* in which a person organized her whole life around her sense of rejection by her one and only son. The God of such a person is too small. In a day such as this, when religion in the minds of mainline religionists is equatable with a particular denomination or sect, the religious life of that person may become constricted to the outer boundaries of that denomination or sect. The particular religious group becomes "a flat earth" to the believer. When that person is called upon to relate in depth and sincerity to people who are "other than and different from" his or her particular group, then genuineness and depth of relationship tend to cease.

Gaining breadth of sympathies and sentiments for the basic human condition of all people everywhere without losing the solid integrity of commitment to one's own personal values is the tension which the mature person of faith takes upon himself or herself. He or she lives with a comprehensive religious faith.

"Seeking"

The transcultural quality of curiosity manifests itself in the healthy religious faith as a "seeking" or heuristic quality. Deep convictions are held by the person of a healthy religious faith but they are held with a sense of "knowing in part and prophesying in part." They are held with a sense of openness and quizzical searching, always with the awareness that convictions have many dark and mysterious corners that need exploring. Similarly, new persons are met with a sense of adventure and are joined as "fellow seekers." This is not the opposite of dogmatism. It is the antidote for dogmatism. The healthy religious faith is in itself a way of learning, a way of knowing. The field of mathematics gives this a formal name, "heuristic." By this is meant a specific approach which one takes to solving problems. As Jerome Bruner says, "A sharp line can be drawn between 'rote drill' and 'understand,'" especially in the field of mathematics. It is one thing to learn of the rote solution of isolated problem after isolated problem. It is another thing to discover a principle that enables one to solve all such problems when they appear. He continues to say, "The mastery of the fundamental ideas of a field involves not only the grasping of general principles, but also the development of an attitude toward learning and inquiry, toward guessing and hunches, and toward the possibility of solving problems on one's own." In order to do this one must include "an important ingredient . . . a sense of excitment about discovery—discovery about regularities of previously unrecognized relationships and similarities between ideas, with a resulting sense of self-confidence in one's own abilities." (Jerome Bruner, *The Process of Education,* pp. 20 and 27; Random House, Inc., Vintage Books, 1960.)

In the realm of emotional health and maturity, such a faith that is willing to plunge into the unknown stands in contradiction to the religion of infantilism on the part of growing persons and the religion of nostalgia on the part of people who have reached chronological maturity but are living in the past. These distinctions become very serious in assessing the difference between the sentimental religion that is imbued with magic and the multiple security operations of defense that are often found in mentally ill persons. Such persons have, as I have indicated before, lost curiosity. They have begun to stagnate in terms of their willingness to be challenged by the unknown, by fresh adventure, and by a willingness to grow.

Ambiguity Tolerance

The person of a healthy religious faith tends to have an appreciation of the ambiguity of human existence and a capacity to tolerate that ambiguity. He or she appreciates the many-colored spectrum of truth. He or she does not live in a world of harsh contrasts of black and white that is ignorant of the wonderful world of color. He or she appreciates the ambiguity of human goodness and is capable of seeing the possibilities of human frailty even in the greatest protestations of goodness. The Danish theologian, Søren Kierkegaard, said that there are three modes of human existence: the aesthetic, the ethical, and the religious. He insisted that cultural religion rarely if ever gets beyond the either/or absolutes and the realm of human morality and ethics. But as we break through the barrier of the ethical prisons that we build for ourselves we develop a wry sense of humor. The ethical inconsistencies become evident and amusing. We are given the gift to see ourselves as others see us!

This capacity to tolerate ambiguity in human experience also is a basis for forgiving those whom one would otherwise harshly ostracize. It is another way of describing human patience with human frailty. It is the source of empathy which is genuine, based on a hard-nosed realism about human behavior that is accompanied, nevertheless, with a sense of patient tolerance and understanding. The apostle Paul called this the ability to restore people overtaken in a fault with a spirit of gentleness looking to ourselves lest we also be tempted (Gal. 6:1–2).

A Sense of Humor

The healthy religious faith tends to produce a sense of humor that is free of ridicule, a sense of play that is free of imposition on others, and a life of music that translates emotions into the nonverbal alchemy that only music can provide. Religious faith at its best has produced these in human beings. Laughter, play, and music are the stuff of which celebration is made. Healthy religion is marked by its realism in facing and not denying the reality of pain and suffering in death. It is marked by the dynamic for facing these realities "nose to nose" and rising above them as a "significant surviving self."

However, such seriousness in the face of human suffering is only one side of the healthy and genuine religious experience. Celebration is the other side. The sense of community is created as laughter, play, and music combine in producing the element of joy and ecstasy. The Puritan ethic has obscured a considerable portion of this particular dimension of a healthy religious faith in its attempt to produce disciplined persons. But the rhythm of life requires an alternating sense of balance between the discipline of duty and the joys of laughter, play, and music.

"Graduation"

A healthy religious faith permits the believer to "graduate" from one level of spiritual growth to another without being rejected by and disowned by the fellowship of other believers. Many persons who are described as dropouts are essentially not "dropouts" from a religious community but "kickouts" in that they have been rejected and disowned because they have grown beyond the level of simplistic religious faith which they enjoyed at a more immature level. They have taken advantage of the education and larger associations that even religious colleges and universities afford. They have developed a larger world view. They have developed new rituals. They have developed new languages. They have become related to new persons. All of this leaves them strangers to their relatives. However, quite often one discovers communities of faith that encourage "graduation" from one level of spiritual growth to another. One finds religious groups such as may be found within the Catholic Church, the Episcopal Church, the Pentecostal groups, and the small disciplined communal religious groups who make room for the graduation of their people into new and exciting expressions of their ancestral faith. Very few mainline religious groups, however, are as honest about their refusal to permit graduation or as consistent in their practice about preventing it as are the Hutterites. The Hutterites developed a constant and coherent community that reduces the necessity for graduation to the barest minimum degree. However, in a pluralistic religious society such as the American religious scene presents, we need a new approach to the upward social mobility and intellectual mobility brought about by education, travel, and affluence. We need an approach that will permit a growing person to move from one level of spiritual complexity to another without being rejected by his or her family of origin.

These are a few of the parameters of a healthy and genuine religious faith that calls for a larger world view, a sense of adventure, a capacity to grow out of the "low-vaulted" past into the more stately mansions of the human spirit. I am convinced that, translated aright, they are the stuff of which good emotional health is made. My reader may well ask why I have not mentioned love as the supreme ingredient in a healthy religious faith. My main reason is that the word "love" has been drained of its ethical and religious meaning. The word too often connotes a puddle of sentimentality. If love means a serene trust and trustworthiness in God and us; if love means growing in knowledge and perception; if love means accepting responsibility for ourselves and others as direct answerability to God for justice to ourselves and others; if love means the capacity to forgive others and the steadfast refusal to become an idolater of past wounds, injustices, griefs, and losses; if love means maintaining our fidelity in a relationship even when betrayed by others; if love means staying by the unchangeable results of our own freely chosen actions and decisions unswervingly; if love means casting out fear and deception as the source of all demonic power, then I will include love as the *summum bonum* of a healthy religious faith. Love keeps us sane in a fickle and sentimental world that is likely to call anything that scratches us where it itches by the name of love.

EPILOGUE

As I indicated in the Prologue, the substance of this book does not attempt to cover the whole range of mental disorders. To the contrary, the two that represent the largest incidence of psychiatric illness—depression and schizophrenia—have been dealt with in considerable detail.

In the unfolding of all the aspects of the religious care of the psychiatric patient, I hope that several things have been clearly evident. First, I hope that the distinctly *human* plight of the patients mentioned will be apparent. As Harry Stack Sullivan often said, we are all more distinctly human than otherwise. If the reader has experienced kinship with the persons described here, then I hope he or she will conclude that this confirms the personhood of the mentally ill and does not need to set off an alarm system. Second, I hope the reader is also aware that I am not implying that the more or less ideal interrelating of the various mental health professions to one another, which I have experienced and which I describe here, is the rule everywhere. Ideal relationships do not exist everywhere. Cooperative relationships do, however, exist in enough places for me to be sure that such creative dialogue in the care of psychiatric patients can indeed happen.

One of my fondest hopes is that the intensive attention I have given here to psychotic behavior profiles will be given by other persons to the neurotic, to people exhibiting behavioral disorders, to the organically impaired, etc. Persons with psychophysiologic disorders also need similar attention as do those having problems of intractable and unremitting pain. My hope is that we will get out of the realm of generalities about pastoral care, status anxiety about the competitive roles of different professions, and the special pleading of persons insecure in their own discipline's relevance to the needs of the patient. To the contrary, I hope that other disciplined observers of the needs of neurotic and antisocial persons will become those persons' advocates as I have sought to be the advocate of the depressed and schizophrenic person. Then I will profit from the record of their disciplined observations.

I use the concept of observations that are disciplined and recorded. I do not in the preceding pages assume that this is in any way what might be called confirmatory research that "proves" that in every instance and in any population what I have said here is so. Rather, I am confident that persons from another culture with a different religious heritage will produce both confirmatory and contrasting views from that presented here. Yet, in all instances I have sought to give myself wholeheartedly to the discipline of writing down and systematizing to the best of my ability what I have seen in concert with my colleagues. These observations will, I hope, serve as hunches and propositions to be tested for their universality of application by more refined research methods. My one source of serenity about the accuracy of the observations in this book is that I am speaking from having been with patients in the process of treatment from the point of admission to the point of discharge and in outpatient follow-up. Yet I ask myself each time I see a patient terminate his or her relationship to the hospitals in which I work with my students: "Will there be anybody out there in the life of the churches and synagogues to become a life support to this person in the heavy adjustment of the return to the larger community from the hospital? What is the purpose of the church and its ministry when viewed from within these persons' needs? Is there any balm in the fellowships of faith to provide an ongoing community with this person? If such a balm is supplied, will the patient have enough capacity for commitment to respond to the outreach of the spiritual community? Or does the loss of self-respect run so deeply in the life of the patient that the gift of community will not be received?"